The Secrets of Self-Hypnosis

The Secrets of Self-Hypnosis

Harnessing the Power of Your Unconscious Mind

Adam Eason

www.adam-eason.com

Copyright 2005
Adam Eason
All Rights Reserved

Library of Congress Cataloging-in-Publication Data

Eason, Adam

**The Secrets of Self-Hypnosis:
Harnessing the Power of Your Unconscious Mind**

Includes Bibliographic References

ISBN 0-9709321-9-7

1. Autogenic Training
RC499.A8.E643EE 2000
1.7.-dc21

Printed in the United States of America
Network 3000 Publishing
3432 Denmark Ave. 108
Eagan, MN 55123
(612) 616-0732

Typeset by TW Typesetting, Plymouth, Devon, UK

This book is dedicated to Dennis and Leslie Eason.

For teaching me the meaning of unconditional love.

For that I am eternally grateful.

Contents

Section 1

Essential Background Information

1

Who is Adam Eason?

I want to share a story with you, which tells of an important experience in my life.

It was an extremely hot, humid morning in Israel as I clung to the back of the tractor being taken to my first days work in the banana plantation. I had to squint as the sun was coming up and this helped stop the dust getting into my eyes.

When travelling in the early 1990s I had decided to go and live on a kibbutz for a few months. A London based company called project 42 organised for English people to go and do this and made it a lot easier to get accepted to join a kibbutz. Kibbutz's were originally to help build and restore Israel and were very much mini communes that were self-sufficient. The majority of kibbutzniks (people who lived on the kibbutz) were Israeli, but they welcomed volunteers from all over the world and in return for their work and skills, they would provide shelter and food and a minimal wage, kind of like pocket money.

I chose to attend a medium sized kibbutz just south of the city of Haifa, a place called Nachsholim. It was traditional, which meant I could really get a deeper understanding about the culture and ideology. It was also in central Israel so that I could travel to Bethlehem, The Golan Heights, Nazareth, the sea of Galilee, have adventures in my spare time as well as get to Egypt, Syria and Jordan after my minimum period of time was up serving on the kibbutz. They ask for a minimum period of work so that there is consistency and stability within the kibbutz.

Upon arrival in any kibbutz, they firstly show you to your accommodation, which you have to share with another volunteer. Next up, the Kibbutz volunteer organisers allocate you a working

3

role. I was told that fruit picking was hard work but good hours and as I liked to be outdoors I agreed to do this and fancied it more than kitchens, wash rooms or other indoor environments that you get allocated when new. You had to work your way up to better jobs!

You could work in the fields with Lychees, Avacados or Bananas. Part of the year was spent reaping the crop; part of it was in maintenance of the fields and the fruit. Some of the work was spent readying for future crops. I said I wanted to work on the banana plantation. It was picking season when I was there, and I had an image in my mind that this would be nice. I imagined myself roaming freely around the plantation with a basket in one arm, lazily filling it with bananas while conversing with fellow workers about their interesting journeys and how they came to be at the stage they were now at in their lives.

This image began to be shattered when I was told by several of the Kibbutz elders that I would not be able to cope with the banana plantation work. It was the time of year for picking the crop and was very physically demanding apparently. They told me that after the picking season was over, in a few weeks, I could work there tending to the baby trees. Some rather ragged Arabic workers from Yemen who were hardened to Banana plantation work also advised the kibbutz elders I that I was in fact too thin, and that coming from England, unused to manual labour, I would not be able to handle it.

This made me want to do it even more. I was sure that this would be good for me to do. I insisted and persisted and finally they gave in and accepted that I needed to be shown it and told me I could come back after the first day to change my mind when I wanted to be assigned elsewhere.

Upon telling my newly made friends among the kibbutz at a welcome meal they held for another new volunteer and I that evening, I was starting to feel apprehensive hearing all the banana plantation horror stories that I was being told. I got picked up at 5am the next morning. We went out in the early morning sunrise on a truck followed by tractors filled with workers.

Now let me explain some basic facts here; Bananas are picked when they are green and hard, they then ripen on their way to the markets for their sale. They are not in a bunch of 5 bananas as I buy them in the supermarkets here in the UK. Far from it, they hang in the trees in bunches that weigh 50–100kgs. Some bunches weighed as much as I did. Finally, have you ever seen a banana tree? They are tall. The bunches of bananas are up high in those trees.

So knowing that, let me now explain how they are picked. The head guy, in this case was a short stocky man wielding a long stick with a shortened scythe-like blade on the end, chooses which we field we work in, then he walks up the lines of banana trees and us pickers follow him in line. He spots a bunch that is at the right time in its life to be picked. The first worker in the queue then has to stand underneath the bunch and catch it when the leader cuts its stem with his long scythe.

These bunches are hard, they are heavy and they are falling at some pace. You then have to put the bunch on your shoulder, carry it all the way across that particular field of banana trees (the pathways are covered with thick and dense foliage and long, fallen banana tree leaves) to where the tractors are. You hold out the bunch with quivering breath, straight, out held shaking arms at full length, a bit like an exercise of endurance that you see on the world strongest man competition, while they are tied to a rail to hang. Then you go back, join the line of pickers and you do it all again. It is done for several hours until the sun comes up fully and it is too hot to work and then you go home to the kibbutz, stained with banana leaf juices and bruised, fatigued and extremely tired. Banana picking is the part of the season that is fairly brief and so it has to be done quickly, rapidly to bring in as much of the crop as possible in as short a period of time as possible.

Another factor worth bearing in mind at this point is that the banana plantation is highly valued as a main source of revenue for the relatively poor kibbutz. Any damaged crop represents a significant loss. Being stuck in the back end of Israel at a young age with 12 Arabic workers and 10 further Israeli kibbutzniks who I did not know and had never seen before except on films at that stage in my life, who were all scrutinising my every move, I suspected that I might not arrive home if I dropped a bunch of bananas or did not catch a bunch right. The only training I received was having the privilege of going last in the line and watching all the others do it. I was so nervous. It was extremely humid too, not conducive to calming down.

At this point, I noted the skill, I followed the technique, I even did some mental mock-ups of how I would do this. Catching it on the chest and shoulder, easing the fall and then shunting the load on to my shoulder to be carried.

So, there I am; pale skinned, lanky, redhead English guy, perspiring through nerves, standing at the foot of a banana tree with a bunch being cut methodically above me. My feet were positioned as correctly as I could get them. A bunch that must have been 70kg comes flying through the air and lands directly on the bone of my shoulder and the entire bunch snaps in half across my shoulder. My legs give way and I stumble, slip and fall to the floor covered in a bunch.

I am sworn at, shouted at, cursed at in a variety of tongues. In fact, the group leader screamed at me. Additionally, one of the Arabic Yemen workers told me in his pigeon English that he did tell me so. I then had the extremely hard task of carrying a broken bunch of bananas (effectively two bunches) to the tractors. I was advised by a more sympathetic co-worker to sit out until the break and then I would get a lift back to the kibbutz to be assigned some other work.

No way. I decided to walk back to the workers line in the field, under the shade of the large banana tree leaves and joined the queue again. I was wet through with sweat. It was pouring off me; everyone else was as dry as one of the fallen, brown leaves crunching and rustling beneath our feet. No-one spoke to me at all. In fact, if anything I got hostile looks from unshaved, yellow tooth men with scars who all looked more like mercenaries than farmers to me at that naïve stage of my life. My fear had gone, I had already taken my life into my own hands and no way was I going to spend the next 3 months seeing all of these guys around the kibbutz having them think:

There is that bloke who could not hack it on the banana plantation, we showed him the meaning of real work . . .

The leader of the team looked at me with such apprehension and I could see I irritated him, when he cut the next bunch for me, I could tell he was hoping it would weaken my resolve and beat me into submission. I felt like I had a place in a Rocky film at this point.

Now, I caught the next flying heavy bunch of bananas and gripped onto it tighter than I have ever held anything. I carried it down to the tractors and it was very painful, very hard and I questioned my ability to be able to do this for the next 4 hours.

But I did.

I carried those bunches in silence, save for a few groans and expletives, for the next four hours. I even carried on while the other workers had their smoking breaks. At one stage I even had to hold my left arm up with my right arm, as I got ready to catch a bunch as my left arm felt so tired and numb.

At the end of the shift, Fauzi, the guy who bemoaned me in the morning, assembled a small gas cooking stove on the ground in what became a daily ritual and he heated up water and made coffee that was quite unlike anything I had ever tasted before in my life, it was like coffee flavoured medicine with a thick layer of tough grit at the bottom. It also had an effect on me that meant despite being heavily tired and fatigued, I also was now wide-awake and wired up.

We sat in the sun sipping our tiny glasses of coffee and they chatted in their home tongues and I looked around and felt good. No one said much to me that day, there was certainly no 'well done' or anything of the sort, I had not done anything more than they had to do every single day after all. However, I became one of the 'banana team' as I called it. The other volunteers from across the world were amazed that I had survived. When we walked into the dining hall that lunchtime (the working day for me was 5am– 1pm) it was with a real sense of achievement and pride. The kibbutz elders looked on and chatted to my fellow workers about my efforts and they did not mention it again.

I worked there six days a week doing this kind of work.

I always had a red face following my work, partly due to my exertions and partly due to my natural complexion and colouring. This combined with the fact that I was quite a livewire at social functions and traditional gatherings meant that I was nicknamed 'The little devil' by all the kibbutzniks and received a lot of respect for my work and effort. I was regularly invited to private meals with families and learned a lot about them and myself during that time. I talked about my work to the others as if it was something that I just did and in fact, I developed some camaraderie with my fellow banana team members.

This story of mine demonstrates huge amounts of self-hypnosis being used in many different ways that were unknown to me consciously at the time. At that stage in my life I had no idea what self-hypnosis was as I had not yet discovered it. Yet the experience was one filled with self-hypnosis, internal communication and drawing upon resources that already existed within me. We all communicate with ourselves in our own way, it is just that we are not always progressive with ourselves or positive in the right ways. We all do things that require our resources to be channelled from time to time. This book shows you how to do it consciously, all the time; how to achieve excellence at will, that is; to know that you are doing it.

This is a book about stress management, it is a book about natural childbirth, it is a book about how to be a non-smoker and it is a book about how to be in control of your size, shape and weight. This book is about how to increase your confidence, it is about how to sleep better, how to distort your perception of time and of course how to relieve pain. This book is about communication and language and how to use them for the best with your self. You see, all these things are within your abilities to be in control of; with the right tools. This book gives you those right tools.

You are going to learn what self-hypnosis is and what it is not. You will learn that self-hypnosis is something that you are already very familiar with and that you are learning to utilise and actually start using the vast resources that already exist within you. You are going to learn how to enter and leave hypnosis and a lot about how to use language to make the most powerful of changes in your life. You are then going to learn about the practical applications of self-hypnosis and how to incorporate it into your life and be in charge of your own life.

No one has the right to control you. Not your friends, not your family and not old, outmoded ways of doing things. Self-hypnosis is a tool to help you take control of any or all the areas of your life.

2

How to Use This book

I don't think of work, only of gradually
regaining my health through reading, rereading,
reflecting.

Rainer Maria Rilke

I had a man referred to me once by one of London's top
psychiatrists, he strolled into my treatments room and let out an
enormous and dramatic sigh and slumped into the chair.

'I am taking seroxat, I was on Prozac. I have been diagnosed by
several Doctors as having clinical depression for the last twelve
years and have been seeing one of London's top psychiatrists for
the last 5 years. He referred me to you. I think I am going to be
very difficult for you to deal with' He said.

I could not help but laugh. Right there in front of him. He
frowned and looked at me and said in a less apathetic, more
serious tone and said; 'Don't you think you should be taking my
problems a bit more seriously Mr Eason?'

'No way.' I replied, 'You are taking your problems too seriously
for the both of us. If I wanted to be really good at being depressed,
I would take it really seriously. There are other therapists around
here who will pander to you in that way and take your problems
very seriously; but I won't.'

We both sat for 3 very long seconds of silence.

'Look . . .' I said, 'I run marathons, half-marathons and other
long distance races regularly and I consider myself to have a lot of
endurance. But that is nothing compared to the level of endurance
that you must have to have gone to the same psychiatrist for 5
years! Having gone for two years and having little success, what
on earth possessed you to go for another 3 years?'

I knew that he and I were making stunning progress when he came into my clinic and met me in the reception area four weeks later and he made a joke at my expense, that's right, he openly mocked me. I knew he was making progress.

Firstly, let me explain that every chapter of this book is punctuated with my own particular brand of humour. Lots of it is tongue in cheek, please bear that in mind. I like to have fun; self-hypnosis should be fun and really is fun. Every single paragraph of this book is written with that in mind, so please be aware of that if you think the manner is unusual from time to time or that I am labouring a point from time to time.

Maybe you are about to experience self-hypnosis for the first time; maybe you have amassed large amounts of experience and knowledge about it already. You may want to use self-hypnosis for a very specific reason, this book helps you to achieve those things regardless of whether you are a beginner or experienced.

This book is not the law! You do not have to follow every single letter of this book to the law. Please just allow yourself to use it in a way that resonates smoothly with you. There may be some aspects of it that you don't agree with or don't like where as other parts seem to resonate with you deeply and wonderfully. The aim of this book is to facilitate, **not dictate** your experience and skills with self-hypnosis. I have been told a certain story several times by differing people as I have made changes in my life and it goes a bit like this:

A young man is running down the street with a violin under his arm. He frantically stops and asks an old gentleman nearby 'how do I get to the Albert Hall?' The old man looks at the desperate young man and somberly replies, 'Practice, practice, practice.

Self-hypnosis is the same. I spend a lot of time each day in hypnosis. Part of my work is that of therapist and consultant and I often have to spend time with people that are emotional, distressed or ill. After most client consultations I use my self-hypnosis to 'wash' myself of that session's effect on me. For many years I have been using self-hypnosis daily and to get the most from it, I recommend you do the same.

Athletes train and practice their skills and we do it with most other things that we want to become not only competent at, but excellent at. I recommend also that you do want to allow yourself to become excellent with self-hypnosis because it is something that can help you achieve some seemingly miraculous things in your life and your experience of life. What's more, anyone can be excellent at using it, employing it in their lives and create more excellence for themselves in whatever way they interpret that to be.

Follow this book methodically and in the right order. It is in the order that it is for specific reasons. Learn about the phenomena and develop the correct expectations, then practice getting into the state of self-hypnosis, controlling it, acquainting yourself with it and developing it, then begin using and utilising it for relatively simple things and create success as a wonderful foundation for you to build upon to move on to achieving the seemingly miraculous stuff. The more thorough you are the more thorough and profound your results are sure to be.

Be relaxed when reading this book, read it often again and again and pick up things that may not have sunk in the first time, consider taking notes and jotting down ideas and when reading allow the information to flow over you, let it wash over you in the same way that waves of warm soothing water wash over your feet when you paddle in the sea on holiday. Allow it to access your deeper unconscious mind so that the things you are learning about become inherent in your life and so that you do not have to think about employing these skills and abilities consciously, they just become part of the way in which you naturally are.

There are going to be times when I ask you to do certain exercises. The most success will be achieved with self-hypnosis by those that do complete these exercises. Do not allow this information to simply be read and stored within you along with all the other stuff that you learned and don't use. Do the exercises. Notice how they make you feel and how that when you actually 'do' things they become far more usable than the theory of doing them. I want to help to show you how to really do some amazing things with your life and I can only do that if you follow the instructions in the correct order and do the exercises. I thank you in advance for doing that and I know you'll thank me in the long run when you have done them.

If you have some particular issue that you wish to deal with, a reason that you invested in this book, you might be tempted to race to that section. Please read this book in the order it is presented, I can't stress this point enough and that is why I have repeated this point in this opening. This is a guide to success. Allow yourself to be guided correctly and you'll discover some wonders.

As you are going to find out, hypnosis is a natural phenomenon; a usual state that you are going to use to instruct and direct the vast resource and capabilities of your unconscious mind to unleash the resources that become finely honed skills that allow you to be in control of reducing stress, controlling pain, letting go of old fears, achieving excellence and altering unwanted habits.

On one of my self-hypnosis courses that I ran in 1998, an eighteen year old girl named Natasha sat timidly and quietly throughout the entire two day seminar. She followed the course well; became adept at taking herself into hypnosis, then mastered the structure of self-hypnosis, learned the use of powerful and evocative self-hypnotic language and how to write and create powerful suggestions and programmes, all the things that this book is going to show you how to do. Natasha called me the following Wednesday (the course had finished on the Sunday) to tell me that she had been to the dentist and had her wisdom teeth removed without any anaesthesia what so ever.

Her dentist thought she was crazy at first, and then was amazed. In fact he was so amazed that he came on the course I was running the following month with his wife and gained so much from it that he eventually trained to be a hypnotherapist to be able to teach his patients self-hypnosis techniques to help themselves too. This is how powerful this stuff is when applied thoroughly and in the order presented. Every time I think of Natasha, it sends a warm feeling down my spine. She was amazing. Thank you Natasha.

I wish you all the very best with this book and I just know that having come this far, you really can do it, and make the changes or updates that you want to make or develop in the way you want to or achieve the success that you know you are capable of and do deserve.

3

What are Hypnosis and Self-Hypnosis?

*Examine for a moment an ordinary mind on
an ordinary day*

Virginia Woolf

Before you begin experiencing self-hypnosis and start using it to make wonderful, beneficial changes in your life, this chapter is designed to perhaps to answer a few questions you may have and also to dispel a few myths and misconceptions about hypnosis.

You know, I still meet people that come to see me as clients that believe that experiencing hetero-hypnosis is like being unconscious. I always reply, 'What would be the point of that? Spending money and time to be unconscious in someone else's company? If I wanted you to be unconscious we would simply bash you over the head!' So it is important that you also know that hypnosis is not about being unconscious. It is equally important that you have the correct expectations about the hypnotic experiences that you are going to have.

In order to understand hypnosis, it is important to understand and differentiate two levels of mind. For the purpose of easy understanding, I am going to continue referring to the mind as two distinctly different things; the conscious and unconscious mind. By that I am referring to our conscious mind, where we are now, and just below that level of awareness is our unconscious mind (also known as and often referred to as the subconscious mind).

The conscious mind is where we usually spend most of our waking time, you know that internal dialogue we have that thinks 'hmmm, what shoes shall I wear today' well, that is your conscious mind. Your conscious mind basically does four things;

Firstly, your conscious mind analyses. What is that? Well that is the part of us that looks at problems, analyses them and tries to create solutions to those problems. It is that part of us that makes decisions all day every day 'shall I open the door?', 'shall I have something to eat', even though they are automatic behaviours, we make a conscious decision about whether or not to do these things.

The second part of our conscious mind is our rationale, the part of us that, especially in western cultures, always has to know 'why' things happen and 'why' we behave in particular ways. This can cause us many additional difficulties as we give any problems that may exist more and more credence and power. More conventional and traditional methods of counseling or psychotherapyEare oftenEvery much concerned with looking at causes of our problems and it is my opinion that all this does is teaches us 'why' they happen as opposed to giving us the skills required to changing unwanted habits and behaviours. The more we think about 'why' we do things the more we seem to embed the unwanted behaviour into our psyches! Though there are times when we need to reflect, it is not always neccesary to do so.

The third part of our conscious mind is will power; that teeth-gritted determination that so many of us are proud to demonstrate. How many times have we used our will power alone to make changes and found that our will power weakens and that change is temporary or non-existent?

Think for a moment, if you were suddenly overcome with ecological fervour and decided you wanted to save the planet and one of the ways you were going to do this was to stop driving your car and cycle everywhere or use public transport. In fact, you felt so strongly about this, that you wanted to forget the entire process of driving. So you sit down and tell yourself over and over again that you have forgotten how to drive. I suspect that even if you told yourself this over and over, it is unlikely that you would actually forget, you see that will power does not always get to the part of us that believes. We shall be coming on to this in more detail.

If a relative was to call you on the telephone and say 'Oh, guess what, your cousin is pregnant . . .' It is highly likely that you would choose to believe it. You are allowing that thought to alter your beliefs; there is no reason to not believe it, is there? That relative has altered your belief. Now, compare that to if you came to see me in my capacity as therapeutic consultant, hypothetically, to stop smoking and all I did was take five minutes to say to you 'You really should stop smoking, it is very bad for. All done; that will be £200.00 please.' I doubt you would allow those words to go into the same part of you as the relative's words telling you about your cousin being pregnant. One of our main aims with using self-hypnosis is to access that part of ourselves where we hold our beliefs and begin to install new and powerful modes of how and what we believe.

The final part of our conscious mind is your short-term memory. By that I am referring to the things that you need to remember to function on a day-to-day basis, so that when your phone rings you know how to answer it rather than stare at it wondering what it is, or ensuring that you cross the road without being run over for example.

That is the conscious part of your mind, it is logical, rational and analytical, a bit like Mr Spock from the Start Trek series and as much as it pains me to say it, our conscious mind is frequently wrong about things.

Your conscious mind is wherever you happen to be pointing it at any given time. It is where your attention is. I am sure you have been in a busy, noisy environment, such as a restaurant or a bar and have been engaged in a conversation with another individual, and all the sounds going on around you just seem to blend into the background. Then, someone else ten metres away can punctuate their sentence with your name and you pick it out as if it was being spoken to you. This illustrates that unconsciously, you are aware of many, many pieces of information every second of your life; sounds, colours, thoughts etc, yet your conscious mind allows you to focus upon what is pertinent or relevant to you at that moment and exclude the other things from your immediate focus.

If you take that conscious awareness and point it inside of yourself instead of outside into the world, you begin to become aware of your inner self, your unconscious self, which is the part of you that we work with in hypnosis and the part of you that you are going to become more and more acquainted with as we progress through this book.

Your unconscious mind is tremendously powerful and automates as much behaviour as it possibly can so that we do not have to think about it. For example, there was a time in your life when you had to be shown how to tie your shoelaces, and you concentrated on doing this. I suspect that by this stage in your life, as of today, you know how tie your shoelaces very well and you don't even think about doing it; you just do it automatically. I have a lonely Auntie who as a boy, my mother would ask me to phone on a weekly basis as she thought this would make her happy and I vividly remember hearing her lighting up a cigarette and heavily exhaling the smoke while on the phone, she didn't even think about what she was doing, she just associated smoking with being on the phone. It happened on auto-pilot.

We are amazing learning machines and we learn behaviours and habits and then our unconscious mind automates them and does them on auto pilot so that we do not have to think about doing them.

Your unconscious mind has within it all your long-term memory. Just about every blade of grass that you have seen in your entire lifetime is stored away in your long-term memory that serves as an amazing storage centre. These memories affect us in varying ways, some more than others. Sometimes our ability to remember them is not as fluid as we need, as it is often not necessary to have all our memory in the forefront of our minds. For example, right now you are unlikely to be thinking about everything that happened to you on your last birthday; however, me just mentioning it, you can dig into your unconscious, long-term memory and remember or at least get snippets of what it was that you did.

Profound or highly emotional events like weddings or the birth of a child will stand out in your life more than what you had for dinner 9 years ago. Unless of course it was a truly magnificent lobster thermidor! Or maybe just a divine plate of beans on toast. However, you will know whether you have had that lobster thermidor or not. What's more, you pretty much always know and remember whether you like certain foods or not even if you have only had them once and that one time was a long time ago.

Another example is if you have ever seen a live stand up comedy show. You watch the comedian and laugh (or not as the case may be!) heartily as you listen to lots and lots of jokes. Then when you leave the venue, you can remember none of them, or one or two at best! Then, a week later, a friend that you were with can say to you 'do you remember such and such a joke from last weeks comedian' and you think 'oh yeah!' as you bring that information out from your long-term memory. You know that you know the joke, it was just not at the forefront of your conscious mind, and it was tucked away in the deeper unconscious.

Your unconscious mind knows more about you than you consciously know that you know. Sound confusing? Well, just think; as you are reading these words, you are breathing, your heart is beating (I do hope!) you are digesting, your body is regulating it's temperature, it is doing a vast range of wonderful things without you having to consciously think about it. You are not sat around thinking 'I really must remember to breathe.' We are not machines; there is an intelligence within us that knows how to do these things, and it is that intelligence that we tap into with self-hypnosis.

Your unconscious mind is where you get your gut feelings, your instincts and intuition that communicate with you sporadically from time to time. Like when sometimes, someone can be saying all the right words to you, but you get a different feeling about them.

I worked with a lady a while ago. All the time she was sat opposite me, really still, except for the action of playing and fiddling with her wedding ring. She was sliding it up and down her finger and every now and then she took it off and tapped her leg with it. While doing this, she was telling me how happily married she was. My instinct, my intuition, my gut feeling told me something else. She was behaving one way and talking another, there was incongruence. Upon further discussion, it became apparent that she was not happily married. My gut feeling told me something over and beyond that which I was hearing in the open.

It is like when I used to have to go and see my bank manager a lot in the initial days of my first business being set up. He told me all the right words; he told me everything that I needed to hear. However, there was something about him that made me want to give him a sideways, slanted look and treat him with suspicion. That was my instincts, my gut feeling. That is your unconscious mind communicating with you as it sporadically does.

Your unconscious mind is a bit like a computer, it is a magnificent biogenetic computer. Throughout your entire lifetime it has been programmed with all your experiences, relationships, interpretations of the world, influences and all this has culminated in your computer functioning with that programming. Self-hypnosis is simply a way of accessing that computer and updating that programming so that it becomes instinctive and intuitive for you to make the changes that please you.

Your unconscious mind is the seat of your emotions and where your behaviours exist and it is the part of you that we work with in self-hypnosis. Hypnosis is a way of us stepping over your conscious mind and accessing the unconscious mind to make powerful and profound changes.

Now, I am sure that you have experienced natural trance states many times before, in fact I know it. For example, when you have been driving in a car and thought to yourself 'ooh, how did I get here?' I remember driving to Oxford one time and I had to drive through Newbury, I recall seeing a signpost that stated 'Oxford 5 Miles' and I thought to myself 'What happened to Newbury?' I had driven through it without really realising that I had done so.

It is like when you have been reading a book and you've turned the page and thought 'I have no idea what I have just read, I am going to have to read it all again.' I can remember being at school watching my history teacher teach me, yet my mind was a million miles away wishing I was doing something else. These examples are all common experiences; they are daydream-like states that we all experience, many times a day. The only difference between these naturally occurring states and those that we use in self-hypnosis is that with the hypnosis, you **intend** to enter the state, you are in control of it and it is just like a slightly amplified, deeper version of the state. That is it. Sometimes it is simply like sitting in a chair with your eyes closed, not the magical, mystical or unusual experience that some people are led to believe it is.

It is important here to know that with self-hypnosis or especially hetero-hypnosis (whereby one person facilitates another going into hypnosis), you cannot be made to do anything that you don't want to do. This is very important. I had a guy that a doctor referred to me, came to see me and said to me 'my doctor told me come and see you as I have emphysema and am going to die of it unless I stop smoking'. I said to him; 'well I presume you want to stop,' he said 'oh, no, I love smoking; it is one of my last few remaining pleasures.' I had to send him away as I cannot make him do something that he does not want to. Can you imagine if I could do that? Wow. I could go and see my bank manager and make him give me million pounds without returning it! You never read about 'baddy hypnotists' making people rob banks or anything else absurd; because it cannot be done.

A young lady had booked an appointment to see me to free herself of her phobia. She had had claustrophobia for 20 years and I think it took us 20 minutes of working together to free her of it, she still emails every now and then to tell me how well things still are for her. When she arrived for that appointment, she followed in her boyfriend who was accompanying her. As soon as he walked in he said; 'I don't believe in all this hypnosis nonsense . . .' And mumbled some more under his breath. 'Well . . .' I said, 'good job I am not working with you then. You sit down here in the waiting area and I shall go and work with your girlfriend.' 'Oh, no' he replied, 'I am coming in with you both.' I was rather puzzled by this and asked 'Well, what do you want to come in for?' and so he told me; 'You might make her do things she doesn't want to do. or make her pay more money than she's supposed too.'

I smirked mischievously and added; 'When you came in here, you told me this was all nonsense and you did not believe in it. Now you are telling me that you believe I can make your girlfriend do things she does not want to do and make her pay me more money! If you believe that, surely you must realise that I would be able to do the same to you too . . .' I explained some more; I explained that if I was that kind of a person and if I really could do such a thing then I would choose someone like Richard Branson or Donald Trump to hand over the contents of their bank account rather than them, and he was fine eventually. His girlfriend still jokes with me about it.

People usually then say to me 'OK Adam, I hear and understand what you are saying and it all makes sense'. 'However, I have seen stage hypnosis and seen people dancing like chickens, are you telling me that they want to do that?' I am saying that these people are not being made to do things that they don't want to do.

When someone buys tickets to a stage hypnosis show, they are already being permissive to the notion that they are going to see hypnosis for entertainment; they expect certain things to happen, they are expecting entertainment. Secondly, when the stage hypnotist asks the audience 'who wants to come on stage' the people that agree to do so or put their hands up are saying 'yes, I **want** to be hypnotised', they are not being made to do anything they don't want to do.

There are not big, burly men with cattle prods forcing people up on stage! The stage hypnotist ensures that the individuals on the show are receptive and follow a large number of compliance exercises and it begins to create the illusion that these people are doing things that they don't want to do, when they are not. The hypnosis can help to step over the inhibitions of the conscious mind to a certain extent, so that the individuals behave with more openness, they just cannot be made to do things they don't want to do.

Often a stage hypnotist may suggest a certain technique to assess the individuals for compliance and suitability. It does not mean that the people not responding to that technique cannot be hypnotised, it simply means that they are less responsive to that method. That is all. If someone were going to take me into hypnosis and started asking me to imagine being sat on a pink fluffy cloud, I would start to think 'what? Are you going to bore me into hypnosis?' I am just not a pink fluffy cloud kind of person. However, the people that come along to my centre for the guided visualisation meditation evenings run here love all that kind of stuff. It does not mean that they can be hypnotised better than me, just that they respond to certain things better than me. With self-hypnosis, you get to choose what you respond to. You can do whatever you want in your own mind.

Anyone can be hypnotised. I work with a very wide range of people for all manner of issues; insomniacs, heroin addicts, schizophrenics, people experiencing chemotherapy, and many more; these are often people that are convinced that they cannot relax or cannot be hypnotised, and as long as they want to, they all can and they all do.

All that is required is that you have an open mind, that you expect it to work and have progressive, motivated thoughts about the processes, you follow the structure (initially) and allow yourself to help you to help yourself to make the changes you want and deserve.

I am sure that during self-hypnosis sessions there will be times when you'll be thinking 'hmmm . . . am I in hypnosis, what am I supposed to be thinking or feeling.' That is your conscious mind thinking that thought and interfering; we are going to be discussing this is more depth later in the book. There will be times in the self-hypnosis practice sessions or your early practice when IEask you toEimagine things. Imagining things does not have to mean visualising. If I ask you to think of a favourite place, you can imagine what it would be like, you don't have to be seeing a picture perfect cinema version of it in your mind.E You can imagine, sense, think, or just know it without seeing it or picturing it in every detail. If I asked you to imagine the sound your feet make when you walk across gravel, you know the sound I am talking about and you can imagine it, but you are not necessarily hearing it in your ears, you can imagine it. That is all you need to do.

I am going to touch lightly on an idea now for you to remember – the unconscious mind often does not know the difference between imagination and reality. More on this later. So, hypnosis is not like being unconscious, it is almost like having heightened awareness, it requires you to want the change, have an open, positive mind, as best as you can, and allow whatever happens to happen, without trying to grasp at what you think **should** happen, just letting it happen and letting it happen with focus and intent.

Hypnosis is just an altered state, just like excitement, nervousness or confusion are all altered states.

4

Natural and Intended Trance States

I am light with meditation, religiose
And mystic with a day of solitude

Douglas Dunn

As you are going to be learning, self-hypnosis is the communication between two levels of mind; conscious and unconscious. The conscious mind, as you have already been reading, is the questioning, analytical, intellectual part of the mind. The unconscious is the emotional and autonomic part.There are 2 types of hypnotic communication that we distinguish between in order to have a fluent understanding and use of self-hypnosis; natural hypnosis and intended hypnosis.

Natural hypnosis

Natural hypnosis is natural communication – it happens all the time you are awake to some degree or another. It is like the examples I have already mentioned when you are driving in a car, reading a book, sat in a boring classroom (or an exciting one) or simply when you are daydreaming.

With naturally occurring hypnotic phenomenon, you are usually not aware of the communication that is going on. I can remember attending a business networking function in Bournemouth once, it was a very early breakfat meeting and I was half asleep and also rather bored. I had been cornered by a couple of local businessmen and I can recall a moment when they were both loking at me expectantly; they were awaiting my reply from a question one of them had asked and I was blissfully unaware of! 'I'm sorry, could you repeat that . . .' I felt very embarassed and rude. This is a

22

naturally occurring hypnotic state, much the same as when you are 'tranced out' in front of the television, not focussed in a business meeting or at a restaurant. I find that many of the activities I do tend to send me off somewhat; when I am running especially.

The quality of naturally occuring hypnosis varies. Everyone experiences natural, hypnotic trance states many times a day, we often are not aware of them or just do not label them as a hypnotic trance state. Many hypnotherapists would state that the best hypnotic communication and experience of hypnosis is when we are relaxed and the conscious mind is less active, exactly like when we are daydreaming for example. However, it is not absolutely essential to be in a deep relaxed state to benefit from self-hypnosis, it can make it more pleasant and enjoyable though. We shall explore this is more detail later.

There is also a powerful communication between the two levels of mind when we experience intense emotion. Like if someone ran into the room and started shouting 'Fire! Fire!' you'd feel panic or some other intense emotion demonstrating a lot of communication going on with you, your state would be altered.

Here are some examples of Natural trance states;

Driving, Going to sleep, Waking from sleep, Cooking, Relaxing, Laughing, Crying, Panic, Exercise, Fishing, Making love, Learning, Listening, Talking, Watching TV, Listening to music, Reading, Dreaming, Playing an instrument, Swimming, Walking, Talking on the phone, Eating in a restaurant, Sitting in the bath.

Please take a piece of paper and a pen and make a note of at least 10 times that you have experienced naturally occuring hypnotic, trance-like phenomena.

Believe me when I say that you have literally millions of examples to choose from in your life, you just have not called them that before.

Intended hypnosis

When hypnosis is used therapeutically or by ourselves for self-hypnosis, it is intended, we are doing it on purpose instead of drifting into it without our knowing.

Intended Hypnosis is simply natural hypnosis with awareness. So, the great thing is, you now know that you have experienced hypnosis many times before (at least on the 10 occasions you have written down) and now all you need to do is learn how to use it with awareness.

The reason that Intended Hypnosis is the best quality of hypnotic communication is simply because you use it with awareness, control, safety, intention and depth. All hypnosis is natural, there is nothing unusual about it, it happens to all of us all the time, and it has just developed some rather unusual connotations over time. Hypnosis is an experience common to all human beings, we all know how to do it and have experienced it before, we just did not think of that experience as hypnosis.

OK, here is the next exercise for you to do. Underneath your previous list, now write a list of things that you or anyone does that has no level of hypnosis or trance involved in it at all. Make sure you do this before reading on.

On your list, you may have many things or you may have a few. The point I want to impress on you now is that there can be only one thing on your list. Here is an important point to remember: **the only time we are definitely not in hypnosis at some level is when we are in undisturbed, natural, non-dreaming sleep.** Hypnosis is simply communication between the minds and that is always happening, even when we are in dreaming sleep. Get this idea firmly lodged into you mind; hypnosis is not some strange, unusual state that renders you 'zombie-like.' You are experiencing some kind of communication within you, even when you are concentrating hard on something or doing something very active.

That's right, non-dreaming sleep is the only time that there is no communication going on between your conscious and unconscious parts of your mind. Hypnosis is the communication between two levels of mind, which occurs anytime that we are awake (or in dreaming sleep). Intended hypnosis then, is entering this state with intention, awareness and control.

Intended hypnosis diminishes the conscious, analytical, intellectual part of the mind in order to improve communication with the unconscious, emotional, creative part of the mind that we have learned about previously. Intended hypnosis utilises that part of the mind responsible for deeper levels of change. Intended hypnosis works when your unconscious mind is totally convinced (rather than your conscious mind), and so works when willpower and determination cannot, this is the reason that we need to learn about how to go about the process of entering this state , controlling it and using the most beneficial forms of communication to allow the changes we want to take place.

Remember: **The only time you are not in hypnosis of some kind is when you are in non-dreaming sleep.** There is always communication of some kind happening within you.

5

Further Understanding the Conscious and Unconscious Minds

On Earth there is nothing great but man; in man there is nothing great but mind

William Hamilton

Ever since reading *The Power of Your Subconscious Mind* by Joseph Murphy as a younger man, I have always loved the idea of imagining my mind as a garden and that I am the one responsible for its upkeep. We plant seeds of thought and belief in our garden, sometimes without even knowing we are doing it, as you add the elements as well with your internal environment, those seeds develop.

Imagine that your unconscious mind is richly fertile land and the thoughts and belief that you sow will grow regardless of whether they are good or bad. So this book is about learning how to sow the right seeds for you to experience life with happiness, goodwill, prosperity, health and well-being.

I am sure that you have experienced an occasion when you listened to a song on the radio and you could not remember the artist, then a couple of days later you were lying in bed and '**Shazam!**' you remember, it just appears out of nowhere. Your unconscious mind will continue working on the instructions you feed it, so best to feed it well and sow powerfully progressive seeds.

Maybe you have trees in your garden, a marvellous sight to behold is a leaf spiralling from a tree, amazing how that tree knows how to let go of what it no longer needs. In that garden, flowers often grow, you know that watching flowers grow can be a bit like noticing progressive change happening in your life, if you sit and watch too closely, you don't notice much happening at first. But as you get on with your life and sow the right seeds, those flowers bloom more beautifully than you may have imagined.

Up in those trees, birds may sing. I love the song of a bird. I wonder, how hard do you think that bird has to think about what note to sing? Of course, it doesn't, it just does it. That bird already knows more than it knows that it knows. Now how much more creative and resourceful are you than that bird? More than you realise, exponentially more, so how much more do you know than you know that you know? Confused? Well, maybe it is time to sing your own song, fill your garden with beautiful sounds without thinking about what note to sing.

Within the structure of self-hypnosis, in this book, you will see that your conscious mind becomes the director of your self-hypnosis, the director of your unconscious; it directs and sends orders to the unconscious. Your unconscious will follow those orders and directions.

We are going to focus on the language of self-hypnosis later in the book in more detail, however think about how you define yourself linguistically or with your conscious thoughts. I run seminars on confidence building and very often I get someone in the audience that says boldly to me 'I am just not one of those confident kind of people.' That is some statement. That statement is sent off into the depths of the marvellous data processing system and becomes reality. The more it is said or thought, the more it resonates with the unconscious and becomes an order, almost like you are giving yourself a directive.

Statements of 'I am this . . .' or 'I do this . . .' whether they are spoken out loud or thought to yourself, exclude the opportunity to be anything else when persistently sending the message to the unconscious. If you say you can't do something, you are perfectly right. When you say or think you can't do something you end up shutting down the opportunity for your unconscious to do anything else. Remember; whatever you believe to be the truth is the truth for you.

If a regular member of the public (does such a thing exist?) steps out of the shower in the morning and sees them self in the mirror, I am not talking about someone who berates or criticises themselves, they see them self and think 'Ooh, I am overweight

27

. . .' Now that person is telling himself or herself every morning that they are overweight and they learn to believe it and that way of communicating in their own mind becomes belief and continues to happen regardless of what fancy diet they are subscribing to at that time. It is the same with someone who smokes; when they light up during a smoking break at work, take a drag on their cigarette and utter to themselves 'Aah, I needed that . . .' They are telling themselves that they **needed** that. That is a powerful message to consistently be sending to your unconscious mind. This is self-hypnosis occurring without thought; you are sowing seeds with your thoughts, feelings and beliefs.

This is fundamental to understanding your unconscious mind; if you think good, good will happen, if you think bad, bad will happen. It is not always as black and white as that, but get that notion into your head as we progress on to more complex things. Once your unconscious mind accepts an idea, it begins to execute it. It executes whether it is a positive or a negative idea.

Despite treating the conscious and unconscious mind as two separate entities, for the ease of understanding here in this book, please note that they are simply two spheres of your mind and so are very much part of each other.

On the self-hypnosis seminars that I run, when I take someone into hypnosis as an example for the others to observe, I often ask the class afterwards to tell me what they think I was doing when I took that person into hypnosis. Here are some of the replies that I get:

You changed your voice . . .
You asked them to focus on their breathing . . .
You stared at them in a funny way . . .
You made them focus on one particular thing . . .

Now, all of the above could possibly have been true. However, I always then ask them the question:

What makes you think I was doing anything at all? What if I was not doing anything? Have you considered that? Maybe, I was doing very little . . .

Have a think about that for a moment. It is a belief of many in these and related fields that all hypnosis is self-hypnosis. The idea here is that the individual actually takes them self into the state of hypnosis, it is simply **facilitated** by the hypnotist. When I was born, I was not born with a magical gift that I could wield at anyone and render them into a state of hypnosis at will; you are the ones that take yourself into hypnosis, the hypnotist facilitates you taking yourself into that state. With this book, we are taking away the hypnotist from the equation and you become your own hypnotist. You are always in control; it is your hypnosis. This notion may well seem contrary to your previous understanding or belief; however, I am hoping that this section of the book has now given you a better understanding. That mysterious aura about hypnosis is not really deserved; it is natural, usual, you experience it all the time, we are learning how to use it with intention for ourselves.

6

Glossary of Terms

Books usually have the Glossary of Terms at the rear of the book, however I just wanted to confirm the words that I will be using throughout the course of this book and thought it better to let you have those now. Here are some of the words and phrases you will be getting used to during the course of reading this book and what I mean by them in the context of this book;

Conscious: The analytical, rational, intellectual part of the mind.

Deepener: Words and ideas that give an impression of drifting deeper into the state of hypnosis.

Emerging from Hypnosis: The process of exiting the hypnotic state. Please begin to start using the term **emerge** rather than **awaken**. **Awaken** implies that you have been asleep and we are not learning about how to sleep here. Many in the field of hypnosis refer to hypnotic sleep, I think this is confusing for understanding self-hypnosis, so shall not be referring to hypnosis as sleep in any shape or form as they are different things.

Hypnosis: This phenomenon of a heightened state of awareness, increased openness to accept suggestions, similar to day-dreaming and can be induced in many ways. A state of focused concentration.

Hypnotherapist: Someone who utilises hypnosis for therapeutic purposes.

Hynotherapy: Utilising the state of hypnosis for therapeutic purposes.

Imagery: The natural way of using memory or past experience or our minds natural creative ability to create or recreate pictures in our mind's eye.

Induction: The process of going into hypnosis using a script.

Intended Hypnosis: Intended, controlled natural hypnosis.

Metaphor: Language or imagined representation that uses one thing to represent another. 'I am as calm as a still pond.'

Natural Hypnosis: Moments of deep communication between the conscious and subconscious. Trance states that occur in your day-to-day life.

Neuro-linguistic Programming (NLP): The study of excellence and the interrelationship between our communication with ourselves and others, learning abilities and responding to our own environment.

Post-Hypnotic Suggestion: An instruction given to your unconscious mind during hypnosis, which works outside of hypnosis, when you are no longer in that formal trance.

Programme: A series of suggestions formulated and strung together. We shall be learning about how to create powerful programmes.

Repetitive Loop: A method of writing hypnotic suggestions to make them more powerful by looping. We discuss this further later on.

Suggestion: An instruction you give your unconscious mind.

Taking Control: Taking control of the hypnotic session. E.g. 'I am in deep hypnosis and in complete control, giving hypnotic authority only to my intended suggestions, I am fully protected from random thought, sound and image having any hypnotic effect.' This will make more sense as we progress.

Trance: Used to describe the state of hypnosis. In the context of this book, it simply is another word for self-hypnosis or hypnosis.

Trigger: Something that activates a post-hypnotic suggestion.

Unconscious: The emotional, autonomic, irrational part of the mind. Also often referred to as the subconscious.

Zap!: Self-Hypnosis!

There was a young girl who attended a self-hypnosis course with her mother and used her imagination and combined it with self-hypnosis to 'Zap' away her persistent headaches with an imaginary space tool. The term 'Zap' kind of caught on and was used by my teacher and I always use it too. If I refer to 'zapping' something, then I mean to apply self-hypnosis to it. You'd be amazed how many times I have 'zapped' away problems.

7

Getting Settled and Prepared

Damn braces: Bless relaxes
William Blake

Prior to your session of hypnosis, there are some considerations to bear in mind. So before we get on to actually going into the state of self-hypnosis, we just want to think about the time immediately prior to that session.

Self-hypnosis can and should be done anywhere. I have used it outside offices before job interviews, on busy trains, before presentations, during football matches and many, many other situations that you might not have thought conducive to the hypnotic process. I am sure that you have read a book in an airport, on a plane, on a train or with other people around you and you managed to block out all other sounds and distractions and tune in to your book. I used to have a clinic in Harley Street, London, which is supposed to be prestigious; it is really busy and my office overlooked the street with constant road works and courier motorcycles travelling up and down it, it was very noisy. However, it would not distract my clients if they were guided into hypnosis in a way in which they were able to filter out other sounds.

For some sessions however, most people find themselves a comfortable quiet place for their self-hypnosis sessions. I would recommend this especially with your initial sessions. It may be impossible to guarantee that you won't be disturbed, so do your best to find somewhere to be free of distractions. I even unplug the phone when I want a really nice, deep and peaceful self-hypnosis session, especially if I am using that session for a life change rather than an on the spot state change. We are going to be learning

33

about instant hypnosis later in this book for when you need something speedy; if you bang your finger in the door and you want to stop the pain, you don't really want to have to find a quiet room and lie down for a while before you can get on to stopping it hurting.

Once you are better and more comfortable entering hypnotic trance states, you can progress to using it in a wide variety of places regardless of distractions.

Again, in the initial sessions, I recommend having your hypnosis sessions indoors and more private. Those wonderful outdoor sessions in the sunshine will come later. I would also recommend subdued lighting, though again, this is not essential, it does lend itself to the process until you become more and more acquainted with the state of self-hypnosis. The most important thing at this early, embryonic stage is that you feel comfortable and safe and are unlikely to be interrupted. This process, simply by its very nature is already showing you that you are important to you by scheduling some time to do this.

I mentioned already that practice is going to be what leads you to excellence with self-hypnosis; the amount of time as well as the quality of that time that you invest in your self-hypnosis is important. As you will learn, there are a lot of things to do outside of trance to enhance your self-hypnosis results. However, the periods of time that you spend in the state of hypnosis will of course vary, there is no real optimum period of time to spend in the state. My average length of time spent in hypnosis is approximately 15–20 minutes each session. Achieving certain objectives may take longer while others are shorter. Ensure that you can keep focused for that length of time. Many objectives may be comprehensively met with one session of hypnosis achieving the desired result. However, I have worked with many people that needed to repeat the session many times over for it to really work its way into their life. Again, be flexible and do what is best for you. Repetition is indeed a successful strategy; the more you enter self-hypnosis, the better you become at entering it. The more you focus on achieving a certain objective, the more those self-hypnosis sessions are likely to yield a successful reaching of that objective.

Prior to any hypnosis session, you want to ensure that you have an open and progressive mind with the right kind of expectation.

Build in success before you start by having an expectation of success; expect it to be successful and you are opening your unconscious mind to the possibility of that happening. If you think you can't do something you are perfectly right and you close down the opportunity to achieve that result.

When entering hypnosis, I have found that people get better results when they are seated comfortably rather than lying down. Your unconscious mind associates lying down with sleeping and you want to gain the most from your sessions. Being asleep in not conducive to making unconscious changes. Your unconscious mind especially associates your bed with sleeping, so it is really best to avoid lying down on your own bed to go into hypnosis, unless you are using your self-hypnosis to get off to sleep.

Ensure that you have your legs and arms uncrossed with your feet, ideally, flat on the floor and your hands by your sides or on your lap ensuring that they are not touching each other (your hands that is). Just ensure you are comfortable.

When you are ready to begin, you then allow your eyes to be comfortably closed. You can of course use self-hypnosis with your eyes open, however, you are more likely to be distracted or disturbed and receive stimulation visually. Your unconscious mind associates having your eyes closed with being relaxed and so you can allow them to be comfortably closed.

Quieting your internal dialogue

In preparation for a self-hypnosis session, you may want to begin quietening your mind. This is not absolutely essential; complete inner silence and peace is something Buddhist Monks take a lifetime to attain. So many people that have been on my self-hypnosis seminars or courses ask me about their internal dialogue and what to do with it. Many people say that their minds start chattering away just when they don't want them to, especially if they have had an active or stressful day. It is also very important to be aware of internal dialogue if it is not being very nice to you.

Internal dialogue is the term for the voice(s) people speak to themselves with. Internal dialogue is often out of consciousness, but as you start to become more aware of it, it becomes much easier to hear it consciously. In some eastern traditions, internal dialogue is referred to as 'the chattering monkey', and years of practice are spent in meditation with the aim of getting the monkey to stop chattering. The reason for this is that they believe that internal dialogue can be a barrier to clear perception and enlightenment.

From a personal development perspective, internal dialogue is often the channel people use to 'berate themselves', reinforce limiting beliefs and generally stop themselves having more fun in their lives, so it's nice to know that you can get more control over it and make it quieter before self-hypnosis begins, then you can use your internal dialogue and conscious mind to take control of the session. Please be assured that even I, with the many years of self-hypnosis experience that I have, still chatter away to myself throughout hypnosis sessions, so any quietening down is good and simply having an awareness of it can be very useful indeed. The really good news is there are ways to show you how you can do this quietening, fast.

Think about this notion for a moment; your mind and body are one system. So, the first technique to switch off internal dialogue is one I learned a few years ago on a training course I attended. I've used it consistently ever since.

Firstly, you stick out your tongue and grasp it gently but firmly between your thumb and your forefinger. Wait a few moments as you continue to breathe. You may well become quiet inside. Simple eh? Though others may think you have gone mad.

This works on the basis that your mind and body are one system. Tiny micro-muscle movements of the tongue and the larynx accompany internal dialogue. When these movements are restricted by your thumb and forefinger, the internal voice stops. Now, I know what you're thinking – it's not very practical to go around with your tongue clasped between your fingers, so there is another method.

Now, if the first exercise works well for you, gently place the tip of your tongue against the roof of your mouth just behind your front teeth (continue to breathe easily.) You will stay quiet.

I use this approach when I'm doing one to one work with people in therapy or coaching for example. It allows me to quieten down on the inside so that I can put all my attention on them and what they are saying and doing. It also allows me to really watch and listen, because I'm not inside my head having conversations with myself abou't what I think is going on.

When I catch myself talking to myself when I should be in watch and listen' mode, the mode you should be in when you begin to enter self-hypnosis too (watch and listen to yourself) I simply do the next exercise.

With a soft, gentle and patient tone, go inside and use your internal voice to say to yourself 'Shhhhhhh, shhhhhhh', like you would if you were soothing a little baby. Allow yourself to smile on the inside, or at least imagine that you have a smile on your face and really feel a sense of patience with the monkey. It may take up to a minute before you go quieter inside. Remember, you do not have to completely silence yourself, just settle yourself down on the inside.

The next approach is one of the first interventions I ever learned, and is incredibly simple. Go inside your mind and imagine that you have the volume control for internal dialogue (usually either a dial or a slider.) If you can't find one, just imagine one – it will work just as well for our purposes. Now turn the volume control up and hear or imagine the dialogue get louder. Then, of course, turn it down and hear it get quieter. Then turn it all the way off. Nice and quiet. Zip.

The final approach is one I learned from Richard Bandler, the co-creator of Neuro-Linguistic Programming. I only tend to use it when I'm trying to pay attention on the outside but some nagging thought keeps drawing my attention inside. It goes a bit like this; in a firm but loving tone of voice, say '**Shut the **** up!**' inside your head. Repeat as necessary. It is funny how many that I have worked with in my time that tell me how they tell themselves to be quiet in this manner.

No one approach works for everybody, but each of these approaches will work for some people. Practice when you are relatively relaxed and have some time, and you will find the ones that work best for you. As you begin to get into the habit of using them systematically and consistently, you will really start to reap the benefits and be priming yourself for you self-hypnosis even better.

Your breathing

Now, because we spend our entire lifetimes breathing, many people take it for granted and we all just assume that we are doing it correctly. There are of course many ways of breathing and different types of breathing. Hard and fast breathing forces us to inhale deeply and quickly so that we can rapidly restore consumed oxygen and expel carbon dioxide; the waste product of our exertions. This kind of breathing is mostly noted when we exercise or partake in rigorous exercise. There is another kind of deep breathing and that is the deep breathing of relaxation, which is slower and occurs when we rest or are not partaking in physical exertion.

Your usual, every day breathing rate is likely to be shallow and rapid as with most people. It usually involves the chest expanding and moving outwards, however, the chest and ribs do not really have a vast amount of capacity to stretch and expand.

As a pre-cursor to self-hypnosis and as part of any healthy routine, deep breathing originating from the diaphragm region is healthier and comes right from the abdomen. A good way to get used to this is to push your tummy outward when you inhale and imagine that you are breathing from that area just beneath your belly button. This area is known as the *Hara* in many eastern health practices. Below your lungs is a large and wide membrane called your diaphragm. As you allow your abdominal muscles to pull the membrane downwards, your lungs draw in more air to fill that space.

I can remember being at school during sports practice and being told my physical education teacher to thrown my shoulders back and breath deeply from the chest and keeping my stomach flat, military style. This was not good advice. It may look good, however it limits your breathing capacity. Practice slow, deep breaths from your lower tummy area, push your tummy out when you inhale, regardless of how it looks and notice the difference in your breathing.

Renowned cardiologist Dr Herbert Benson (1976) coined the term **'relaxation response'** for the response that our body has to this deeper breathing as the deeper breathing triggered a series of reactions in the body to stimulate the body's parasympathetic nervous system and instigate relaxation. This is the opposite to that well-documented 'flight or fight response' which is that rush of nerves and adrenalin when our body prepares to fight or flight in response to anger, stress, anxiety or fright.

When you consciously reproduce one part of the relaxation response, by breathing deeply from the tummy, the body notices and responds with more additional agreeable, relaxing physiological changes such as slower heart rate and increased blood flow to all parts of the body. This is a wonderful state to be in and to begin to instigate when entering self-hypnosis and can contribute to it being a better overall experience.

Sounds simple doesn't it? Asking you to breathe properly. Breathing; we all have to do it. Just how aware are we of our breathing and the effect it has on how we live our life? Even when not used a precursor to self-hypnosis.

> When you breathe, you inspire. When you do not breathe, you expire.
>
> Is a quote from an 11-year-old's science exam

John Grinder, co-creator of Neuro-Linguistic Programming talks about the link between respiration, physiology, internal state and high performance. He calls this 'the chain of excellence'. I once read a book by Osho, the wonderfully non-PC mystic and guru. In the book, Osho instructed the reader to pay attention to their breathing rate when they were happy, and notice the timing of the in-breath and out-breath. He explained that next time they were sad, they could re-induce the happy state by merely repeating the breathing pattern.

So, to get into the idea of understanding your breathing and how it affects you and your life, physiology and your psychological state. Here are several exercises for you to heighten your awareness of your breathing and subsequently enhance your ability to get into a state that optimises your experience of self-hypnosis.

Firstly, when you are experiencing a powerful, positive state in your life, this can be anything or anytime when you are positive and happy, then allow yourself to become aware of your breathing rate. Pay particular attention to the timing and rhythm of your in-breath and out-breath.

Second of all, next time you are in a neutral or negative state, start breathing at the rate and rhythm from the first part of this exercise, and usually, within a minute or so, the positive state should begin to return.

Many gurus advise people to do breathing exercises regularly. I know Tony Robbins does in his marvellous book *Unlimited Power* he advises that you start each day with a breathing exercise of inhaling slowly and deeply, then holding it for twice as long as the inhalation and exhaling in a controlled manner in twice the time as the inhalation. It really is invigorating and a great way to get motivated at the start of the day, especially if you are looking to do some things with your day that require motivation.

Breathing is powerful, our life force, and is a major factor influencing our state of mind (if you are uncertain about this, hold your breath for two minutes and re-read this sentence). This being the case, please use your common sense when doing any of these exercises (if you have a respiratory condition, please check with your health advisor first.) I do not want any asthmatics complaining that they did themselves harm following the exercises in this book!!

So, thirdly, start breathing comfortably but deeply, in through your nose and out through your mouth. Imagine that you are breathing from that area of your abdomen just beneath your belly button that I mentioned earlier. Make the in-breath last to a count of 5 and the out-breath to a count of 6. Continue for at least 2 minutes, and notice what happens.

This 5:6 ratio seems to be a simple yet powerful way you can induce a relaxed state at will. The art of Yogic breathing is called Pranayama. Pranayama offers many different approaches for cleansing the mind and body through breathing exercises. Next up is one of them that I learned from the work of Robert Anton Wilson.

Here we go, (this may seem a bit odd to do, I'd recommend not doing this in front of friends or at work!); Lie on your back and pant like a dog, breathing shallow breaths rapidly in and out through your mouth 20 times. Then, breathe slowly, deeply and gently in and out 20 times through your nose. Once again, do the mouth-panting 20 times, then resume gentle nose breathing. Notice what happens.

This technique is referred to as the breath of fire, and typically results in a state of. well, you find out!

These techniques can be very powerfully utilised when wanting to get in control of your state if you are going through a period of change such as reducing your weight, stopping smoking or developing more confidence. Tune in to the way that your breathing affects you and begin to use it to settle yourself and create a nice state to proceed into your self-hypnosis session.

Please remember that most people don't breathe nearly enough. Start to breathe more deeply and notice how much better you feel. Have lots of fun with this. Notice how good you can make yourself feel when you breathe differently and how comfortable you can be as you prepare for self-hypnosis.

Engage in the moment

The only way to live is to accept each moment as an unrepeatable miracle, which is exactly what it is – a miracle and unrepeatable.'

Margaret Storm Jameson

In preparation for getting into self-hypnosis, people often comment to me that they spend lots of time thinking about the past or what might happen in the future. These are fine in the correct context. To get yourself into a good state of self-hypnosis, something that can enhance it further is to really engage in that moment. Feedback to yourself what you are experiencing at the moment. It might sound strange; however, see what happens when you tell yourself what it is that you are experiencing. You can just do it in your own head, as you are settling, breathing, beginning to relax, just engage in the moment.

Being engaged in the moment does not have to be exclusive to the time immediately prior to a self-hypnosis session; it can also enhance your business and life experience in general.

I spend lots of time working with individuals, corporations and businesses to get them engaged in the present moment. The centre that I own and run here in Bournemouth on the south coast of England (at the time of writing this book) used to sell a wide range of books and one that I used to stock was a book called *The Power of Now* by a man called Eckhart Tolle. Lots of people that came to classes, workshops and consultations at the centre would often tell me how great it was and give me snippets of information about its content and for a number of years I would occasionally think

'Yeah, I really should read that book' then kept on deciding that I would wait until later (yes, I am fully aware of the irony in this!). Nevertheless, I am already sold on the power of the present moment, for a number of reasons.

Firstly, if you really think about it, only this present moment exists. I think this is by far the most compelling reason to put your attention on the present moment. Yesterday doesn't exist, except as a memory, with all the unreliability we know to be true of memories; when you experienced yesterday, it was **now**. Tomorrow doesn't exist either, except as an imaginary construct; when you experience tomorrow, it will be **now**. And as it's all that exists, it is a good idea to experience it.

A great way to do this is to begin with sitting with your feet flat on the floor, in a comfortable, aligned position (spine straight, hands on your thighs or at your sides, breathing comfortably). With your eyes open or closed, allow yourself to become aware of the different sounds, sights, smells and sensations around you. This is the present moment.

That's right. This is the present moment, and there are a number of good reasons for keeping your awareness in the present as much as possible (in addition to the first reason I gave.) especially with regards to the state you want to be in when you enter self-hypnosis. Again, this is not essential, just something else to enhance your experience of self-hypnosis. What's more, I am just referring to the time immediately prior to and at the beginning of your self-hypnosis session; there may well be times during your hypnosis when you might want to reflect on the past or imagine the future; engaging in the moment as I am explaining it now is for getting into a good, receptive state at the beginning of a session.

Another great reason for encouraging you to engage in the moment more is that there is a whole lot more of it ('it' being 'now') in store for you. If you stop for a moment, you will realise that all the experiences of your life will take place in a present moment. The more comfortable you are with the present moment, the more comfortable you'll be with those future presents.

Also remember that the present is where you are. If in doubt, look at your hands. Your hands only exist in the present moment. Rub your fingers together, feel how it feels to be in this moment.

Because this moment is where your hands (along with the rest of your body) are located.

In addition, the present is the only time you can take action. You can wish you took action yesterday (so many do; they rue the day that . . .), but yesterday no longer exists, so it will remain a wish. You can plan to take action in the future, but when you take the action, it will be in the present moment. The only time you can take action is in this hot second.

Bear in mind that wherever you are heading to, you presumably want to enjoy it when you get there. Get in the habit of enjoying the present now and you are sure to be even better at enjoying the now when you get there.

I took some amazing insight from my running experiences with my younger brother Ben. When we ran and trained together and competed in races, he always enjoyed the race and commented on our surroundings whereas I always had my eye on the finish line. So much can and has been said about enjoying and engaging in the journey rather than always focusing on the future. My running experiences became much more enjoyable when I concentrated more on the experience rather than the end result all the time.

Life and work today seem to operate at a faster and faster pace. People have lots of demands on their time, and need every advantage they can get to be more effective. When 'I do corporate and business consultancy, one of the most common challenges' that people want to deal with is being focused and making progress on important business objectives or life goals.

As I have investigated more and more how people avoid being focused, I have found that, they are often not centred in the present. Instead, they are thinking about what is happening tomorrow, or what happened yesterday, or running through a list of things that they need to do later. As a result, their attention is not in the present.

I used to work in Victoria in Central London and if you have ever been there during the rush hours it is a hectic place. What I find interesting is that you can tell who is engaged in the moment and who is thinking about their day or the next day. Those people whose awareness is within their heads, mulling over their day or dreading what's in store tomorrow are the ones bumping into people or veering off in wrong directions. Whereas those people whose awareness is outside their heads and engaged in their surroundings are those that are balanced, poised and agile, like a panther!

When you bring your attention and your energy into the present moment, you can accomplish things more quickly, solve problems more effectively, and enjoy the process more than you might expect. So, have a go at connecting with the moment more and more in your days and especially during that time immediately prior to your self-hypnosis sessions.

You can even stop just before starting an important task, and take a moment to centre your self and relax. Then, get clear about what you want to accomplish, and then begin. Do this prior to your self-hypnosis session for more clarity about what you want to achieve from that session.

Physically and mentally relaxing

One of the real basic methods of relaxing is that of progressive relaxation and it is a way that most people find easy to follow and easy to do. Now, I do not want to sound like a scratched record here; it is not absolutely essential for you to have to be deeply relaxed straight away, or even deeply relaxed all the time, however, it will help you at the beginning before you become more and more acquainted with the state of self-hypnosis. If you find these basic methods are not for you then you can find some other way of relaxing in a way that is for your best and a way that is congruent with your likes. One of the main reasons for creating a relaxed body at this time is because of the idea that if your body is deeply relaxed, your mind will find it hard to be anxious or focused on what you don't want it focused on and it is easier to remain focused on the main objective of your self-hypnosis session, whatever that might be for you.

So, practice this progressive relaxation method. Firstly, allow yourself to get comfortable sitting or lying in a comfortable position. This process involves you tensing and relaxing your muscles. The action of doing so places your awareness on that particular muscle. As you do this more and more often to aid your 'settling down' process, you'll become better and better at it as your unconscious mind becomes more familiar with what to expect.

To start with, make a fist with one hand and clench the fist really tightly, feel the muscles tensing, take a nice, slow deep breath as you do this, you may even want to consider doing it with your eyes closed. Use your imagination and maybe imagine the tension that is in that clenched fist as a colour or as water or electricity, something that represents the tension well for you.

Once you have held this clenched fist as you inhale slowly and deeply, then relax you hand as you exhale even more slowly. Then imagine the muscle tension changing in colour, or structure in your hand, imagine it dissolving and disappearing or melting away. Notice the difference between the hand when it was clenched and the wonderful relaxation and sensations in your hand when the tension is released. Imagine all the muscles softening in your hand and do the same with the other hand. In the future, you might want to do this with both hands at the same time and work through your body symmetrically.

Now proceed to do this with the muscles in the arm. Really tense them, imagine colours, shapes or whatever you want to imagine the tension, then release, imagine the change, soften the muscle and enjoy the new state that now exists within that muscle. Good feeling, eh?

Proceed on to the toes and legs, tensing the main muscles and then releasing them. Allowing the muscles to develop a floating sensation. Follow with your tummy, chest, back, shrug your shoulders and release, tense your neck and let go and your facial muscles. Really scrunch your face muscles up when you do this, it feels so good when you release and focus on them relaxing.

Run through this entire exercise twice or more and notice how your entire body feels at the end when you allow yourself to just be still.

Another form of progressive relaxation is to partake in a similar action, but without physically tensing the parts of your body. Instead, you can use you imagination and imagine a colour spreading through your body, bit by bit. Really imagine that colour going into every cell as it moves through your body relaxing you. Be sure to use a colour that relaxes you. Or just imagine each muscle softening as you place your awareness upon it and move your awareness through your body.

More feedback

As we did before, feed back to yourself what you are experiencing to heighten the sensations. By that, I mean describe to yourself in your own mind what exactly it is that you are experiencing. This will then become easier to remember and more and more easy to achieve again and again. Notice the areas of your body that relax first and the easiest and recall how they feel and imagine those feelings spreading all over you into every fibre.

To summarise

So, get yourself in a comfortable position, breathe well, engage in the moment, relax yourself and lessen your internal dialogue and you have created a marvellous foundation for yourself to begin to experience self-hypnosis.

Section 2

Language and Structure of Self-Hypnosis

Now you are all ready and waiting with baited breath to start experiencing hypnosis and enjoying the state that I keep referring to. We have some wonderful things to do and learn about before we reach that stage. Before we can begin to get into the state of self-hypnosis, we need to ensure that while we are in the state of self-hypnosis, we know what to do when we are there and we need to know the right kind of language to use when in self-hypnosis and how to be in control of the state of self-hypnosis. It is learning this information and preparing well for self-hypnosis that yields the most magnificent success when you start using self-hypnosis.

1

The Self-Hypnosis Model

First of all I am going to give you a structure, which you can follow that will form the basis of every self-hypnosis session that you have. It is a map to ensure your success in each and every session and it is really easy to follow. I have put this structure in a step-by-step model that I am going to explain. Before I start to explain the model and structure of self-hypnosis, I want you to allow yourself to use your imagination for a moment and follow these rather strange ideas. They may seem strange and irrelevant; I assure you that there is method to my madness.

OK, I would like you to imagine that a few feet away from you is a bright green alligator. Got that? A bright green alligator, just a few feet away from you. Now, whether you can see these things, imagine them, or just sense them, do whatever is right for you. This alligator is unusual in as much as it has three eyes. Yes indeed, it is a three-eyed alligator. It's first eye is signalling it's true intention; it is frowning and leering, as if it is looking at you like you are it's dinner. However it's second eye is completely different, it is safe and welcoming, giving you a look of safety. The alligator's third eye is twitching; it is blinking 1–10 times every 20 seconds. Really get that idea into your mind, this idea of the three-eyed alligator with it's three eyes doing those different things. If you need to, re-read the paragraph until you have that picture in your mind as best as you can.

Beside the alligator is a huge barrel. Like in the old pirate films, it is a big wooden barrel with black cast iron trimmings. On top of the barrel is a plate of chips. I know, I know 'What on earth is he going on about ...' bare with me here, just use your imagination, conjure this up in your mind. There is a plate of chips on top of the barrel. Next to this plate of chips are four bottles of sauce. The first sauce is spicy and hot, the second sauce is mild and cool, the third sauce is indifferent, nothing special about it and the fourth sauce is extremely pungent, I mean it smells strong! Got that? Next to the plate of chips are four sauces; hot, cool, indifferent and pungent.

Now, on the other side of the barrel is a cat. You can imagine whatever kind of cat you like, maybe the first one that pops into your mind right now. This cat is just continually digging away in the ground. Surely, that is the behaviour of a dog!? Nope. This cat is continually digging beside the barrel with the chips and sauce on top, seemingly oblivious that there is a three-eyes alligator on the other side! Suddenly, who should arrive on the scene, but a postman! The postman delivers a gift, a gift that he leaves there beside the barrel, cat and alligator. The gift is an ornate egg. The alligator and the cat both say 'thank you' to the postman, that's right, they can talk too. Inside the ornate egg are five smaller items. The first item is a doll, the second item is a mini-sized room for a doll (like they used to make on kids TV shows out of a cereal packet for your doll or action man to live in) the third item is an ornate ear, the fourth item is a small ornate gift box and the fifth item is an eye.

Really get that into your mind. Create that strange scene in your imagination. Get that entire scene in your mind and please, please do not proceed with reading any more of this book until you have that scene in your mind. Run through the previous paragraphs as often as you need to get a really vivid idea of that in your mind.

Are you sure you have done that? Please stop and go back if you didn't. I am asking for a very specific reason. I am not just being randomly mad, I assure you.

Now then, the following is the model of self-hypnosis and what I mean by that is that it is the structure for you to follow for every self-hypnosis session you have, for now. Later on in the final chapters of this book, I will be showing you how to abandon the structure and really advance your self-hypnosis. However, you need to learn the structure first so that you can abandon it. It is important for you to have this structure so that you can really get used to being in control of your self-hypnosis sessions and not just allowing your conscious mind to keep wandering off all over the place.

So, what you are going to be doing, is finding somewhere comfortable, going through all or any of the settling down procedures that suit you the most and then going through the following structure, following this path to manage your self-hypnosis session. The way to get into hypnotic states is in a following chapter, and the way to formulate and deliver your suggestions to your unconscious when you are in hypnosis is in yet another chapter.

It may seem a little confusing at this stage, however, just begin to get an idea of this structure for applying later.

Overview

Your control of your self-hypnosis resides in your conscious mind. So, you are going to have some triggers that reside in the conscious mind that when you successfully activate them, will notify you that you are entering hypnosis. Then you are going to take control of the state, then deepen your hypnosis and then deliver your programmes or suggestions for change and then exit. That is the basic structure of a self-hypnosis session.

So please remember these two fundamental following points:

• Your access to self-hypnosis resides in the conscious part of the mind.
• Your self-hypnosis can only be accessed by using the 3 triggers. (all explained later)

By that, I mean you go into self-hypnosis by using your conscious mind to activate an internal 'switch' which acts as a trigger for you to alter your state and enter hypnosis. You are going to have three triggers in total that all must be activated for you to enter self-hypnosis.

For any of you reading this that does not know the alphabet, the following model could possibly be confusing. However, if you do know the alphabet it is very easy. You don't even have to know the entire alphabet; you only need to remember A–E. The first five letters of the alphabet are all that you have to remember. Do you think you can remember those first five letters? The five structured steps of the self-hypnosis model are as simple as A–E. Each step of the self-hypnosis model is a letter from A through to E.

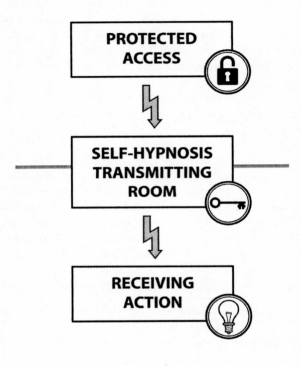

The self-hypnosis model

'**A**' stands for '**Access**'.

That refers to accessing hypnosis. This first step is whereby you enter self-hypnosis. We access self-hypnosis by using these 3 Triggers;

The first trigger is you must: **Be in a safe place**.

Right, firstly you need to be in a safe place. By that I mean that it is not really considered safe to be entering a closed-eye sate of self-hypnosis when at the wheel of a car, or when mowing the lawn, or when teetering on the edge of a cliff top. The same could possibly be said about lying in the bath, so just be aware of that.

The second trigger to enter hypnosis is that you: **Have the intention.**

You are entering hypnosis with awareness and on purpose. This second trigger is that you have the intention to enter self-hypnosis, so you choose to do so and it does not happen by mistake, not like drifting into natural hypnosis states when you day dream or read or do any of these things we mentioned earlier in this book.

The third and final trigger for entering hypnosis is: **Count from 1 towards 10. Entering hypnosis only between the numbers 6 and 10.**

That is then it. The third trigger is that you count from 1–10 entering hypnosis between 6–10 on a number you decide on before hand. You can count in your mind or out loud or imagine watching the numbers.

So, to access the state of hypnosis, you intend to do so, you ensure it is safe to do so and you count from 1–10 entering hypnosis between 6 and 10. Having counted to your chosen number; you are officially in self-hypnosis. I'll show you how you do this later in the book, be patient.

That is how you Access hypnosis; Be safe, have the intention to enter hypnosis and count from 1 through to 10. Those triggers mean that when you run through this properly, by this stage, you are now officially in the state that you refer to as 'self-hypnosis.' You may well not feel any different at this stage in the early sessions, in fact, you are unlikely to. We are just beginning.

'**B**' is for '**Being in control**'.

So, we need to get in control of our mind and of the self-hypnosis session. This is very simply done by saying in our mind with our conscious internal dialogue voice, the following;

I am in deep hypnosis and I am in full control, responding hypnotically only to my intended suggestions. I am fully protected from random thought, random image and random sound becoming hypnotic suggestion.

By doing this, you remind your self that you are in Control, you are in Hypnosis, you give authority to your Intended suggestions or programmes and you are fully protected from random thoughts, sounds and images from influencing. The key areas can be remembered by thinking C-H-I-P. OK? Control, Hypnosis, Intended, Protection.

I am in **control**, I am in **hypnosis**, I give authority to my **intended** suggestions and I am fully **protected** from random thoughts, sounds and images. So, this step '**B**' was for '**Being in control**'.

'**C**' stands for '**Continually Deepening**'.

Having entered hypnosis and taken control of the session, we now want to deepen the state for ourselves. Depth really is a misnomer and of course only exists within our minds; this is a discussion for another time and another book. Think of ways, and be as creative as you can, to deepen your state of hypnosis. Use a method that focuses your attention and gathers your attention in a relaxing way. Use something of interest to you. There are lots of examples coming up in the book.

One of my favourite and most inspiring books is *Jonathon Livingstone Seagull* by Richard Bach. I love that book and always loved the idea of being a seagull perfecting the art of flying, gliding a few feet above the waters surface and then rising up and diving down at speed. You might use some of the following methods of deepening your hypnosis experience:

- Imagine walking deep into a forest.
- Imagine climbing a mountain.
- Imagine being by the sea or even imagine diving in it.
- Going down Stairs or travelling down an Escalator or going down in an Elevator
- Counting down from 100 and letting every number down take you deeper into hypnosis.
- You may want to give yourself a deepening suggestion like 'every time I say the word NOW to myself I drift to deeper levels.'
- Take yourself on an outer space journey.
- Imagine and remember a time when you were really relaxed.
- Remember a favourite place, what does it look like, sound like, and feel like to be there?
- Imagine that you are candle that is melting and your muscles are melting too.

You get the idea. Some imagine skiing down mountains, some just sky dive. Be as creative as you like, or use your breathing; 'Every breath is taking me deeper' and then each time you exhale, imagine sinking deeper into whatever it is you are resting upon. There is no limit to what you can do in this section of the session, just keep your wits about you and do your best not to wander off.

If you were being hypnotised by another person, then it is fine to wander off. However, when using self-hypnosis, you have to maintain control and focus of the session. If you want to randomly wander off, then using self-hypnosis for safe, controlled hypnotic relaxation is covered in a later chapter.

'D' is for 'Deliver Your Suggestion'.

Having sufficiently deepened your state of hypnosis, it is now, at this stage of the session that you enter or deliver your suggestion or programme for change (a series of suggestions to form a programme). We shall be covering how you actually deliver your suggestions later on in the book, there are several methods.

Before we proceed into more detail later, here are some important things just to bear in mind about entering your suggestions and delivering them to your unconscious right now:

- **Enter your suggestion using your chosen method**; as I said, there several methods and these are discussed later, choose what suits you best.
- **Be enthusiastic and sell it to yourself**; show yourself that it is important. If you have written a programme about stopping smoking or reducing weight and you want to install that programme in a self-hypnosis session, you have got to show yourself that you mean it.

Remembering to be enthusiastic about a programme for change is important, you want to let yourself know that it is important to affect the change that you want to achieve, so ensure that you deliver it with an open mind and with enthusiasm. Have the correct progressive and positive expectation about the success of the programme too.

Before you then exit hypnosis, take s moment or two or whatever period of time you like, to **thank your unconscious mind**. Either say thank you in your mind or you can do what I do which is to imagine embracing my unconscious self as if it were a person or a friend. This is all part of nurturing the relationship with yourself; with your unconscious mind. You want as wonderful a relationship as you can with your unconscious mind so that you are tuning in to what it responds to the most and creating a good level of harmony within you. As with any good relationship, as it develops, you get more from it.

My teacher was taught by an Australian hypnotherapist and always referred to his subconscious mind as 'subby.' My teacher refers to his unconscious mind as 'subby' and he even says 'thanks subby' at the end of each self-hypnosis session. I have worked with many people that have had names for their unconscious, which made it easier for them to develop a wonderful acquaintance and relationship with their unconscious mind. You may want to do the same. I think this is a lovely idea. The notion that you are really getting to know and appreciate yourself and what makes you happier and happier.

Finally, 'E' stands for 'Exit'.

Coming out of hypnosis simply involves you counting from 1–5. You can count aloud or in your mind, whichever way you do so, when you count 5 and open your eyes you signal the end of that self-hypnosis session. By counting from 1–5 you end that session of self-hypnosis, and get used to what each of the numbers represent and what you want to return to usual, you may even want to say the following, I would certainly suggest that you do say it to yourself the first few times you enter hypnosis, so that your unconscious knows what it is doing each time you count from 1–5 in future sessions:

When I count 1, I have full control, flexibility and coordination throughout my entire body, from the tips of my toes to the top of my head, from the tips of my fingers and thumbs to my shoulders, any feelings of lightness and/or heaviness return to their true and correct perspective.

So, here we put all our bodily sensations back as they should be. Sometimes, prolonged stillness in hypnosis can alter our sensations of lightness or heaviness within our limbs for example.

When I count 2, I position myself back in the place where I entered hypnosis, remembering and recalling what was to my left and right, above and below, remembering and recalling some features of the place.

This is important if you spent some time in a favourite place or using your imagination vividly to be somewhere else. You are ensuring that you connect with the place you are actually in once again.

When I count 3, all sounds are in their correct perspective and have their true levels of importance.

Some people have found that while in hypnosis, their hearing can become altered slightly. For example I took a lady into hypnosis and she commented how my voice seemed like it was background noise even though I was sat right beside her and that the traffic on the road outside seemed like it was the main sound rather than the noise it was. We can sometimes change our focus to make a sound seem nearer or further, so here you put it all back into place as you expect it to be.

When I count 4, I am keeping and bringing with me all the wonderful benefits of this hypnotic session.

That's right. All the good stuff that you have been delivering during your hypnosis session, you want to remind yourself to incorporate it and integrate it into your life. Make sure that even if you have little conscious awareness of the benefits, that all your intended benefits and desired outcomes of the session are surely sealed in, kept and integrated into your unconscious mind.

Finally, 'When I count 5, I open my eyes to be fully emerged from this session and fully out of hypnosis.

You count 5 and open your eyes and it is all done for that session. It is as simple as A–E. That is the basic structure that you follow each session of self-hypnosis. Really acquaint yourself with it, learn that structure, so that you can simply get into hypnosis and follow that outline every time.

So, the sharp ones among you will now have worked out what all that nonsense was about the alligator. 'A' is for **Access** (Alligator), you access self-hypnosis with 3 triggers (3 eyes), you have the intention, it is safe and you count from 1–10 entering hypnosis between 6–10 (you know the reason for this is that we Exit hypnosis with 1–5).

'B' is for **Being in Control** (barrel), you take control by remembering C-H-I-P (and the plate of chips of the barrel). You remind your self that you are in **control**, (cool sauce) you are in **hypnosis**, (hot sauce) you give authority to your **intended** (indifferent sauce) suggestions and you are fully **protected** (pungent sauce) from random sounds, thoughts and images.

'C' is for **Continually Deepening** (cat continually digging) and you deepen in any way that suits you and resonates with you the most. Use your imagination and have fun with this.

'D' is for **Delivering Your Programme or Suggestion** (postman delivers the gift). At this stage remember to thank your unconscious (like the cat and alligator remembered to thank the postman).

'E' is for **Exit** (Egg-sit. The ornate egg). You exit by counting from 1–5 (5 gifts inside the egg). You put everything in your body back as it should (doll) and then position yourself back in the place you entered hypnosis (dolls room) then allow all sounds to return to their true perspective (ear) and then keep and bring with you all the wonderful gifts and benefits of the session (gift box) and then open your eyes (the eye) to fully emerge from hypnosis.

Easy to remember, eh? Keep practising the imagery and running through A–E so that you fully know the structure of self-hypnosis before starting to use it. Then, when you are sure that you know that process and not before, you can proceed to the next chapter of the book. If you ignore my advice and plough straight on regardless, you will not get as much from this book as you want and your success will not be as profound. This is just the model, it is the structure that you follow for your self-hypnosis sessions, and how we actually do each component part of it we are now going to learn. It really is important that you know what the **A–E** self-hypnosis model all stands for before you proceed.

2

Introduction to the Language of Self-Hypnosis

My English text is chaste, and all licentious passages are left in the obscurity of a learned language.

Edward Gibbon

There are ways that a hypnotherapist utilises language to elicit certain responses within his client and the emergence of Neuro-Linguistic Programming and other modern innovations in the field of language have made its use wonderful and powerful when dealing with others.

With self-hypnosis it is very different. You are communicating to yourself. You have to be specific and emotive. You want to seduce your unconscious mind, you want to elicit the best results from it and that is going to depend on the kind of language you use and the associations that you have with the language you use. Think about words that elicit the best responses.

The way language is used baffles me, have a think about some of the things that people say. For example, here in England it is so common when asked 'How are you?' for someone to respond with the answer 'not too bad, thanks.' What, what, what?! Was the question 'Hello, what degree of bad do you feel?' and the answer is 'Oh, not too bad thanks.' This is madness. You see, the language that people use every day often defines the way that those people are. Whenever anyone says to me 'Oh, not too bad.' I always reply 'So, what, you are just moderately bad or averagely bad, just not **too** bad.'

Think about other expressions that are used as well. There was once a television commercial for a washing powder called Daz.

The advertisement stated 'nothing works better than Daz.' Yeah? Well use nothing then. If nothing works better than Daz, use nothing.

Have you ever heard someone say 'I told myself that the last thing I would do before I left is forget my keys.' And so the last thing that person did before they left home was to forget their keys. Amazing self-hypnotic programming going on there without even knowing it!

What about when people say 'I have a brain like a sieve' or something like 'Oh, he is my best friend; it was the least I could do.' Well, if he was your best friend, why don't you do the most you can do instead of the least!

It is these finer distinctions in language that really matter. Especially when you are communicating with yourself and especially when using self-hypnosis. So, before we finally start going into self-hypnosis, we need to start to be aware of the suggestions that we are going to give ourselves when we are there and how we are going to form our programmes for change.

3

Guidelines to Writing Programmes

Not so much a programme, more a way of life!

So what is meant by '**Programmes**'? What I am talking about here is a script that you write that you can then deliver to your unconscious. Remember step '**D**' in the self-hypnosis model stands for '**Deliver Your Suggestion or Programme**', well it is that part of the self-hypnosis session that we are dealing with now, because before you can deliver a programme or suggestion to your unconscious mind in your self-hypnosis sessions, you need to create your programmes. Before you can create and formulate your programmes, you need to be aware of the best kind of language to use and how to really get the most from the programmes you create for yourself.

You can buy lots of books filled with scripts and I have included some scripts in this book. However, I recommend highly that you use the golden information in this chapter and create your own scripts, your own programmes for change.

If you have invested the time and energy in doing that, you will know at all levels that this is important for you to want to make that particular change. Also, my scripts or the scripts of another writer may not be the kind the language or expressiveness that resonates with you. Its components may not be congruent with you if someone else has created the script. We are all unique individuals and respond to things differently and you are the one person who knows how best to push your own buttons and what you respond to the best and most powerfully.

So, you are going to forge these programmes like a piece of prose and I will be showing you how to deliver them to your unconscious mind in a later chapter, all we need to focus on for now is the programme itself and how you want to deliver the change to yourself in the most effective way for you.

Here are some guidelines for you to follow when creating your own programmes for change. Please do remember, this is not the law! You do not have to follow everything here to the letter. Your programmes will be most successful when they are congruent with you and your style. All that I am suggesting is that these guidelines that follow may well enhance the effectiveness of the programmes and are things to be aware of.

Before you begin writing your programmes for change think about what the outcome is that you most desire, think about how you would like to be, think of what the benefits will be to you and bear in mind these following guidelines.

Write it down and read it through several times

Once you have written out the suggestion, put on your editing hat. Have any words entered without your intention? (We will be coming on to use of words in the next chapter.) Are you happy with the finished result? Do you get a good feeling about it?

Remember that during this early period as a self-hypnotist, one suggestion per hypnosis session can be more successful than giving many. Then work your way up to more complex programmes of change.

Keep it simple

Be specific, concise and precise. It is best to be specific about the outcome and vague about how exactly how you will achieve it. Other than suggestions for comfort and safety, it is better to leave it to your unconscious. Trust that your unconscious knows how to get you what you want.

If you are going to write yourself a really simple programme to begin with to ensure some success; hypothetically, let's call it **my programme for making a cup of tea for my wife or husband**. You may have been going to do this anyway; however, you write a programme to make sure you do this gesture as it will make your husband, wife or partner very happy. What a nice programme!

Now, when you write this programme, you do not need to writing things like:

when I awake in the morning, I sit up in bed and move my body around, and toss my bed covers away from me, I then put my feet over the edge of the bed and put on my slippers, I then stand up and walk step by step to the kitchen to put on the kettle . . . etc, etc.

This is just not necessary at all. You can simply state, 'In the morning, I make my wife (or husband or partner) a cup of tea.' It is a simple instruction to the unconscious mind. It does not have to be made complicated; I encourage simplicity with your programmes.

Want it to work and expect it to work

The more you want it to work, the more effective your suggestion will be. If in doubt, write down the pros and cons. Do you really want what you have asked for? Any programme or suggestion that you deliver to yourself will be rendered impotent if you do not want it to work. Have the highest expectations of it too, this really is then like sunshine and rain upon your seeds. Really wanting a programme to work is sometimes all you need, as long as you really it to work, expect it to work and you put some effort into achieving the results you want, then you can often ignore all the other guidelines; you'll be assured of success.

Make it work

Now this might sound obvious, give yourself the suggestion that you will make yourself and your spouse a cup of tea when you get up in the morning. As I suggested in one of the earlier guidelines. Now you might have done that anyway, however if you used your hypnosis to ensure it happening you are beginning to align your conscious and unconscious minds. You are generating success from the start. When you create success, you have more firm foundations to build from. Your unconscious mind will associate successful implementation with your self-hypnosis and begin to really supercharge the programmes you create and deliver to yourself.

Think it through

Do not proceed if there is any doubt about your programme or the suggestions contained within it. When in doubt, think about your programme. Do what you can to remove the part that you are not happy with and only then proceed.

Think of all the possibilities of what your suggestion could mean and the consequences of it. Your unconscious is very literal and will give what you ask for. For example, you might use your self-hypnosis one morning before work and tell yourself 'everything that happens to me today makes me happy.' Sounds like a nice idea doesn't it? Unless you arrive at work to be told by your boss that his dog died in the night. You and your career do not want this to make you happy, it could have detrimental effects if you start skipping around and being happy as a result of their sad news. I exaggerate of course, however, it is more likely to be remembered by you that way.

Ask for what you want, not what you do not want

State your goals and the objectives in the positive. Your unconscious responds accurately when given specific instructions. I really want you to think about the difference between 'moving away from' what you don't want and 'moving toward' that which you do want. Whatever you focus on the most will be what you'll get more of regardless of whether it is positive or negative.

Someone may want to reduce weight by no longer eating cream cakes. So they tell themselves over and over not to eat all those lovely cream cakes. They are painting their internal environment with the message of the cream cakes. It is like driving towards lamppost in a car, staring at it, accelerating and saying 'I hope I don't hit that lamppost.' Whatever you focus on you stick yourself to. If you keep focusing on what you don't want, even if it seems that you are pulling away from it, you'll keep being pulled back towards it.

Instead, it would be better to focus on achieving and maintaining the size, shape and weight that pleases you and moving towards the goal of how you want to look and feel; being your ideal weight.

So, this idea that you can't not think of a pink elephant. This is because negation is processed differently by neurology than it is in language. If I say 'Don't smile', your neurology has to process the meaning of the word 'smile' even to understand what I'm talking about. Human beings are goal-oriented; our neurology and our physiology are adapted to move towards the 'ideas' (pictures, sounds, feelings) we hold in our minds. For this reason, it's important to be selective about the 'ideas' you keep in your mind, because you get what you focus on. It is true.

If you are unsure what you've been focusing on in your life up until now, there's a quick way to find out: look at the results that have been showing up in your life. On some level, the results that you've been getting are a reflection of what you've been putting your attention and energy into.

Firstly, stop and think and then figure out what you've been focusing on: make a list of the main results that you've been getting in your life.

The results you've been getting are an accurate measure of what you've been focusing on. If you have a bulging bank balance and are experiencing lots of material wealth, well done! You have created that result by focusing on the abundance in your life. If you're deep in debt, congratulations! That could sound like I am being ironic. I am not I assure you. This still marks quite an achievement. You have managed to create that result by focusing your energy and attention on lack of material wealth. This is how powerful your mind is. The notion of material wealth is just to illustrate this point by the way. As far as this book is concerned, I hold no position on what your interpretation of wealth is.

At this stage, review your list and identify the results that you are most pleased with. Congratulate yourself for having achieved these results. Show gratitude to yourself.

You may find certain things on your list that you are really happy to have in your life, but that you didn't make a conscious effort to bring about. Perhaps you have some great friends who you really care about, or a happy relationship. Maybe your health is particularly good, or you experience a deep sense of peace a lot of the time. Whether you are conscious of it or not, these are a result of what you have been focusing on.

Identify the areas where you'd like to change your results. It may be that there are some areas on the list that you are not yet happy with. Happy or not, these are the results you have been getting.

So the next thing to do is accept that your current results reflect your current reality. When you accept this, then you can begin to move in another reality, otherwise you are trying to kid yourself and there is little value in not being true to yourself.

Your current results are the way it is, but not necessarily the way it will be. Once you accept things as being how they are, then it is a much, much easier task to change them to how you'd like them to be. Acceptance of your current reality is a quick way to meet yourself at your own map of the world, which is the best place to start for creating something new.

Next, decide how you want it to be. Begin thinking about how you are going to use your self-hypnosis to create this. In each area that you are not yet happy with, decide how you want it to be. For example, if you are single and want to be in a relationship, then that is how you want it to be. If you are in the red and you want to be in the black, then that is how you want it to be. If you are a smoker and you want to be a non-smoker . . . you get the idea.

Then, learn to pay attention to your thoughts. Every time you catch yourself focusing on what you don't want/don't have, stop and focus on what you do have in that area. When you create programmes of change for yourself and use self-hypnosis, be aware of the great things you do have and concentrate on what you want, what you want to move towards.

If you want to increase your wealth, every time you catch yourself worrying about bills, focus on the pennies, pounds, dollars or drachmas that you do have (no matter how few.) If you want to get into a relationship, every time you find yourself moping about how you are not in one, stop and think about the relationships you do have (or have had). The most useful emotion to access when you are focusing on what you wish to increase is . . . gratitude. Then you move toward what you want to have more of. Please remember this point when you are writing your self-hypnosis programmes for change.

Use emotive language

Use language and words that elicit emotions within you. We shall be coming on to the use of words much more specifically in the next chapter. However, think about what words you really like, which ones appeal to you or words that have certain positive feelings associated with them when you hear them or think them. How would you describe the most enjoyable experiences of your life? Use those words in your self-hypnosis. The more good feelings that you can pour into your programmes, the better.

Say exactly what you mean and mean what you say

Use clear language, free from ambiguity. Be sure to ask for exactly what you want, because you are likely to get exactly what you asked for!

When I first trained as a hypnotherapist, there was a lady on my course who was unable to complete her homework each month. She kept telling the teacher and her classmates that she did not have the time. She kept on insisting that she needed a break to catch up with her work. 'I need a break . . .' she would keep on repeating this whenever I spoke to her. A few weeks later, she fell and broke her leg whilst at a supermarket and had to have 10 weeks off work and so she got to take time off and catch up with all her studying. So do think about what it is you continually ask your self for. She was not even using formalised self-hypnosis; she was influencing herself hypnotically with her constant insisting of how much she needed a break. Now, this could all be coincidence and it is a rather unusual case, however, I urge you to say what you mean and mean what you say.

Your unconscious is literal, you are likely to get what you asked for, whether you want it or not! In addition, in order for something to work, ensure that you mean it.

Set a time to start and finish

Programmes should all have a time to start and in some cases, a time to finish. If you are writing a programme for dealing with driving test nerves for example, for enhancing mental calmness during your driving test, it can have an end when the test has finished.

When do you want it to begin? Most of my programmes have the beginning and ending in the first sentence, I often write 'from this moment and lasting throughout my entire lifetime.' I often want that programme to last my entire lifetime, so the sentence is sufficient.

Later, we are going to be learning about time distortion and how to alter our perception of time. Now, if you have altered your perception of time for a plane journey, so that when you step off the plane it feels as if the journey just zipped by in a flash, you will want that experience of time to stop when the plane journey ends. You don't want to then wake up one day and think 'Whoa, I am 90 years old, my entire life has just zipped past me . . .' I joke of course, but I am sure you understand the importance of this.

We are also going to be learning about how to use self-hypnosis for pain relief; again, you will want that pain relief to end after a period of time. Pain is there for a reason, it is a signal, you do not really want to be pain free for longer than a set period of hours at any one time.

So please remember to give your programmes a beginning and ending.

Label your suggestions: give them a title

Title your programmes. This makes altering, boosting or removing them easier. You can then refer to them when you use your self-hypnosis to alter an existing programme. This is much better than going into self-hypnosis and saying to yourself 'ok, that programme I delivered to my unconscious a few weeks ago, about excelling in my exams . . erm . . . that programme is now changed to . . . er . . .' You can understand where I am coming from with this can't you? If for any reason a programme is no longer valid or it has expired, then it can be removed if it has a title and a way of removing it.

When I first started using self-hypnosis after my first training course with it, I wrote loads of programmes and put them all on disc and had them filed with their titles and I always tell the students on my self-hypnosis seminars and courses to do the same.

On one such course, I had a lady who was not thoroughly impressed with this notion and she asked me:

Adam, are you not worried that with all this programme writing and installing that you are doing, that you are just becoming robot-like and too programmed?

I replied instantly (some might say smugly) with a smile:

No, I am not worried, if that ever concerns me, my programme for spontaneity just kicks in.

Remember your achievements using hypnosis

Success breeds success, continue to remind yourself and others of the things that you are achieving. Again, feed this back to your unconscious and your self repeatedly.

Use your senses and imagination

I was running a training course a little while ago and I had asked all the delegates to go and get into groups to do an exercise involving making pictures in their minds. As is usual, I had a gentleman who told me that he could not make pictures in his mind and he carried on making himself believe that he could not do it. I asked him if he could remember a time in his childhood when he was happy and he replied that he could remember a time. I asked where he was on that occasion and he told me he was in his bedroom playing with his model aeroplane. I asked him to describe the room and he told me that it had blue walls and he began to explain the room in detail. He got so into his description that he even fashioned shapes with his hands during his description. When he stopped with his description I asked him if he still believed he could not make pictures in his mind. I think you know what the answer was. He carried on happily with the exercises from there on.

If I were to ask you what colour your front door is at your home, when you answer, how do you know it is true? How did you arrive at your answer? A natural way to do this is by imagery in our minds and by using our imagination and range of senses.

We often do not realise how much we use our senses with our imagination, and I suggest that using your senses and imagination with your self-hypnosis is a sure way to increase the power of your programmes and of your sessions with self-hypnosis.

Imagery is far more than just pictures. We often use imagery to recreate and remember emotions as well as using imagery with our senses of smell, touch, hearing, and even taste. Have you ever been hungry and imagined what it would taste like to have your favourite food at that moment? Your memory may be so vivid that you can taste it in your mouth.

It is like if I asked you imagine holding a fresh lemon in one hand. You know the smell of a fresh lemon right? Imagine slicing it in half with a knife and then slicing it in quarters and having some of the juice running out onto the surface. Then imagine picking up one of those lemon quarters, placing it into your mouth and really sinking your teeth into it, with the juice running over your gums along the roof of your mouth and over your tongue. Notice how if you really imagine that you can make your mouth begin to water and even taste that lemon taste.

Most people have a preferred sense that they use more commonly than the others; touch, sight, sounds, smell or taste. It will usually be sight, sound or touch. Think about which of your senses you respond to the most and use that sense more in your programmes. You want to bring your programmes to life and add dimension to them.

Of course, we overlap senses all the time but visually oriented people will be primarily concerned with what their imagery looks like. Auditory people will be more concerned with sounds and voices that they associate with their imagery whereas kinaesthetic people will be primarily concerned with how their imagery feels and the associated physical sensations of them. You will of course respond to all senses and I would suggest that you use as many of your senses as you can in all your programmes.

A really good way to develop your ability to create imagery with more clarity is to look at pictures and images and then close your eyes and make sure that you can still see them in your mind, and then keep on looking at the picture and forming it in more and more detail in your mind.

Your imagery and imagination skills will develop the more you use them. Imagery and imagination is worth pages and pages of written suggestions within the programmes you create, keep this in mind. Imagery really is the language of the unconscious.

Imagery is another reason for you to create your own programmes and use your own language. If I asked 100 people to describe a beach scene, every one of those people would describe something different and unique to them. The aspects that appealed to them each the most would be personal to them. You respond to the finer distinctions and details of your own imagination rather than that of somebody else. I am going to be giving some scripts in the book, however use them for ideas and getting a sense of structure rather than using them verbatim.

In addition to this, be aware of the difference between association and disassociation in your imagination. If you imagined seeing yourself riding on a roller coaster, it would be a very different experience compared to if you really imagined **being on** the roller coaster and going along in it. To add to the experience or desensitise from an experience in your mind, consider the differences between really associating and dissociating with what you are visualising.

What you ask for is exactly what you get

Remember that I mentioned the girl on my course, who kept stating that she needed a break? That was an example of doing this without really knowing.

Let me give you an example of something that happened to me: I used to work in a busy town and had to drive into work. Each day I would get stuck in one particular traffic jam where two lanes funnelled into one and at morning rush hour, the queues were horrendous. A friend of mine pointed out a shortcut that I could take; by taking a little road that not many people knew of, I could take 20 minutes off my morning journey. I had a dress rehearsal one weekend and then when the week came, I was in such a state of early morning auto-pilot that I kept on driving past the turning that following week and getting stuck in the traffic jam as I had been before.

So, I decided to write myself a programme and use my self-hypnosis to help me remember the turning. I wrote a programme for myself and it included within it these words:

... each time I drive past the turning, I remember the shortcut ...

Seems reasonable right? I delivered the programme to my unconscious mind using my self-hypnosis that evening and went to work. Of course, guess what happened; I **drove past** the turning, and then I remembered it! I joined the traffic jam once again. What I needed to write in my programme was that every time I **approached** the turning, I would remember it and take the turning to help me get to work quicker.

I am not suggesting for one minute that your unconscious would be quite so pedantic, what I want is for you to think through the possibilities and be aware that you will often get exactly what you ask for. Your unconscious mind is very powerful and also very literal.

Avoid ambiguity

Hypnotherapists use ambiguity a lot to help other people to enter into hypnosis. However, with self-hypnosis, it is more important to be precise of meaning. There really is no point in having a term or a phrase being ambiguous if it is yourself that you are communicating with. You know what you want to achieve and so that is precisely what you focus on whilst being precise.

When I say avoid ambiguity in your self-hypnosis programmes, what I mean is avoid phrases that your unconscious mind could interpret in a way or ways that you were not intending. You may want to reconsider referring to 'the whole of your head' when treating a headache. Your unconscious mind may interpret this to mean **your mouth**, as in the 'hole of your head.'

In addition to that, referring to 'tomorrow' or 'the day ahead' is also ambiguous. This is because your unconscious mind is experiencing **now** and 'tomorrow never comes' when you are experiencing **now**.

Avoid hallucination

Now, this is something that you may turn your nose up at if you are at college. I would have done too. However, I mean a naturally occurring kind of hallucination. Have you ever thought that you could not find your keys? You looked on the table on several occasions; in fact you stared at it on several occasions and could not see your keys. Yet, later on there they were on that table. That is simply a negative hallucination.

Be aware when you are writing your programmes that you consider using phrases such as 'I am seeing things more clearly each and every day.' It might cause things to become invisible!

Reward yourself

That's right. Give yourself the rewards you deserve. Include rewards in your programmes: As a result of stopping smoking I am healthier. As a result of having more confidence, I enjoy social occasions more. When I stop biting my fingernails, I feel more beautiful. When I achieve and maintain my ideal weight, I can wear those clothes that I have not been able to wear for years.

You get the idea. Think about how you will benefit from achieving your goal.

Provisional clauses

If I was to write in to a programme something to do with having better quality sleep; I might want my sleep to be more and more undisturbed. However, I would want to put in a provisional clause, something along the lines of:

> My sleep is more and more undisturbed. Undisturbed that is unless there is an emergency and an emergency as I know is anything that requires my immediate attention. Should en emergency exist or occur, I awake and deal with the emergency in the most appropriate way. In the absence of such an emergency, my sleep continues to be so wonderful and deeply refreshing and invigorating.

I added a provisional clause where necessary to cover all eventualities.

Give thanks to your unconscious mind

At the end of each self-hypnosis session, take some time out to thank your unconscious mind. This is nurturing your relationship with yourself. You might even want to imagine embracing your unconscious mind as I mentioned earlier in the book.

To summarise

Again, I am going to say, these guidelines have been suggested here to optimise the programmes you write. They do not have to be adhered to by the letter. They are not laws that you have to follow. They are simply guidelines to give you ideas to enhance your programmes and allow them to be more effective.

4

Use of Words

Hold fast the form of sound words
The book of Timothy, The *Bible*

Words are just a part of our lives aren't they? Why do we need to think about them? The words that you use carry a lot of connotation and a lot of deeper meanings for you as they do for everyone. What one word means to one person can mean something completely different to another.

Think about an occasion in your life that was a wonderful occasion; maybe a happy birthday, the birth of a child, a wedding or a celebration, maybe a time when you achieved something, when you succeeded or maybe a time when you felt the full force of joy or love. Really think about that experience. Remember what you saw, remember and think about the sounds that you heard and think about how you know and how you knew you felt so good then. Whereabouts in your body were those good feelings? Now, as you really think about that memory and immerse yourself in it, think about the words that you would use to describe that experience.

These are the words that are going to elicit the most powerful response from within you when you use them in your self-hypnosis programmes and when you spend time in hypnosis without working on a specific programme.

Have a think about these questions; what words make you feel good? Which words give you good feelings? Make a list of the words that appeal to you. You can use a thesaurus to help. Ask yourself; how would I like to feel?

Remember; suggestions work best when you have intense emotion combined with your self-hypnosis.

Here are some good words you may like to use in your suggestions:

Healthy, Peace, Balance, Harmony, Relaxed, Confident, Good, Happy, Powerful, Joyful, Calm, Unison, Assured, Vibrant, Loving, Progressive, Better, Beautiful.

You get the idea. It is really important though that you use words that have a good meaning to you and make you feel good.

Now, I am going to add a couple of words here for you to think about. Think about the words 'more and more' and 'increasingly.' These words are going to be important to create growth, power and fluidity in your programmes. Let me explain how.

Consider the sentence 'as a result of achieving my ideal weight I am happy.' This is a nice way to remind yourself that achieving this particular goal (whatever it might be for you) you are happy. Great. However, we can make that more powerful by changing a rather static 'happy' to 'more and more happy.' I don't know about you, but I would never want to think that I ever reached the pinnacle of happiness and could not go any further.

'Happy' is static. In order to supercharge your programmes and the way you utilise language in self-hypnosis, you can mobilise the words and get them moving onwards and upwards for you. You can change 'Happy' to 'Happier and happier' or 'more and more happy' or 'increasingly happy' or 'progressively more happy' or 'more and more appropriately happy. ' Use whatever feels right for you, just use other words to develop and power it up.

Words to avoid

Again, this is not the law. I keep saying this I know. Some of these words may seem fine and feel fine to use for you. I am just giving you ideas and considerations when using these words in your self-hypnosis. When writing your programmes, my recommendation is that you consider avoiding the following words and types of words;

Words that elicit bad feelings. Words that are ambiguous. Words that are limiting, restrictive or disempower you. Words that you are uncomfortable with.

When you have prepared your programme, ask yourself these questions: Is there another phrase or word that is better?Is there a word or phrase I find more pleasing? Is there a way in which you can put your energy and power into this suggestion in a better way?

So, firstly, I want to point out some words that can elicit bad feelings:

Try, can't, won't, don't, should, shouldn't, must, mustn't, jealousy, temper, no, lose, will, sad, difficult, but.

I want to point out a couple of these words in particular. The word 'try' sends a shudder down my back. I use this word in therapy often to ensure that people won't do what I am asking them, for example I might say 'try to resist the urge to relax.'

When you are trying to do something, you are not doing it. You build in failure by using the word try. So just remove it from your programmes. You will have heard that expression 'if at first you don't succeed, try and try again.' Yuck. Awful stuff. It really should read 'if at first you don't succeed, try and try, and try and try and try and try . . . etc, etc.' You want to do the things you want to do, you want to achieve the things you want to achieve; you don't want to try and do them or try and achieve them.

The word 'Will' is another one to avoid if you can. Will is not actually happening, it is something you will do rather than actually are doing. It never occurs. You know, you can put almost any sentence together with the word will in and simply remove that word to make it more progressive and positive for your self-hypnosis requirements. Have go at doing that. (I realise that there is likely to be at least one wise-guy who now uses the word as in 'last will and testament' yes, very clever. I have not heard that one before.)

Here are a couple of examples:

As a result of stopping smoking I will be healthier. Now becomes;
As a result of stopping smoking I am healthier.

I will successfully achieve my goals is transformed into I successfully achieve my goals.

Here we have just removed it to make it more progressive. You see, it is those finer distinctions that I keep referring to that can really make a difference to the way you use language, and you may as well really use it more and more powerfully while you are in the state of self-hypnosis.

Lots of people tell me that they want to '**Lose**' weight. I always tell them that no one loses when they come to see me. Think about what else you lose in life. Generally, it is things that you would rather have kept like your keys or your wallet. You generally lose things that you want to find again. Lose has many negative connotations. Instead of losing weight, reframe it with the words 'achieving and maintaining the size, shape and weight that pleases me.' This is much more progressive. It is focusing on what you want, not what you don't want too, as we learned about earlier.

Finally for this section, I want to mention the word '**But**'. This word can often be seen to be negating what has come before it; I would really like to come out tonight, **but** I have to wash my hair. Of course I really love you, **but** I need to pursue my career. I had a great time, **but** that guy sitting next to me was rude. This might not always be the case for you; however, it is for you to be aware of when addressing your own unconscious mind in self-hypnosis and within the words in your programmes.

Secondly, I recommend that you really do avoid using words that are put-downs. They don't really have a place in self-hypnosis at all. Avoid the following words and words like them:

> Untidy, Dirty, Smelly, Ugly, Stupid, Lazy, Hopeless, Disliked, Unkempt, Smelly, Idiot, Embarrass, Ridiculous.

I know you know lots more. I don't really like even having to write these in this book. Your programmes and self-hypnosis sessions are better without these words.

This next set of words is for you to keep aware of and avoid if you feel they limit you or your programme in any way. I am referring to words that are absolutes. These are words that have no flexibility, that are final. For example:

> Always, totally, closed, never, finish, impossible, definitely, completely, death, cancelled.

You may for example, state in a self-hypnosis programme that you **never** smoke again. Which is fine and good for some people. However, you may have one too many glasses of sherry at

Christmas and have a sneaky puff on your friend's cigar. Now this does not make you a regular smoker again, however, it has negated the sentiments that you wrote in your programme. It has made your programme less credible to you because you wrote that you would **never** smoke again and you just did, albeit only one puff, by writing that you would **never** do it, you leave no flexibility and you leave no room for interpretation of particular circumstances that may arise. That may be fine with some, just bear it in mind.

I mentioned the subject earlier within the guidelines for writing programmes and that is the notion of ambiguity. With self-hypnosis and the programmes you write for use in self-hypnosis, it is best to avoid words that are ambiguous. Words such as:

Maybe, Desire, Growth, Positive, Negative, Normal, Whole (as mentioned earlier).

You might well use the expression that your **desire** to stop smoking is increasing. Again, this sounds fine on the surface. However, do you want your **desire** to stop smoking to increase or your **actual ability** to stop smoking to increase? If you only increased your **desire** to stop smoking, it might become a very frustrating experience.

Also, you might want to consider referring to your personal growth increasing. It could be referring to something growing on your body somewhere!

Think about the word **normal**. Who is to say what that is? Do you know specifically what you mean when you refer to anything as being **normal**? If you are going to use the word **normal**, I would recommend that you define what that means to you also, be specific about it or just substitute it for the word **usual** if you can.

Finally, on the topic of words, I would like to point out to you the use of the '**Able**'. It is one thing being able to do something; it is another to actually do it. If you are going to increase your **ability** with something, then also ensure you do it:

As a result of this programme, I am more and more able to stop smoking, and so I do stop smoking.

Note, the addition to the end of the sentence; '. . . and so I do stop smoking.' This carries out the action that you are **able** to do.

I realise that this book has offered up many considerations so far. These are just that; considerations. You can allow yourself to find the right solutions and methods for you. As you get more and more used to being in hypnosis and discovering the kind of suggestions and words that have the most powerful effect for you, then you can fine-tune your use of them.

5

Mind Mapping

Map me no maps, sir, my head is a map, a map
of the whole world.

Henry Fielding

When you know what it is that you want to write a programme about, you may not know where to begin. Not knowing where to begin can sometimes prevent us from actually getting into the frame of mind to take action. This is where mind-mapping can be very useful for you. Make a map diagram with your chosen goal in a circle in the centre. Then, branching out from the circle, list all the important points associated with your goal. Sights, sounds, smells and other senses may play a part.

Put down on paper all the areas that you want that programme to cover and related ideas next to that. The object of the exercise is to cover every aspect and describe every detail. It is a great way of committing your thoughts to paper. You then have something real and tangible to begin to work with. When you have put lots and lots of your ideas about that programme onto a mind map, you can begin to formulate your programme and order the ideas ready to write out the programme.

Then you can write the programme out in rough, check the words, check it against the guidelines mentioned in this book and really craft a work of art for delivering to your unconscious mind in a self-hypnosis session.

6

Looping

Thy firmness makes my circle just,
and makes me end where I begun.

John Donne

Now, this is a sure fire way to rocket fuel your programmes. Think about the power of a circle. I am sure you have seen the symbol of eternal life with the snake consuming itself in a circle by eating its tail. Circles are powerful and we often get on a circle the wrong way. Think about when someone has found themselves in a vicious cycle; someone who is, in their own opinion, overweight for example. They eat more because they feel lonely or bored or in need of comfort or for whatever reason. Shortly afterwards they feel worse as they are contributing to their own condition of being overweight and often end up eating more to feel temporarily better. It is a vicious cycle.

So, with the programmes that you write and create and formulate for yourself, you want to create a virtuous circle. You can create a virtuous circle within your programme so that each element of the programme leads to the next and then the last element of your programme leads to the element that the programme began with. This might sound confusing, so here I have enclosed an example to illustrate this idea of looping your programmes.

See in the diagram how one element feeds the next.

Here is an example of a programme that loops relating to the diagram above. This programme is very one dimensional, it is just prose; it is here for illustration purposes. This programme is for enhanced mental calmness and developing inner strength. It is very generic and non-specific. The importance is to note how each

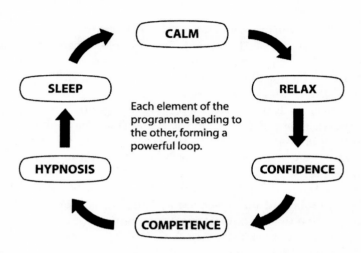

CALM

SLEEP

Each element of the
programme leading to
the other, forming a
powerful loop.

RELAX

HYPNOSIS

CONFIDENCE

COMPETENCE

element of the programme leads to the next (these transition points are in bold) and how this programme starts and finishes on the same theme. It is for illustrating the looping:

This is my programme for strengthening and enhancing my inner self. From this moment forwards and lasting throughout my entire lifetime, I find that I am feeling and being progressively more and more mentally calm. I am more and more calm in my thoughts, more and more calm in my feelings, more and more calm in my reactions, more and more calm in my responses. Progressively feeling and being more and more calm with place and person, time and event, circumstance and situation, so wonderfully, naturally and easily calm and beautifully and gently relaxed. It's like I have more time for my thoughts, more time for my self, my inner self.

And mental calmness is the ability to experience events, circumstances and situations in my life in their true and correct perspective and so progressively I do find from this moment forwards that I am experiencing each and every aspect of my life in its true perspective, experiencing each and every event in my life in its true perspective, as it should be; free from distortion of events and happenings of the past.

I am so much more mentally calm and what this means is that I have the ability now to deal with and to cope with each and every aspect of my life in a more and more calm way, having time for my thoughts and my feelings, my reactions and my responses.

And **because I am more and more calm, I am more and more relaxed.** More and more physically relaxed, for example, when I am walking upstairs, I am using the muscles that are required to climb upstairs, and the muscles I am not using are resting and relaxing, easily, gently and naturally. And on the occasions when I am resting all my muscles, each of my muscles in turn are relaxing easily and gently, conserving and reserving the energy and the life force that flows through my system. Giving me more natural energy at the times I require it and need it the most, enhancing my belief in myself, my enthusiasm and my motivation for life.

And you know, **there is a by-product, a natural benefit of feeling and being more and more relaxed and feeling and being more and more calm. And that is that I notice, I truly notice, that I am becoming, feeling and being more and more confident,** more deeply self assured and this is natural because two of the main ingredients of increased confidence are mental calmness and physical relaxation. When I am calm mentally, when I am relaxed, physically, I find that I am naturally feeling and being more and more confident, and so I am from this moment forwards being more confident in each and every aspect of my life.

I am more and more confident with place and person, more confident with time and event, more confident with circumstance and situation, so much more confident in my self, really believing in my self and my abilities to achieve the goals I set my self in life. A deep-rooted self-belief in my self. More and more confident in relying on my self to help my self get the very best out of each and every aspect of my life, getting the most out of each and every situation. Instinctively and intuitively depending on my intuition and my instincts and my inner, natural, creative abilities to help me make the most out of each and every aspect of my life.

As I am and feel more confident, more deeply self-confident, so those around me can feel it and how wonderful that feels, how naturally my self-esteem is enhanced more and more each day and night, night and day. Growing and enhancing within me.

And because I am becoming more and more confident, so it is that I am becoming more and more competent. More and more competent in each and every aspect of my life that pleases me. I am better and better in more and more aspects of my life, better and better at making changes in my life that please me, better and better at achieving goals. Better at relying on my self in a way that promotes, endorses and encourages the results I am looking for, the effects that I wish.

Because I am becoming better and better in each and every aspect of my life, of course, this means that I am becoming better and better at using hypnosis. I find that my hypnosis is of a better and better quality. Each and every time I choose to enter hypnosis I find that it is easier and easier and more natural for me to enter into hypnosis. I find that I go deeper and deeper so naturally and easily. As a result of this I find that my hypnosis sessions are more powerful and beneficial for me and to me.

As a result of my continuing better quality hypnosis, I find that the quality of my sleep is also becoming progressively better and more natural. Each and every time I choose to sleep, I drift easily and simply into sleep, each and every time I choose to enter into sleep I enter into a deeper and deeper, more natural, more beneficial, refreshing, invigorating and relaxing sleep. I find also from this moment forwards and lasting throughout my entire lifetime, my sleep is progressively more and more undisturbed. Undisturbed, of course except in case of an emergency and an emergency, as I know, is anything that requires my immediate attention and should such an emergency occur or exist, of course, I wake and deal with it in the most appropriate way.

In the absence of such an emergency my sleep continues to be so wonderfully refreshing and relaxing that I wake at the time I set myself, feeling and being so wonderfully calm, refreshed, relaxed and at ease, often waking with enthusiasm, sometimes with excitement, and always, always with this wonderful, gentle beautiful mental calmness. **(Remember, this theme of mental calmness is the theme we started with at the beginning of this programme. The end of the programme leads to the beginning. It loops and powers itself up.)**

This is my programme for strengthening and enhancing my inner self. It is a natural hypnotic programme always working effectively and efficiently for me and to me, each breath that I breathe and with each beat of my heart, I am strengthening and enhancing this programme, ensuring that it is working even more beneficially and progressively for me. I thank myself and my unconscious mind for allowing me to benefit from this deep hypnotic session, knowing next time deeper, next time even more progressive.

So you can see, if you continue to loop the content of your programmes, you can make them more and more powerful. You use the power of a circle to your advantage. The simplest way to do this is to get the last line of your programme to relate with and lead into the first line of your programme as illustrated in the last programme for mental calmness.

7

Quantum Looping

*The eternal in man cannot kill, the eternal in
man cannot die*

Katha Upanishad

When you invested in this book, I bet you had no idea that you
were going to be learning about something called 'quantum
looping.' Well, you are. What a very clever thing you are going to
be.

In fact, quantum looping is very, very simple.

Having used the power of looping in your programme, we are
now going to use the power of looping like a powerful backbone
running through all your programmes.

The way to do this is to firstly write your programme in a loop.
Secondly, include the following into every suggestion you write:

- Better Quality Sleep
- Better Quality Hypnosis

By doing this, you create a commonality in every programme you
create. This will promote, endorse and encourage better quality
sleep and better quality hypnosis with every loop of every
suggestion you write. Because each programme has a common
element in it, when you are powering up this element in one
programme, you are powering it up in the others too. You begin
quantum looping. You then take your rocket fuelled programmes
and send them all into space as far as their success for you is
concerned. The success is contagious and spreads into every aspect
of your life.

The common element in each programme ensures that if it is
working well, then the common elements in the other programmes

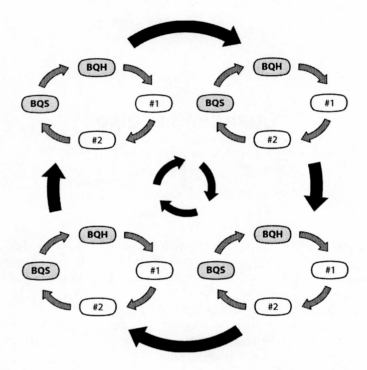

are working well and so they are creating momentum and developing more and more success. The diagram on the previous page illustrates what is meant by quantum looping; each of the smaller circles are your programmes and the elements within them. Notice how each programme then powers up the next and so on.

8

Delivering Your Programmes

Load every rift, of your subject with ore
John Keats

Now that you know how to write, create, forge and craft these wonderful programmes for change, personal development and enhancement, you can now learn how to deliver these programmes to your unconscious mind. Then we are going to be going into hypnosis; 'hooray.'

Remember step 'D' from the self-hypnosis model. 'D' stands for delivering your programme and then remember the postman delivering to the cat and three-eyed alligator? Good.

Here, I am going to show you the three main and most commonly used methods of entering your programmes. You may develop other ways for yourself in addition to that which you learn here.

Method 1: Pre-session entry

With this first method, have your programme written nearby. You initially have to have the intention to enter hypnosis and ensure that you are in a safe place in order that you can activate step 'A' for **accessing** self-hypnosis.

Then, immediately prior to entering hypnosis, read the programme aloud and with enthusiasm. Reading aloud makes it more real and tangible than reading it to yourself silently in your own mind. Again, be enthusiastic, let yourself know that you mean this and want it to work.

Then, as per the rest of step 'A' count from 1–10, entering hypnosis only after 6 on a number that you have decided on before hand. I always enter hypnosis on 7 as I was born on the seventh day of the month and is my favourite number. That was the 7th August by the way. You don't have to send me a birthday card.

Next, you take control as per step '**B**'

Then you deepen the state as per step '**C**'

Once you have sufficiently deepened your state of hypnosis to the level that you are happy with, you then use your inner voice, your conscious minds voice to say to your unconscious the following words:

> The programme entitled <programme title/name>, which I read out immediately prior to entering this hypnotic session, has now been entered into my unconscious and from this moment forward has full hypnotic authority and effect upon me.

Or you can use your own words to have a similar effect and meaning. Simply, you are moving the programme from where it was in you short term memory from having read it aloud immediately prior to the session and delivering it to your unconscious mind with those words.

Then, you thank your unconscious.

Proceed to step '**E**' by counting from 1–5 in your mind or out loud to signal the end of this hypnotic session.

Remember that you can increase the effectiveness of your programme, by asking your unconscious to give it more power and make it more effective.

Method 2: Open eyes

With this method, simply enter self-hypnosis by going through steps '**A**', '**B**' and '**C**'. So you are accessing your hypnosis, being in control and continually deepening. Again, have your programme written and nearby.

When you are happy that you have deepened enough, say to yourself in your mind:

> When I open my eyes, I remain in deep hypnosis and read my suggestion.
>
> This suggestion has full hypnotic authority and has full effect on me as I wish it to. After reading my suggestion, I return to deeper hypnotic state.

Then open your eyes, remaining in hypnosis and read your suggestion to yourself or out aloud.

Thank your unconscious.

Then, you just Exit as usual with step 'E' counting from 1–5.

Another important point to remember here is that when using this method; make sure that there are no other words in your field of vision (including peripheral). So if you have posters on the wall or writing in any other form, make sure you have fully protected yourself from its influence or remove it totally from your vision to be safe and sure that nothing unwanted is being taken on board during this session.

Method 3: Record your suggestion

The majority of my own programmes are recorded so that I can listen to them whenever I like and relax while doing so. Here is a simple way of doing so.

When putting the tape or CD together, leave your first 60 seconds on the tape or CD blank. You will see why shortly.

Secondly, you then record steps 'B' to 'E', which includes your programme. What is the reason that we would not record step 'A'? Think about it. Step 'A' is for accessing self-hypnosis; can you remember what step 'A' comprised of? In order to enter hypnosis, it must be safe for you to do so; a recorded version of you cannot know that. You must also have the intention to enter hypnosis, again, a recorded version of you cannot have the intention for the real you to enter hypnosis, only you can have the intention to enter hypnosis.

Then of course, you have to count from 1–10 to enter hypnosis between 6 and 10. It is you that has to do that, not a recorded version of you. So you record steps 'B' to 'E' including your programme in there.

When you record your programmes remember to use second person, for example: 'Adam, you are in deep hypnosis' and **not** 'I am in deep hypnosis.' Usually, when you use your self-hypnosis you use the first person tense as you are talking to yourself, however, when recording, you use the second person. This is because if you settled down and got into to hypnosis to listen to your recording and benefit from it and the voice on the recording started saying 'I am in deep hypnosis and I am relaxing.' etc. You will just think to yourself 'Hmm. That is nice for you. What about me?'

You can use music if you wish in the background to enhance the relaxing aspect of the programme or any other aspect that you wish to emphasise.

Then, when you are ready, run the tape or CD from the beginning and enter hypnosis in the usual way, by having the intention, being in a safe place and counting from 1–10 entering hypnosis only on or after 6.

Upon entering hypnosis, give control and full hypnotic authority to your voice on the tape. You may even want to say something to yourself along the lines of 'I give full hypnotic authority to the voice on the tape and the programme has full effect upon me in the way that is for my highest good.'

Then, you can just lie back and enjoy the ride!

Music can be a very powerful aid to your hypnosis, do remember these two important rules when using music: Firstly, only use an instrumental piece – sung or spoken words may have hypnotic influence. Do not use an instrumental piece that has memorable words associated to it, even if it has no words your unconscious mind may still associate the word with it. For example, the instrumental version of 'I'm not in love' by 10cc may have a detrimental effect on your marriage!

At first, use all 3 of these methods of entering your programmes and see which works best for you. When you choose your favourite, you can use your self-hypnosis to even make sure that all the other methods work just as effectively.

Above all, enjoy your time in self-hypnosis and sell your programmes to yourself, let yourself know that they are important. Here is how you want to lay out your recording.

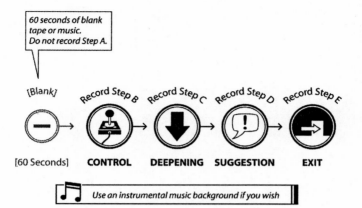

60 seconds of blank tape or music. Do not record Step A.

[Blank]

Record Step B · Record Step C · Record Step D · Record Step E

[60 Seconds] · CONTROL · DEEPENING · SUGGESTION · EXIT

Use an instrumental music background if you wish

Section 3

Hypnotic Technique

Now that you know how to get yourself settled, you know the structure of the self-hypnosis session, you know how to create programmes and the best language to use in self-hypnosis; you are now ready for the next step. The next step is of course actually going into hypnosis and getting used to the experience of it. Hold tight, here we go . . .

1

Getting into Hypnosis: Inductions

The real way to travel! The only way to travel!
Kenneth Grahame

Sound the fanfares! Whoop out loud! The time has arrived to finally start going into hypnosis and creating some trance states to enjoy.

An induction simply means to induce trance (self-hypnosis) in yourself. The induction is a simple procedure (many methods enclosed herein) to follow to induce trance in your self.

The induction is the initial stage of the session and is what creates the state of body and mind to enter hypnosis. Often, when the body is relaxed the mind can begin to focus on the state necessary to create the state of self-hypnosis. However, physical relaxation is not absolutely essential; it does help though, especially in these early stages. If you are the kind of person who fidgets a lot, you may need to work on some very active relaxation before inducing deeper states of self-hypnosis.

We are going to progress from eye fixation techniques, to visualisation techniques, to awareness techniques and other forms of induction to get you really aware of the varying forms that your self-hypnosis can take and you can discover what works best for you. If you are hyper aware on one occasion, or maybe anxious or analytical, during a session, you may need to use a different technique.

Be aware of falling asleep during your sessions; avoid self-hypnosis on your bed unless you are using it to enhance sleep and keep your mind focused on the objective that you want to achieve from the session. Remember, deep, non-dreaming sleep is when there is no communication going on between your minds.

Those of you who relax really easily, or possibly fall asleep easily need to look at the inductions that keep you curious and interested in the process and keep your mind active. So again, you may not want to use some of the long or lengthier induction methods and instead go for the shorter, snappier inductions that keeps you tuned in and sharp.

The techniques

So, to begin, use the techniques and strategies to ensure you are settled as we learned in the chapter of the first section of this book. Be aware of yourself, relax, breathe well and have a good sense of expectation and optimism.

The following chapter includes some sample scripts to use or you can create your own ways of going into hypnosis when you get good at doing the basic ones presented here.

There is a very particular structure to this section of the book. Here are several ways of developing trance states for yourself along with scripts to follow and for you to practice going in and out of trance states. While you are practising, you do not have to concern yourself with delivering programmes or suggestions for change, in the early stages just get acquainted with and get good at taking yourself in and out of self-hypnosis and enjoy those trance sessions.

Then, when you are really happy that you can get yourself into a trance with those methods, you can take yourself into hypnosis and use the programme for self-hypnosis I have enclosed at the end of the next chapter. This programme for self-hypnosis is designed especially for you to use to install the model of self-hypnosis into your unconscious mind. Then, you can begin to structure all your self-hypnosis sessions as described in the model of self-hypnosis and you can being to start delivering programmes and achieving excellence.

So, to recap:

1. Practice going into trances with the methods in this chapter and the scripts in the next chapter.
2. Take yourself into a trance and deliver the '**Programme for Self-hypnosis**' that is given at the end of the next chapter.

3. Start structuring your self-hypnosis sessions as per the model of self-hypnosis.
4. Use your self-hypnosis to deliver your personally created programmes for change.

Some self-hypnosis sessions are going to be on the spur of the moment and will not involve writing programmes; to relieve pain if you hurt yourself, to relax before a job interview or to get to sleep if feeling restless. These are all things that you can enter hypnosis and do without all the programme writing and preparation. There is another chapter all about this 'Instant Hypnosis' coming up.

Here is a range of inductions to get practising going in and out of hypnosis with:

Attention fixation

Having got yourself settled and relaxed and in a comfortable position, focus your attention on an object or a spot on the wall or ceiling, or anything else that is stationary.

Focus all your attention and place all your awareness on that spot or object, really examine it. Continue to breathe deeply while you focus, with purpose and at a nice slow pace. Have all your thoughts on that object or spot.

The idea here is that you are creating a focus that is free from distractions. You are eliminating unwanted thoughts and feelings by not focusing on them. Of course, you are likely to find, especially when first doing this, that stray thoughts pop into your head or that you wander for a moment or two, if that happens, just bring your awareness back to that object and focus and breathe deeply. As you practice you become better and better at focusing your attention and clearing your mind.

If other thoughts do pop into your mind, you don't have to resist them or fight them, just allow them to pass as quickly as they came and focus on your point of focus again. There is no right or wrong here, just experience.

At this stage, you can now begin to start telling yourself how relaxed you are as you continue to focus all thoughts and feelings on that spot. When you feel that you are really nice and focused, you can begin to start giving yourself suggestions such as the following, though you will benefit more from your own language as you get better at it:

> With each, slower, relaxing breath that I inhale, I can feel the relaxation spreading into my shoulders and neck and with each breath that I exhale, that relaxation deepens and the muscles in those areas soften and loosen, as the relaxation spreads down through my body I can feel it spreading and relaxing deeper.

Using your own words of course is better; it is the **notion** that we want to install here. Your unconscious will understand that you want to relax and begin to develop it further.

You may notice your eyes blinking or they may not be blinking at all, they may even water ever so slightly. You can notice this happening and feed it back to your self by saying to yourself;

> As my eyes continue to focus on this spot that I have chosen, they may feel more and more tired. Each blink of my eyes serves to deepen the level of relaxation in my body and sends more of it through my body, softening and loosening more and more.

You may want to allow your eyes to close if you think you would be more comfortable. If you do, initially, imagine that spot that you were focusing on, imagine that you can still see it and are focusing on it even though your eyes are closed. You might want to spend longer with your eyes open in these early sessions, you can decide when the time is right for you to proceed to doing so. You may want to add here;

> I can decide when I want to close my eyes. Just as I choose to allow myself to relax or drift off to sleep in the evenings, so I choose when to allow my eyes to close and develop my hypnotic state.

Continue to give yourself a steady flow of simple, relaxing suggestions, in a variety of different ways or sticking to what is most effective at that time. The repetition will allow your mind to relax and you can drift comfortably into the right state for you at that time. Close you eyes gently whenever is right for you, allow yourself to relax more and more.

When you feel that you are altering your state, you can proceed to enter self-hypnosis this way and then follow the self-hypnosis model as best as you can. Having accessed hypnosis (albeit in a different way than that of the self-hypnosis model; this is just for now) you can now take control, deepen in whatever way is right for you, deliver a simple suggestion if you want to (later you will deliver programmes) and then thank your unconscious mind and exit hypnosis.

Clasping hands induction

For some of you, the only way to get yourself into self-hypnosis might be by using an induction technique that has a physiological aspect that you can notice obviously. These kinds of inductions are often the kind of authoritarian methods used by hypnotists that are commonly used on stage.

Not everyone will find this method useful, however some of the types of people who will do are those who are used to requiring evidence or having something tangible to be aware of what is occurring. Dave Elman was a master of direct induction techniques and his book entitled **Hypnotherapy**, outlines his approach in greater detail. We shall be using one of his better-known methods of inducing hypnosis in the next chapter.

Firstly, allow yourself to clasp your hands in front of you, then do the following:

Press your hands really tightly together, really tightly so that you can feel the palms of the hands touching each other. Press them very tightly indeed. So that it verges on becoming uncomfortable.

And allow your hands to become locked together so tightly that they feel as though they're stuck together with super glue – they are just so tightly and securely locked together. And the harder you press those hands together the tighter they stick and the more securely locked the hands become. You need to be telling yourself this.

Press them together so tightly now that they just won't come apart. Even say to yourself and ensure that you are telling yourself that they just won't come apart. That's it, tighter and tighter – those hands so securely clasped, so tightly clasped, like the hands are held together with super glue and they just won't open at all. You can even pretend that they are locked together and stuck, so that as long as you are pretending, of course they are locked and stuck together. Really imagine in your mind that they are stuck together with that glue.

Then, in a moment, ask yourself to try to open them. You'll try to open them but they won't open at all, because they are so tightly stuck together.

OK so try to pull the hands apart, try, and notice that the hands are just too tightly clasped together that they simply don't open at all. And the harder you try to open them the tighter they feel. When you are ready, relax the hands, stop trying to open them, and just let them open, let them open easily and the hands are moving apart now (Take a look at those hands) – there – they're opening easily now, just relax them by your side and allow your eyes to close and follow one of the scripts or follow another induction to get yourself into a deeper state of hypnosis, as you do that notice how your hands feel and let those sensations of relaxation start to increase and spread through your body. You can take over from here as you continue to give yourself suggestions to enhance this.

Breathing inductions

In addition to the information in the earlier chapter with regards to settling down using your breath, your breath can induce trance and is used all over the world in various practices of meditation. These are often very powerful. You can start to heighten your awareness of your breath even more than you were previously. Noting it as it comes in and goes out, keeping the length of breath the same throughout. You may even want to imagine your breath going deeper and deeper down; a deeper breath is not necessarily a bigger breath or a larger breath, it is simply a breath that goes deeper and deeper down, a breath that relaxes you more and allows your body to ease on down.

Firstly, here is a good induction for focusing on your breathing.

You can begin, as we have done with other inductions, to notice a spot on the ceiling or wall and let all of your awareness be on that single spot for a moment. As you breathe and begin to relax you may notice that your awareness of the spot changes. You can also notice the way your awareness and focus changes too.

As we did before with the other induction, you can allow yourself to notice interesting things about the tiniest details of that spot.

Now you may have noticed that as you are focusing on that spot your body is relaxing a little bit more, (all the time throughout this induction, feeding back to yourself and saying to your self the things to get this notion across) and you can now heighten your awareness of how heavy or light your arms and legs are, just notice them and the sensations within them. Maybe you noticed as well, that your breathing has altered and whether it has slowed down a little or a lot, use your imagination, your awareness and say to yourself that it is becoming beneficially slower, deeper and comfortable in a way that enhances your self-hypnosis.

As your breathing becomes more naturally rhythmic and relaxed, tell yourself that your body is beginning to feel more relaxed and continue to notice is how heavy or light your limbs are right now and the sensations that exist within them. Just continue to notice the spot, and continue to notice how you feel and now also notice how steady your breathing has become as you focus upon it.

Allowing it to happen without you interfering with it. Almost as if you are observing your breath happening; as if you were watching a baby in your arms breathing, or a bird on a tree breathing, just observing your own breathing being so steady and comfortable. Maybe it is the same level of breathing that you had before when you have allowed yourself to relax. So gentle and so easy to just observe your breath, that it can begin to feel as if each breath in naturally leads to the next breath out, and that breath out easily leads to the next breath in. They occur in harmony.

Just get yourself focusing on that idea that each breath in is easily and naturally leading to the next breath out, and that breath out easily leads to the next breath in. SO that it may begin to feel as if your breath is becoming more of a circle of breath, your breathing can be imagined by you as being circular. Each breath continuing to lead to the next; in a circular motion.

Allow yourself to enjoy the natural way this happens, watch it happening passively. Now notice how naturally that happens for you, feeling as if your breath is a continuous, relaxing circle.

Then, continue breathing naturally and let each breath relax your body more and more so that your eyes can be relaxed more and more too. Focus on and imagine your eyelids becoming heavier and more tired so that you find it harder and harder to keep them open. When your eyes get too heavy to keep open, you can just let them close, relax your eyelids even more and let that softening, relaxing feeling travel and spread into all the muscles of your face.

Then, start teasing yourself a little bit by imagining how good it is going to feel when you close your eyes. Then, when you are ready, you can decide for yourself to close them. Notice how good it feels and tell your self how that feels.

Now that you have your eyes closed, you can notice that circle of breath even more, just happening naturally, almost like it has a flow of energy all it's own. Continue to imagine that it is happening all by itself, a steady circular breath that requires absolutely no effort from you.

Focus on the breath totally to the exclusion of everything else; all that exists is that circle of breath. Now from here you can start to use your imagination more if you want to. For example, you can begin to notice and imagine yourself inside of this energy, inside of this circle of breath, feeling the gentle movement and going along with it, you might even want to imagine the colour or sounds of it and make them colours or sounds that appeal to you and your unconscious.

Then, get yourself fully immersed in the freely moving circle of your breath. Many people just use this an exercise for relaxation and enjoyment. The more you practice, the more you get from it.

Then, you can begin to journey inside yourself, into your unconscious mind. Really allow yourself to go deeper inside your own mind, maybe to the place inside you where change can happen, maybe to where you have all the information and resources to achieve whatever you wanted to achieve with this hypnosis session, if there was anything at all. Discover whatever you want to discover, or just bask in the relaxation, concentrate on your breathing or continue to understand and receive information that your inner mind, your unconscious mind, would like you to know.

You can then use this time to deepen the state, to deliver a suggestion or a programme, or just count to 5 and bring yourself out of this state. Remember that in the initial stages, you are just practicing altering your state, getting into hypnotic states so that you can then deliver your programme for self-hypnosis and start to powerfully structure your self-hypnosis sessions and give them more purpose.

Here is a slightly different take on the idea of concentrating on your breathing, I originally got this idea from Terrence Watts, a well-know UK based hypnotherapist and trainer. The idea involves imagining breathing through your hands:

It is an innovative, relaxing and fun induction method, which works well for pretty much anybody. Begin by getting yourself settled down and comfortable, then follow these guidelines as best as you can.

Having got yourself settled and starting to relax, ensure that your hands are on your lap or by your sides and allow them to be free so that you can fully experience the sensations within them. Firstly, allow yourself to concentrate on your breathing for a few moments, let yourself imagine a very unusual idea though. Imagine that you can actually breathe through your fingertips. Just imagine and get yourself involved in that idea that you can actually breathe in through your fingertips. Continue to use your imagination and imagine that you can feel the air moving into your hands. Maybe quite slowly at first. As you experience the sensations in your hands and fingers, you might just notice a faint tingling sensation of some kind as you concentrate on your hands which you might feel on the back or in the palms of your hands. As you focus on that idea that you are breathing through your fingers, progress onto imagining that feeling of the air moving slowly along your arms.

Imagine it moving through your elbows, keep on just imagining that comforting flow of air moving through your elbows into your upper arms. Then imagine the air moving into your shoulders, both arms simultaneously and both shoulders. As you imagine it moving, notice the sensations that you are aware of so that maybe you find again that faint tingling sensation or any other sensation that might be there in your elbows or forearms this time. Keep on with this; imagine the air moving down through the body, down into your legs and through the thighs, through the knees, into your lower legs.

Again, continue to look out for sensations as it moves so that you might feel that faint tingling sensation, just there, somewhere along your legs or just around your knees. Then, allow it move down through your ankles and into your feet and finally out through the feet. You can now start developing the idea as you continue to imagine this. You might want to picture the air moving through you, or colour it, even give it a sound as you allow it to continue rhythmically, slowly and steadily. The suggestions that you can give yourself now can be that you can find a great deal of calmness and easiness in that rather unusual process of can breathing in through your fingers, letting the air move slowly as you can actually feel the air continuing to move through your entire body, in just that one single, natural, steady, unidirectional flow. Now, because it is a unidirectional flow of air, moving through your entire body in one single easy flow, you can give yourself suggestions and ideas to develop the notion that the calmness and relaxation you are breathing in and noticing are not involved in any way with the tensions and stresses that you breathe away from yourself. You can continue to repeat that idea, that suggestion to yourself that the calmness and relaxation that you breathe is uninvolved with the tiniest last traces of tensions and anxieties that you breathe away from yourself.

You may not even want to suggest that there are any tensions or anxieties to let go of, so you might not even want to mention that much. Just continue to remind yourself that with each breath you take, with each thought that you think and with every feeling that you experience, you find yourself becoming steadily and naturally more and more relaxed. Develop and continue with the idea that with each breath you take, with each sensation that you experience, you are steadily, easily and naturally more and more, calm, relaxed and at ease as you continue this rather unusual process of breathing in through your fingers and allowing that soothing, gentle, relaxing flow of air to move through your entire body and out through your feet.

This is then something that you can do for yourself with more and more ease whenever you want to. All you have to do is to simply settle yourself into a comfortable position with your eyes closed then simply imagine yourself breathing in through your fingers. You can develop it further and imagine that flow of air comforting and relaxing every part of your body as it moves. Then you are breathing the air out through your feet. You may even want to suggest to yourself that each time you breathe out you relax a little further, more profoundly or whatever suits you the most and generates the most wonderful feelings within you.

As before, you can now progress to deepening the state in the manner of ways that have been mentioned or whatever way you prefer and keep on practising developing the state until you are ready to install your programme for self-hypnosis.

Visualisation inductions

There are many ways of using visualisation and imagination to enter hypnosis; there are several scripts in the next chapter, some long and some shorter. Here is a nice and quick example of using your imagination to visually induce self-hypnosis.

It is known as the **Candle Induction**.

Start by using your imagination to imagine in your minds eye a single candle, which is lit. Focus your mind on the flame of the candle, notice the flickering and dancing of the flame as the yellows and reds swirl around. Whether you see this in your mind, or whether imagine it, sense it or just think to yourself that you know it is there, whichever of these ways you do this is the right way for you. Just trust that you are doing it in the way that is right for you.

Keep the candle in your mind as you go very gently and very deeply, into a profound state of relaxation. Then enjoy watching the candle in your mind, almost as if you were watching a film, and as the flame flickers and dances, you may notice a halo around the flame, like a natural glow or aura – and if you find your mind wandering away from the flame of the candle, just bring it gently back again.

So you just continue, as you keep the flame of the candle there in your mind, and then you can begin to count down from 10 to 1 in your mind. Tell yourself that each number you count makes you many, many times more comfortable and relaxed than you are now and keep on suggesting similar suggestions to your self.

Then go on to count to yourself or out loud, whichever is most agreeable for you and allow yourself to relax more, and suggest to your self that you are more and more deeply, deeply relaxed.

Once you have finished counting, you might want to go on to something else, another way of deepening further that suits you.

At the end of each of these inductions, when you are then proceeding with the remainder of the self-hypnosis session, it is a good opportunity to create some receptiveness within yourself. When you take control of the state as in step 'B', you can even suggest things to yourself such as 'I am now very deeply relaxed and each and every suggestion that I give myself does go deeply into my mind, to that place where I allow change to happen.' Or something similar along those lines, using your own language to suit you and your preferences.

Stairways and 'Going Down' inductions

This notion that we go **deeper** into hypnosis is one that has led to many methods of inductions to take us in a downward direction. Because of the idea of deepening hypnosis, ideas such as going down stairs, travelling down escalators, descending in an elevator or even skiing down mountains and diving deep into the ocean are ones that are commonly encountered.

Here is an example of a staircase induction to give you some idea and then you can expand or develop the idea to meet your own preferences.

As you sit or lie in your comfortable position, allowing yourself to get very comfortable and very relaxed – you again use your imagination to allow yourself and guide yourself to become aware of a staircase – the example I am going to use here is that of a beautiful staircase with a polished, ornate banister running down alongside and a deep, rich carpet underneath your bare feet.

As you look down the stairs you notice that there are ten steps leading gently down – ten steps leading down, and down, and down; these are the steps that lead you deep into a deeper, more beneficial state of hypnosis, they lead down into the part of you that knows how to achieve all the things you want to achieve – or you may just want it to lead down deep into relaxation, or maybe even toward a basement of relaxation- and then, in the next moment you to walk down those steps, at a pace that is conducive with enhancing and altering your state and as you step down each step in your own pace, you count them off to yourself one at a time.

Give yourself the suggestion that you find and discover for yourself that the deeper down you go and with every step you take, the more comfortable and the more relaxed you do become. So when you are ready to walk down the stairs, imagine that you gently and purposefully place your hand on the afore mentioned banister (get it into some detail in your mind) and begin to slowly descend the stairs as you count them off from 10 to 1 or whatever set of numbers you want, you may enjoy this so much that you want to take a spiral staircase down 100 stairs counting backwards.

With each step suggest to yourself what it is that you want to happen with each step, for example, you may want to say to your self something along the lines of:

10 – deeply relaxed, deeply comfortable, 9 – deeply relaxed, deeply comfortable each step takes me deeper 8 – more and more and more relaxed, letting go even more with every step down 7 – deeply relaxed, deeply comfortable, so calm and at ease 6 – way down now, 5 – more and more peaceful, finding that place of peace and harmony deep down inside me 4 – tranquil and deeply relaxed, deeply comfortable, more so with every step 3 – more and more and more relaxed, moving deeper 2 – almost at the bottom now, just one more step to go, and 1 – going deeper and deeper down into hypnosis now, all the way down – to that deeper, healthier level of mind.

Then as you reach the bottom step you can let the stairs and the usual world, your everyday world, drift further away as you drift further and further down – tell yourself that you are drifting deeper and deeper.

When you then find yourself standing at the bottom of the steps and feeling very comfortable, very relaxed and at peace with the world, you can take it further if you want to. Sometimes, you can imagine that there is the most inviting and comfortable looking bed in front of you that you sink into and allow yourself to dream about a special place.

You may want to imagine that in front of you is a large, oak door. The door is closed, but you can and do open it because of course, you have the key to this door. Maybe it is a door to a deeper level of being. Anyway, ensure that you really want to go through the door and that you want to see and experience what is there on the other side. You can anticipate and expect or just allow yourself to innately know that a wonderful place is there waiting for you.

So, progress on to move now toward the door. Push it open. Push the door open and suddenly the door creaks gently open, and you push it even further open and walk through. Now as you close the door behind you and turn and find yourself in a very special place. You can decide what that place is. Alternatively, you can just then start the process of taking control of the hypnosis session and developing it with the structured model of self-hypnosis.

If you are going to go to a special place, describe the special place to yourself with your language and words. Then also imagine it, hear the sounds that are or would be there, generate the feelings that let you know that this is a special place for you. Really get into it.

These are a variety of different ways to induce the trance state, to induce your self-hypnosis. Experiment with them and enjoy them and really get used to going in and out of those states.

Finally, before moving onto the scripted examples, I wanted to give you a really interesting and well-known technique of entering self-hypnosis. It is known as the Betty Erickson technique as she devised it. Betty's husband Milton Erickson is referred to on several occasions in this book as a renowned hynotherapist and psychiatrist. The technique is entirely attributed to her.

Betty Erickson method

This self-hypnosis method is based on the following premises and ideologies. While there are a number of counter-examples to these notions, they will be of value in understanding and utilizing this process of taking your self into hypnosis. Some of those premises I have touched upon already, we are going to take them a bit further here.

We process information (that is, we think) in pictures, sounds and feelings. In Neuro-linguistic Programming, these sensory modalities are referred to as representational systems. These representational systems are visual, auditory and kinaesthetic.

Firstly, the **Visual System** – by this we refer to the external things we see and the internal images that we create. This includes remembered images ('What does your front door look like?'), constructed images ('What would it look like if it were re-decorated?'), as well as the actual, real things we see about us.

Second of all is the **Auditory System** – the external things we hear, the internal sounds that we create. This includes remembered words or sounds ('Think of your country's national anthem'), imagined words or sounds ('Imagine that national anthem played by saxophone'), and also includes your internal dialogue as well as all of the real, actual, live sounds around us.

Thirdly, the **Kinaesthetic System** – these are the things we feel. These can be actual physical sensations or imagined ones. Can you imagine being at the seaside and paddling in the cool sea?

Most of us have developed greater proficiency with one or the other of our representational systems though we each use all three of them. We usually have a dominant system. Since this is usually the case, an individual who 'thinks' in images wouldn't experience a state of self-hypnosis simply by visualising. However, if that same individual were to experience a preponderance of feelings or sensations, this would be unusual – an alteration of their state of consciousness. When we talk about altered states, what we're really referring to is processing information in a different manner than usual; communication between the conscious and unconscious minds.

Focused attention

Stereotypical images of hypnotists holding watches or other fixation devices for clients to stare at are the result of this understanding about hypnosis. I for one have long ago banished my velveteen smoking jacket and watch on a chain for more modern methods of hypnotic induction. (That was a joke by the way; me in velveteen?!) As we have discussed, the experience of hypnosis is typically an inwardly focused one in which we move away from the environment around us and turn our attention inward. This technique is doing that even more.

The Betty Erickson self-hypnosis technique

Find a comfortable position and get your self relaxed and settled. Get into a position that you will be able to maintain easily for the time you are going to be doing this process. It can be sitting or lying down, though sitting is recommended to prevent you from falling asleep. Get yourself centred, just looking in front of you and breathing slowly and easily. Let yourself relax.

Think about the length of time that you intend to spend in this state and make a statement to yourself about it such as 'I am going into self hypnosis for 20 minutes . . .' (or however long you want) You will be delighted to discover how well you 'internal clock' can keep track of the time for you.

Just for this technique, you can give yourself a purpose. Obviously, when you get fully involved with process of writing your programmes and delivering them, you use that method. For now though, make a statement to yourself about your purpose for going into self-hypnosis. In this process, we allow the unconscious mind to work on the issue rather than giving suggestions throughout, so our purpose statement should reflect that fact. Here's how I recommend you say it: '. . . for the purpose of allowing my unconscious mind to make the adjustments that are appropriate to assist me in _____'. Filling in the blank with what you want to achieve such as 'developing more confidence in social situations.' I know that the text is 'wordy' but that's how I got it when I learned it. The actual words aren't nearly as important as the fact your statement acknowledges that you are turning this process over to your unconscious mind.

Now for the actual process – looking in front of you, notice three things (one at a time) that you see. Go slowly, pausing for a moment on each. It is preferable that they be small things, such as a spot on the wall, a doorknob, the corner of a picture frame, etc. Some people like to name the items as they look at them – 'I see the hinge on the door frame'. (If you don't know the name for the thing, say 'I see that thing over there.') Now turn your attention to your auditory channel and notice, one by one, three things that you hear. (You will notice that this allows you to incorporate sounds that occur in the environment rather than being distracted by them.)

Next, attend to your feeling and notice three sensations that you can feel right now. Again, go slowly from one to the next. It is useful to use sensations that normally are outside of your awareness, such as the weight of your glasses, the feeling of your wristwatch, the texture of your shirt on your body, etc.

Continue the process using two Visuals, then two auditories and then two kinaesthetics. Then, in the same manner, continue (slowly) with one of each.

You have now completed the 'external' portion of the process. Now it's time to begin the 'internal' part.

Firstly, close your eyes. Now, bring an image into your mind. Don't work too hard at this; this is fun, remember? You can construct an image or simply take what comes. It may be a point of light, it may be a beautiful beach, or it could be your car or an apple. I shall not scare you with the ideas that randomly pop into my mind. If something comes to you, just use it. If nothing comes, feel free to put something in your mind.

Pause and let a sound come into your awareness or generate one and name it. Although this is technically the internal part, if you should hear a sound outside or in the room with you, it is OK to use that. Remember that the idea is to incorporate things that you experience rather than being distracted by them. Typically, in the absence of environmental sounds; I often hear whooping hallelujahs from a gospel choir; don't ask me why, that just happens in my mind.

Next, become aware of a feeling and name it. It is preferable to do this internally – use your imagination. (I feel the warmth of the sun on my face) However, as with the auditory, if you actually have a physical sensation that gets your attention, use that.

Repeat the process with two images, then two sounds, then two feelings. Repeat the cycle once again using three images, three sounds, and three feelings.

Then to complete the process – It is not unusual to feel a little bit 'spaced out' or wander off somewhat. At first some people think that they have fallen asleep. But generally you will find yourself coming back automatically at the end of the allotted time. This is an indication that you weren't sleeping and that your unconscious mind was doing what you asked of it.

Most people don't get all the way through the process. That's perfectly all right. If you should complete the process before the time has ended, just continue with 4 images, sounds, feelings, then 5 and so on. It is another way of just getting you acquainted with going in and out of hypnosis before you can then install the programme for self-hypnosis at the end of the next chapter and follow the structure that you have learned in the earlier section of the book.

2

Scripted Examples

Few things are harder to put up with than the annoyance of a good example.

Mark Twain

Further to the inductions in the previous chapter, here are several sample scripts of some of the things that have been mentioned so far. You can doctor them or gain inspiration and ideas from them rather than copy them word for word. Remember and observe that scripts are rather one-dimensional; they do not always carry a lot of emotion, images, sounds or sensations that I suggested you put in to your programmes when you create them for yourself. It is up to you to bring them to life and add depth and dimension in a way that appeals to you.

You want your scripts and programmes to be alive and emotive, with the kind of language that stimulates you and takes you on magical journeys to success and achievement or just creates more and more discovery and happiness within you. These are just ideas for getting into hypnosis, for getting into trance states, when you have then delivered your self-hypnosis programme to your self, you can then progress on to the section of the book which has all the specific applications for using self-hypnosis to make certain changes like stopping smoking, gaining confidence, healing, creating wealth and much more.

These scripts are in the first person tense, as if you were using them for reading them to yourself and delivering them to yourself that way. Remember if you want to record them, you will need to turn them into a script that a hypnotist would use if they were addressing you and use the second person tense.

Firstly, here are some guided visualisation scripts:

Forest Walk

I imagine myself now moving, almost floating in a beautiful forest. It's a crisp autumn day and the dappling sun reflects upon a gurgling stream that runs along the edge of the forest and can be heard gently and softly in the background. I tread carefully into the forest, over the crackling red and golden leaves and broken twigs; pine cones are scattered across the ground – a squirrel runs up a tree – I watch the speed with which it moves, swiftly up and through the branches until it moves out of my sight.

It's a very peaceful life here in this forest; I notice clusters of bluebells and soft green moss. I can detect the pleasant aroma and perfumed, I can almost taste the freshness in the air and feel it tingling on my tongue. The deeper into the forest I venture, the deeper into relaxation I drift – I am drifting more and more deeply into a progressively more and more calm and tranquil feeling.

I watch a leaf falling from a tree as it dances and twirls in the air, before fluttering slowly down to rest with the others. I pause for a while and rest against an old oak tree. I can feel the rough bark of the tree against my fingertips – smell the earthy ground and soft leaf mould – fairy rings of toadstools or mushrooms scattered here and there, and even as I am resting here against the rough bark of the tree, I can feel a deep sense of peacefulness in this beautiful place. And this deep sense of peacefulness is growing and developing within me – it is growing stronger and stronger each and every day. Each and every day I am growing stronger and stronger – as strong as an old oak tree, stronger and stronger each and every day.

Because now, my body knows how to relax more and more naturally, in the way that nature intended. And relaxing like this brings me closer to nature and the wonderful resources that exist deep in my unconscious mind.

Scenic Garden Script

I imagine that I am standing at the top of some steps, which lead down into a long, colourful and beautiful garden. Just standing comfortably and lazily. As I gaze onto the garden, I breathe a deep long breath of pure, clean, fresh air and I can feel that wonderfully healthy air flowing through my body. As I gaze, I stretch and relax feeling more and more increasingly, deeply, lazily and calm.

In the garden I can see a long, lush, green lawn, beautiful coloured flowers, large trees and hedges surrounding the perimeter, ensuring that the garden is private and secluded. I can smell the clean fresh air, and the sweetness of the all the wildlife and nature here in my own special garden. I can hear the sounds of bees humming at a safe and comfortable distance, of birds singing high in the branches of the trees above, the occasional soft breeze rustling the branches.

Every sight, every sound, every feeling serves to take me deeper into a deep hypnotic experience, more and more easily, naturally and gently.

I feel that soft, warming breeze as I enjoy the feeling of the suns rays against my skin, warming my face, relaxing my body, relaxing my mind further and further. I can see at the very far end of this garden is a slowly babbling brook flowing from a small waterfall from higher ground; the sound is so deeply soothing and calming.

All is so peaceful, so calm and tranquil, so enjoyably serene. As I stand enjoying the sights of this beautiful garden, I notice that a colourfully patterned butterfly has landed on one of my arms and seems to be responding to me. It is preparing to take flight and seems more likely to do so with every slower, deeper breath that I breathe, almost as if my deeper breaths were energising the butterfly. I find that after a couple of breaths, the butterfly gently flutters its wings and flies away. I decide that I wish to walk towards the garden and look down at the gentle sloping steps of which there are five. With each and every step that I take, you naturally drift deeper and deeper to the right state of hypnosis for me now. Into a deeper and deeper blissful hypnotic trance now.

So, down the first step, drifting deeper, the second step, relaxing more and more. The third step, wonderfully deeper, really feeling the difference, the fourth step, so much enjoyably deeper, really letting go. And the fifth and final step, all the way now, to the very deepest level of hypnotic trance.

As I begin to walk along the fine, springy lawn, I smell the wonderful flowers and shrubs, noting all the new life around me, new beginnings; I breathe in this new life, these new beginnings and feel it flowing through my system. With each step that I take, I drift deeper to sleep now, until I reach the babbling brook. I enjoy the sound of the clean, clear water passing over the rocks and pebbles around the waters edge. I notice brown, furry bulrushes growing around the outside and see up ahead a large weeping willow tree drips its foliage into the water. Everything is so tranquil, so relaxing, and so calm.

I sit down beside the running water for a moment, just soaking up all that is wonderful here and now for a moment, knowing that there is nothing expected from me, there is nothing that I need to do or have to do, this is an opportunity for me to spend some time separated from the outside world for a little while at least.

Mountain Script

It is a beautiful spring sunny day – the warm sun is shining down upon me – making me feel more and more wonderfully comfortable .I am moving and going on up along a path up a mountain.E I notice that the path is gradually ascending this gentle slope.E I can and do let myself really feel that I am travelling upward and going higher and higher, into the mountain of peace and tranquillity.

As IElook around me now.E I just pause here for a moment, and notice a soft breeze blowing on my skin and on my hair.E I am quite high up the mountain and I have a wonderful clear view below, and across – I can see for miles and miles around.E Here and there I notice wildlife moving and even come across a rabbit or a few mountain sheep or goats.E They live peacefully up here; I continue my journey up the mountain.E

As I go higher, so the mountain becomes a little steeper and in places the path narrows.E Gorse bushes border my path in places, and mountain flowers peep out to greet me.E I can see another mountain, which looks so close that I almost feel that I could walk over to it.E

As I climb higher and higher, ascending up the mountain, I eventually reach a plateau where I stop to rest.EI Just pause there, resting a while, relaxing more and more, and take in, absorbing the beautiful and spectacular view.EAs I look down the mountain I can see how far I have come.E I have come a very long way, up a mountain path that was, at times, difficult, at other times easy, however I continued.E And I can continue now until I reach the summit.E I'm going to just enjoy those last moments as I progress toward the summit until I reach the summit. IEmove closer and closer now towards my goal.

Here is a script just using your awareness of your self to enter hypnosis:

Heightened Awareness Script

I just allow myself to listen quietly to the instructions and suggestions that I am giving myself and of course I am more and more aware of all those other sounds too, sounds within my immediate periphery as well as sounds from outside of it. These sounds all serve to enhance and improve my experience of this session more and more and I continue to heighten my awareness of the quietest sounds. In fact the sounds, even if that means the sound of silence, just continue to help to relax me progressively more, that is right, and while I am listening to the immediate sounds all around me, I just simply allow myself to be as lazy as I could ever want to be. I bask in this awareness of this moment. I realise that the past has happened, I cannot change it, the future is yet to occur, it is not tangible, so I continue to engage myself fully in this moment and I continue to just allow myself to be as lazy as I could ever want to be.

I notice more and more acutely what it is that I am experiencing in this moment. So, that while I continue relaxing here in this comfortable position, I can just be more and more aware of my body. I am more and more aware of my hands where they are resting, noticing even the most tiniest of movements and sensing the weight of them, then allowing my attention and awareness to spread out along my arms, to really experience how my arms are right now, perhaps noticing the angle of my elbows and maybe sensing the weight of my head whatever it is resting on, or however it is balancing on my shoulders.

As I focus and concentrate on my own inner realities increasingly more, I realise, that weight might seem to just gently alter, or vary as I allow myself to relax more and more, continuing to just be more and more aware of my ankles and feet now, where they are placed, and wondering if they will start to feel heavier or lighter too, as I continue to relax further and further. I allow my self to think again about my breathing for a few moments, noticing that my breathing is becoming slower and steadier, more rhythmic as I relax more and more; it is slower, deeper and steadier. I am breathing so slowly and steadily and evenly, it is almost as though I am sound asleep, breathing so evenly, so naturally, so steadily, I almost would not disturb a feather placed immediately in front of me, breathing so slowly and easily, so gently.

Right now, in this moment as I allow myself to relax even more deeply and profoundly, I begin to sense the beating of my own heart, noticing it quite subtly at first and as I concentrate and feel its movement, my awareness tunes into it more and more, I am easily sensing the beat of my own heart and just seeing whether I can use the power of my mind to slow that heartbeat down, a fraction, just a touch, I am just seeing whether I can use the power of my mind to slow that heartbeat down just a little, so that I can allow my entire body to continue to relax and become steadier and easier until it is just ticking over, smoothly, like a well maintained machine of some sort or another, it is just ticking over, more and more smoothly, more easily, quietly, more comfortably, so that I can become gradually more aware of my entire self, my entire self, more aware of my arms and hands, just sensing how they are, again more aware of my legs and feet too, again just sensing how relaxed they might feel, and wondering if it is possible to relax them even more, to be so in touch with myself that I can actually get my entire body, to naturally relax even more, yet remaining totally alert and sharply focused with a better and better clarity of thought.

I am noticing now how even my face muscles can begin to really relax, relaxing and letting go of any tensions that were or were not there, almost, but not quite, completely unnoticed, just being vaguely aware of the skin and the muscles of my face settling, smoothing out, a wonderful feeling, all those tiniest of muscles just melting away, softening more and more wonderfully, letting go further with every breath that I exhale and that feels so good, and as I continue to sense the beat of my heart and my body's natural rhythm, I wonder at the fact that I am so absolutely relaxed and comfortable that I simply drift deeper and deeper into a deep hypnotic state now.

Just allowing myself to enjoy being as relaxed as anyone could ever wish to be, allowing myself to just be, as lazy as anyone could wish to be, and I wonder if I can now manage to relax even more, even though I am already as relaxed as it is possible for most people to be, I am just letting go of the last tiniest traces of tension in my body and softening the muscles, simply, with each easy, gentle breath I breathe, allowing every breath I breathe to relax every muscle, every nerve, every cell in my entire body, as I am drifting deeper and deeper into self-hypnosis now.

Here is a Dave Elman style of induction as I touched upon briefly in the previous chapter, for this one you just need to follow the instructions that you give yourself in your mind and create more and more beneficial suggestions as you progress;

Firstly, take a long, deep breath and hold it for a few seconds. As you exhale this breath slowly, controlled, allow your eyes to close and let go of any surface tension in the body. Just let your body relax as much as possible right now.You may even notice that some parts of your body are easier to relax than others, you can become aware of the parts of you that feel most comfortable and allow all those wonderful sensations to spread as you breathe comfortably and steadily right now.

As you have your eyes closed now, allow yourself to pretend that you cannot open them, that's it, pretend you cannot open them. Keep on pretending and while you are pretending, try to open your eyes. You'll find that is impossible, if you are concentrating hard on your pretence. Now, you know very well that you can open your eyes anytime that you change your mind and stop pretending.

So now, place your awareness on your eye muscles and relax the muscles around your eyes to the point that they just won't work. You have to do this, I can't do it for you, that's it, just relax the muscles around your eyes to the point they just won't work.

When you are sure that they are so relaxed that as long as you hold on to this relaxation, they just won't work, then hold on to that relaxation and test them to make sure they won't work. Stop testing.

Now, this relaxation that you have in your eyes is the same level of relaxation that you want to allow yourself to have throughout your entire body, so just spread that level of relaxation throughout your entire being, let this quality of relaxation flow throughout your entire body.

We can deepen this level of relaxation much more. In a moment, you are going to have yourself open and close your eyes. When you close your eyes; that is your signal to let this level of relaxation become 10 times deeper. All you have to do is want it to happen and OKyou can make it happen very easily. , now, open your eyes.. Now close them again and feel that relaxation flowing throughout your entire body, taking you much deeper.

Maybe you can even use your wonderful imagination to imagine your entire body covered and wrapped in a warm blanket of relaxation.

Now, we can deepen that relaxation much more. In a moment, you are going to open and close your eyes again and double the relaxation you now have. Make it become twice as deep. So once more now, open your eyes.. And close them again, and double your relaxation. good. Let every muscle of your body become so relaxed that as long as you hold on to this quality of relaxation, every muscle of your body is totally relaxed and dormant, still and peaceful.

In a moment, you are going to have yourself open and close your eyes once more. Again, when you close your eyes, double the relaxation you now have. Make it twice as deep. All you have to do is want it to happen and you make it happen so easily. Once again now, open your eyes. and close your eyes and double your relaxation. good. Let every muscle in your body become so relaxed that as long as you hold on to this quality of relaxation, every muscle in your body becomes loose, limp and more and more relaxed.

As you heighten your awareness of how you are feeling physically, noticing the differences on how relaxed you are now compared to when you first began this hypnosis session, you know this is physical relaxation.

With each breath you breathe, allowing yourself to drift into the state that is the right state for you right now. You can then progress to deepen in a way that is right for you.

Variation of candle induction

You remember that induction of focusing on the candle flame from earlier? Well, here is a slightly different, slightly longer version of that induction for you to use and enjoy:

As I relax more, and let go more and more, I can and do allow every muscle in my body to relax more and more profoundly.

I now picture, sense or imagine in my mind a candle, this candle can be any colour I wish it to be. The colour that I have chosen for my candle is a colour that my unconscious knows relaxes me and calms my mind.

I now focus on the flame of the candle. I can see, sense or imagine how beautiful the colours within the flame are. I may be aware of red, blue, yellow, purple, white or maybe another colour, and as I see, sense or imagine those colours within the flame, I relax more and go deeper, as I enjoy these relaxed feelings spreading into every fibre of my body.

I now focus on the wax body of my candle and as I see, sense or imagine the first trickle of melting wax begin to move down the side of this warm and comfortable candle, I see or imagine the melting wax touch the candleholder and merge with it to become part of the candleholder, so I become more and more relaxed, safe and comfortable.

Now, I imagine that I am that candle, a candle of total relaxation and, as I picture it, as the muscles in my body, helping me to relax more and more completely. I picture that which I am sitting in or lying on as a candleholder, and that my muscles, like the wax of my candle of relaxation, are melting into the chair, and that I am becoming, myself, a candle of relaxation.

Inner eye induction

A nice, short way of entering hypnosis As pioneered by Michael Yapko.

In the same way that I have eyes that see the world around me, I also have an inner eye that is known as and called the mind's eye, and it can see images and process thoughts even as I relax so deeply, and my mind's eye has an eyelid, and like my physical eye, that eyelid can close down, as it, too, becomes heavy and tired, wanting to close, and it can begin to close, and as it slowly drops it shuts out stray thoughts, stray images, and can leave my mind perfectly clear, it experiences whatever I would choose and it is closing now, closing more and more, and my mind grows quiet and at peace, and now it closes completely, closing out all stray thoughts or images that I don't want to interfere with how relaxed I am.

This is your programme for self-hypnosis

OK, by now, you should have practiced and practiced more and more of these techniques and should be getting more and more familiar with going into self-hypnosis. You should be using many different ways and deepening the state in your own ways and really personalising your experience of hypnosis. Once you are sure that you are ready to take things on to the next stage, take yourself into a hypnotic state using any induction method you can, then take control of the state (step 'B'), deepen to the right level for you (step 'C'), deliver the programme that follows (step 'D') which is your programme for self-hypnosis, using any of the techniques shown earlier in the book, then thank your unconscious mind and exit hypnosis (step 'E'). Having done that, do it again, then do it again and repeat the delivery of this programme until you are sure that you have firmly embedded it in your unconscious mind and are ready to move forward.

Programme for self-hypnosis

There are three accessing cues that only I can use to activate my self-hypnosis programme. The three cues are:

Firstly, I have the intention to enter self-hypnosis.

Secondly, that I am in a safe place so that I can relax as I am now.

Thirdly, using my usual speaking voice, or in my mind, I count from one toward ten, entering hypnosis only between 6 and 10.

The instant I enter hypnosis, I am deeper than I am now, each time deeper than the time before. The very instant I enter hypnosis, I am in full control, and being in full control means that I respond hypnotically only to my intended instructions and programmes. Being in full control means that I am protected from random thought having any hypnotic influence. Full control means that I am protected from random image having any hypnotic influence. Full control means that I am protected from random sound having any hypnotic influence.

Only my intended instructions are given any hypnotic authority.

While in hypnosis I can give myself any suggestions in any way that pleases me. I can think them, whisper them, speak them aloud, record them or use any other way that pleases me.

When I have finished with hypnosis and am ready to exit, all that I need to do is count to 5. I can count aloud or count in my mind, either way, on five each time, on five, I am out of hypnosis, fully out of hypnosis.

This programme is my control of my hypnosis. Only I can activate it, and every time I use this programme and enter hypnosis, I automatically strengthen it and it works better and better.

I now ask my unconscious to take this programme and lock it away in the very deepest area of my mind, safe and secure. My hypnosis is now of a better and better quality each and every time I enter it.

Take yourself into hypnosis and deliver this programme is as many ways as you like, or in the same way several times, whatever you prefer, just get it well and truly delivered to your unconscious mind and then keep on using the structure of the self-hypnosis model for your self-hypnosis sessions.

From there, you can begin to write and construct powerful programmes for change as you have learned about already, using the guidelines that have been set out, along with the kind of language that you respond to the most effectively and start making some really amazing changes, transformations, updates or just having some more fun and happiness in your life.

3

Instant Hypnosis

Faster than a speeding bullet.
U.S. Radio Introduction to Superman

There are going to be times when you want to enter hypnosis fast; when you do not want to have to relax yourself, count from 1 to 10, take control, sufficiently deepen, deliver a pre-created programme and then exit hypnosis. There are likely to be times when it is not appropriate to do that too. Those times will be when you want to stop your eyes watering if and when you are chopping onions, or if you cut yourself shaving and want to stop the bleeding, or if you bang your finger in the car door, or want to relax yourself immediately prior to a job interview, or making a long, late running train journey zip by; all these things that I have just mentioned, I have used self-hypnosis in an instant, to get the results I wanted at that moment.

Before really getting into the idea of instant hypnosis and 'zapping' yourself into the state for rapid and immediate use, be sure that you are thoroughly and well acquainted with getting into hypnosis in the full, structured method first. It is really important that in order to achieve a profound and powerful level of success with self-hypnosis, that you are fully aware of the state and how you recognise it.

How do you know when you are in a state of self-hypnosis; you will only know when you have practiced the structured methodology over and over and got to that stage whereby you really do recognise the qualities of your hypnotic experience. Once you have arrived at that stage, you can then begin to get into that state more rapidly because you consciously and unconsciously know what it is that you are looking for and you can begin to let it happen and flow more easily without having to consciously concentrate and analyse the state to know if you have it or not.

When you are ready for instant hypnosis and are well acquainted with the self-hypnosis model and it's use, then take yourself into hypnosis with step 'A', take control with step 'B', continually deepen with step 'C' and then deliver this following programme as per step 'D' in whatever way suits you best, remember to thank your unconscious mind and your self and then exit as per step 'E'.

Programme for instant hypnosis

From this moment forward whenever I intend to enter instant hypnosis there are three parts to the trigger. The first part is to have the desire, the intention to enter self-hypnosis instantly. The second part is to be in a safe place. The third part is to say to myself aloud or silently 'Instant Hypnosis Now.'

The instant I enter into hypnosis I am completely protected from random thought, random sound and random image becoming suggestion, and on entering hypnosis my body retains the position that I am in, i.e., if standing, I remain standing, if sitting, I remain sitting.

Once in the hypnotic state I am in full control and can use it for whatever purpose I please.

On finishing with the hypnotic state I count to five as usual to exit from hypnosis.

You can of course create your own version or create your own trigger words to ensure it is congruent with you. Just do whatever you would prefer.

Section 4

Advanced Methodology and Applications

This section of the book gives some specific applications of how to use self-hypnosis, often in conjunction with some other methods, to achieve specific outcomes. Even if you are not a smoker, you will benefit from reading the section on stopping smoking, as there are ideas and information in each and every subsequent chapter that can be used in other ways to great effect.

Before you move on to these applications and some of the advanced methodologies that are within this chapter of the book, please, please, please ensure that you know the structure of self-hypnosis and that you are easily entering self-hypnosis using the self-hypnosis model comfortably.

Ensure also that you are aware of how to write programmes for yourself, that the information presented in this book so far is being used by you, so you are considering your language with yourself and in the field of your self-hypnosis, that you are heightening your awareness of the ways that can and do enhance and advance the effectiveness of your own suggestions and programmes and the power of your self-hypnosis as an amazing self-help tool.

Before you progress, I have a very important thing to add here, this is very, very important; each of the chapters has some scripted examples, some I have written, some are written by others and doctored for our purposes, please, please use them for ideas and

inspiration, not to use directly. Some of them may not contain the kind of language that is right for you to get the success you want and deserve.
Your unconscious mind and your brain deserves better than that. You deserve to spend the right time and invest the right energy in using the material for generating your own ideas. That is important. Please, please do take note of that. Some of the programmes do not have all the elements included that should be included in your programmes; they are for ideas and structure only. They are not for using directly.

1

Safe Controlled Relaxation and Stress Relief

This chapter is about overcoming stress and getting things into their correct perspective. It is also about you having the tools to be able to relax whenever you want, not only when you need to, but before you need to as well.

You know, we need a certain level of stress in order to be able to function at our best; we need a certain level of stress to ensure that we can cross a road without being knocked over by an oncoming vehicle. When stress gets out of control and creates distress is what we want to avoid.

Too much stress can cause emotional breakdowns, fatigue, headaches, high blood pressure, insomnia; it is not good therefore to have an excess of it. Sometimes, just being aware that it is there and knowing that you need to action to remedy it is the beginning of releasing unnecessary stress. You cannot control what is going on around you in the world; however, you can change and alter how you respond to that which is going on in the world around you. Progressive and positive thinking is a solid foundation for relieving and overcoming stress.

There are so many things that you can do and I am sure are already thinking of that you can create with your self-hypnosis; programmes that you can devise to combat too much stress. This chapter gives other additional ideas that you can in addition to those ideas and strategies of your own.

Back in pre-historic times, the well-documented 'fight or flight' physiological response was very useful as it enabled us to be at our peak if a sabre-tooth tiger was on our tail. Our blood would rush to our main organs, we get a surge of adrenalin, unimportant bodily functions like digestion would be ignored and our bodies were able to do just that; 'fight or flight', it was our ingenious survival mechanism.

This mechanism is very much dated in our modern world now, and when we are challenged, by whatever stimulus, maybe by extreme workload or what we perceive as traumatic changes occurring in our life for example, our fight or flight response kicks in and we do not function as we really want to in those given circumstances. Our digestion stops, heart rate increases, we get headaches, circulation is altered, an entire host of unwanted responses.

What we want to be able to do is take control of how we feel when we want to feel it, instead of going on some automatic stress response to having a demanding boss for example.

The following self-hypnosis exercises and self-hypnosis sessions are designed to put you in control of how you feel and show you that you can relax and put things into their correct perspective.

A gentleman came to see me some while ago, his wife had booked him in to see me as a friend of hers had successfully overcome a thirty year phobia of heights with me. The lady told me that her husband was exceptionally stressed in many aspects of his life, mainly at work though. He arrived for his appointment and he instantly said those words that I hear so often 'My boss makes me so stressed.'

A story I was told once mentions that it was not long after the Gods had created humankind that they began to realise their mistake. The creatures they had created were so adept, so skilful, and so full of curiosity and the spirit of inquiry that it was only a matter of time before they would start to challenge the Gods themselves for supremacy.

To ensure their pre-eminence the gods held a large conference to discuss the issue. Gods were summoned from all over the known and unknown worlds. The debates were long, detailed and soul searching.

All the gods were very very clear about one thing. The difference between them and mortals was the difference between the qualities of the resources they had. While humans had their egos and were concerned with the external, material aspects of the world, the

Gods had spirit, soul, and an understanding of the workings of the inner self.

The danger was that sooner or later the humans would want some of that too.

The gods decided to hide their precious resources. The question was; where? This was the reason for the length and passion of the debates at the great conference of the Gods.

I wonder if you've ever considered; What if one of your five senses stopped working? What if you could no longer hear here or anywhere? All the words of any language would simply pass by your ears, unnoticed, like a CD player with no CD in it. Yet, of course, all those words continue to exist, in fact, many more, newer words come into existence.

Then imagine that all of a sudden, you are able to hear again, hear here and everywhere. Each and every word is totally new to your ears, innocence in a sense. Yet they had long existed before you heard them. Isn't it exciting when you discover something just new to you or something you just knew?

This is just like observing the contents of or walking more deeply into your wardrobe full of clothes and suddenly noticing an item you remember being there. Maybe you forgot for a while and finding the once new, forgotten article sort of makes it renew. You may remember where you bought it and when, suddenly re-experiencing that experience of excitedly buying it again, right there in your own wardrobe.

Usually, when you rediscover this item you become keen to put it on again and show it to yourself and others. You try it on and notice how it feels and fits. Perhaps you already have other things you can wear with it and look forward to wearing it with pride and happiness, increasing surety.

Now I wonder what items you have forgotten about, that you possess, reclaiming, renewing, what will you wear with them? It may seem like I have gone off on a couple of tangents here. If you are scratching your head thinking that the last few paragraphs were unusual, that is ok. I just read through it myself and it is meant to be like that I assure you.

Everybody's body and mind knows all that it needs to know about being relaxed, if you fell over and grazed your knee you would not doubt your bodies ability to heal that graze, so with that same sense of knowing, you can trust that your body and mind know how to relax, how to enjoy peace and tranquillity within, and allow your innate abilities to let that happen now, without you having to consciously think about doing it all the time.

It is that conscious inner talk and conscious hyper-activity that used to get in the way, so now, you are letting that go, get that voice to shut up, 'Oi, internal dialogue, stop!', or use some of the techniques from section one of this book, just get your internal dialogue to stop and think your other thoughts, relax, breathe, let go. You know how to do it.

You see, at the great conference of the gods, someone suggested hiding these resources at the top of the highest mountain. But it was realised that sooner or later the humans would scale such a mountain.

And the deepest crater in the deepest ocean would be discovered. And the mines would be sunk into the earth, and the most impenetrable jungles would give up their secrets, and mechanical birds would explore the sky and space and the moon and planets would become tourist destinations.

And even the most wise and creative of gods fell silent as if every avenue had been explored and found waiting.

Until the littlest god, who had been silent until now, spoke up:

Why don't we hide these resources inside each human? They'll never think to look for them there.

Now, that guy whose wife had recommended to come and see me, said that to me and I said to him 'You know what, your boss cannot make you be stressed, no one person or circumstance or situation can make anyone feel anything, you choose how you feel, you learn how you feel and how you respond to any given situation is your choice.'

So we worked together on him finding the resources and establishing the belief to allow him to know that he can choose to relax, and learn how to allow himself to experience the world in a way that he found to be most comfortable.

Imagine a scene; under a hot sun, a little boy is gazing at a young man intently chipping away at a large piece of rock.

'Why are you doing that?'

'Because,' said Michelangelo, 'There's an angel inside, and he wants to come out.'

OK, so the first tool for helping to overcome stress that I am going to illustrate here is that of a 'stress shield.' Take those words verbatim and you know exactly what we are dealing with here. You can create a shield to protect you from pretty much anything and use the script to form the basis of any kind of shield that you would find useful.

This programme is delivered within your self-hypnosis session as per the self-hypnosis model, then, it works all the time while you are out of hypnosis, even at times when you are not consciously thinking about it.

Stress shield programme

As I concentrate on my breathing even more, noticing my breathing, the rhythm of it, gently, just naturally breathing in pure relaxation and exhaling any and all stress and tension in my body, I just think to myself, good riddance to all that was unwanted, I don't need it, what I need is more and more natural, wonderful relaxation, so I feel anything unwanted simply leaving my chest area as I exhale slowly and gently, in fact it just melts away now.

I do really notice now, that some areas, some parts of my body are more easy to relax to a really deep level, while other areas and parts easily happen moment-by-moment, I know that both ways of doing this now are fine, so when I am concentrating, on those areas of my body that I already am finding to be most comfortable, and very wonderfully relaxed then I can and do begin noticing those other areas, and I start recognizing even more what there is about those parts of my body that makes me feel and be so beautifully comfortable, or very relaxed, that's right, what do I notice? I take my time to notice, and if I really want to, I can and do let myself begin feeling all those gentle sensations in those areas, the most relaxed and comfortable parts of your body, noticing it even more now.

The most relaxed parts just beginning to gently spread all around my body, that's right, I am letting my body enjoy allowing my body and mind to relax now, but only as much as I want to, I remember that I am in control now, and as this special feeling of relaxation spreads, I am doing it now, those sensations can become stronger and stronger and more enjoyable, don't they? I am allowing it to continue to gently radiate to all of my body now, into every cell, every molecule and every atom of my being.

I like to imagine this in my mind, to imagine my relaxation spreading to every part of my being, to every cell in my body, maybe like the rays of sun, shining through me, gently warming, soothing, relaxing, or maybe like those circles of water radiating, rippling outwards from a pebble dropped into a gentle, quiet pond, and as I let that relaxation spread to every part of my body, every muscle, cell and fibre, really enjoying feeling more tranquil and more increasing peaceful feelings of relaxation in every part of my body, and with each moment my feelings of deep, gentle relaxation becomes as strong as I truly want them to be right now, only as strong as I truly want them to be, and it feels good to be true to myself right now in this moment, so I am true to myself right now, as well, and every cell of your body understands deeply how important it is for me to enjoy this healing sensation, this relieving, soothing sensation, and this deep feeling now gently, and powerfully, goes out beyond my physical self, right out beyond it, radiating out, right out, all around my, forming a powerful protective shield of energy all around my body and mind, and I allow it to now project out around, below and above me, or I can keep it really close, just like it is an invulnerable second skin.

Now, this protective shield is a creation of my unconscious, I can do with it whatever I wish, I can allow this powerful shield to protect me, in any way, or as many ways as I want to, this shield of energy can act as a filter, to filter out and remove those feelings or things going on around you, things, circumstances, reactions and responses that in the past I used to find stressful, my shield is filtering the way I respond to circumstances and situations, allowing me instead to let in those feelings I wish to let in and experience, and those good feelings build and develop and nurture me, and my shield can act as an amplifier too, to help me understand people, places, to understand how to keep them in perspective and to help people to understand me, more and more easily.

In fact I find that stress as I used to know it, just rolls off me, it drips off me so quickly, it actually bounces off this shield before I even think about it, before I have the time to respond, and I can just know that with each and every day and night, night and day, with each breath that I breathe, I am enhancing this shield, making it more and more powerful and resilient, even on those occasions and during those times when I am not consciously aware of it, it is there, protecting me, being enhanced with every breath that I breathe and with every beat of my heart, I can relax, just knowing that it is radiating this relaxation and energy all around me, protecting me.

Having developed this programme or your own version of it, remember to thank your unconscious mind and exit from hypnosis. Then, really use your imagination when you are out of hypnosis to enhance it, just assume that it is there, working for you and continually protecting you from things that in the past you used to respond to with a stressful reaction.

Another tool that I have found to be wonderfully useful for both myself and those that I have taught self-hypnosis to is that of altering your perception of an issue literally. A way to do this is that if you spend any level of time thinking about something which used to stress you out, then the people, places, characters that exist in your mind you can change. Change the people involved into animals, cartoon characters, insects or fish or film stars that make you like, even characters. It may sound unusual, however, it is a tremendous way to reframe your thoughts and lessen the impact that they were having upon you. It also removes the reality from the situation. You know, a sense of fun and humour is a wonderful way to reduce stress. You are also then opening up the creative parts of your mind to provide solutions and let go more easily of what used to be the problem.

Imagine your issues, the people and the environment at work for example, as animals in a jungle or cartoon characters in their setting or even fish in a tank and imagine them interacting in a way that is amusing to observe. You can then take it further and match the way in which your boss interacts with the other cartoon characters or animals and to take it even further; you can think about how those characters would solve any issues and how that solution would translate itself into your real life. Let your unconscious mind have some fun and be creative coming up with innovative ways to reinterpret old issues.

Now, I know that you are going to find this very hard to believe, but I was a bit naughty at times as a youngster and I used to find that if ever I had been sent to see the headmaster and had to be exceptionally serious in those surroundings, it made me want to giggle. It may have been a nervous thing.

However, I always would think the most ridiculous things. This has gradually found its way into my adult life and I have found it useful to use this to my advantage. I was recently in an important business meeting with my solicitor and bank manager and my brain was about to freeze over with the seriousness and monotony of it all. So, I began imagining the most hilarious things that could happen and how they would react; I am not going to tell you what those things were, just trust me when I say that they were outrageous.

Now, I know that you have experienced a time when you wanted to giggle but it was supposedly inappropriate, everyone has had one of those, I am sure. Use those experiences and create some more of them. Imagine the silliest things and then instead of blurting out your giggles; seal them in.

Imagine them in your body, desperate to get out and escape. Seal in your giggles and imagine them travelling under your skin and trying to escape through the pores of your skin. This is a glorious sensation. Try your very hardest to be stressed when you have giggles under your skin. Do this. Even write yourself a programme to do this more often and in more funny ways and lighten up your old stressful occasions, go ahead and get the giggles and enjoy it and notice how very hard it is to be in a stressful frame of mind when you are bursting with giggles.

Safe, Controlled Relaxation

I want to offer you another programme now to create some stress prevention. Relieving stress before it actually happens is what this is all about. I want you to have access to this tool, which I refer to as **Safe, Controlled Relaxation**, and it is a specific programme for you to use and apply as you want to, it gets you regularly relaxed. Lots of people do ask me 'Why use the relax programme when we have self-hypnosis?'

Well, when you take yourself through the process of self-hypnosis, as you may have been noticing, it involves a lot of work; you have to be aware and concentrate on that which you are doing.

The reason that I suggest using this programme for safe, controlled relaxation is that you are going to be able to enter this relaxing state and allow yourself to just bask in it without having to do anything in particular, you can actually just allocate your self some time to do it and then easily relax and allow your mind to wander off wherever it wants to, knowing that you are relaxed and protected in your own mind.

This programme creates a safe place in the conscious mind, that is, you deliver this programme to yourself in self-hypnosis and then when you use it, it is just relaxation, not hypnosis. It is a form of hypnotic relaxation.

So when you enter safe, controlled relaxation in the future, you are not going to be in hypnosis, because you are going to be in a state of safe, controlled relaxation.

OK, so what is it used for? It is used updating the survival system; this safe, controlled relaxation overrides some of the fight/flight response that we mentioned earlier.

This safe, controlled relaxation programme resides in your conscious mind. By that I mean, that as with your self-hypnosis, you are going to enter the state of safe, controlled relaxation with your conscious mind. You are going to have triggers to enter the state, similar to self-hypnosis.

Before we go further with this, I want you to think about one of the times in the past when you had what I refer to as 'one of those days.' Let me give you an example. I worked for a national newspaper in central London when I was much younger and I commuted from outside of London. One day, I slept through my alarm clock (I had not installed my natural self-hypnotic alarm clock that I use now) and awoke late (stress begins). I was running late and caught the train during the busiest time of the day when there were more people than I was used to with my earlier train (stress rising), I could not get a seat, so had to stand for the entire journey and could not read my newspaper to update myself with them as was an essential part of my job, my routine was disrupted (stress rising).

Upon arrival in the city, I grabbed a coffee (more stress induced) and raced for the underground, which was so packed, I mean it was heaving. I was nose to nose with people that I did not want to be (more stress). I eventually got into work about an hour late. My boss rushed over, would not accept any excuses, told me off (stress is really rising) and told me he expected the report that I had to give him today by 11am. I rummaged through my bag to realise that I had left it on my table at home where I had been up all night working on it (major stress now). So, I have another coffee and ignore all of the messages from my worst clients that are fuming that I am not returning their calls (stress is going for it now).

I went and told my boss about the report and he gave me a full written warning that went on my files (really stressed) and I had to go home and get it. When I got back, people were ranting, boss was not impressed with my report, etc, etc. More coffee, nothing to eat, more stress. My best friend at work, the girl on the next desk, leaned over, smiled in an assuring way and with understanding and asked if she could borrow a paper clip as she had run out, to which I replied; 'Look, can you just get lost! For Christ's sake!' You just know that I put a few more rude words in that sentence don't you? I am not going to put that in a book!

I had things out of perspective. I went into a rage when my best friend had asked me for a paper clip. It was ridiculous, she still reminds me about that day now. The point I want to illustrate here is that we often get things out of perspective. What I am suggesting here, is that if you use the safe, controlled relaxation programme for 10 minutes a day, or even for ten minutes twice a day, then you will counteract that stress. You will be keeping it in perspective and preventing its occurrence in the first place.

What I wanted to introduce with that story of me foaming at the mouth and going temporarily insane with stress, is in fact the concept of **distress**. Dis-stress is when stress goes AWOL. As I previously mentioned, we need to have some stress. When crossing a road for example, you need a certain degree of stress to make sure a taxi does not knock you over.

We often need stress to thrive, many people use stress as their edge. It is when we go over that edge that we need something to combat our unpleasant physiological and psychological responses. We are no longer cavemen that need to run away from animals, although, I did used to consider my boss an animal of some sort when I worked at that national newspaper.

It often seems as though we are not fully equipped to be dealing with the stressors of the modern world. We can sometimes seem ill equipped both physiologically and psychologically.

When we get upset by all things that should not really, we are **Dis-Stressed** and as I mentioned earlier things start to happen to our bodies and minds; digestion stops, body malfunctions, men's testicles move inside their body, we can get tension headaches, our immune system is less effective; your body is reacting inappropriately.

I often ask myself; 'Will this affect my life in 6 months time?' or 'Will I remember this in a years time?'

So, when we are dis-stressed, we are getting things out of perspective. Distress puts our body out of balance, out of kilter, out of ease, which can lead to and can produce disease. Dis-ease.

At the time of writing this book, Eschaemic heart disease is one of the biggest killing diseases in the world. You know what; dis-stress is one of the major contributory factors of that heart disease. That is only one disease.

So, to return to safe, controlled relaxation; to access the state, again you use three triggers, you can guess what two of them might be, I am sure. The first trigger is that you have the intention to enter safe, controlled relaxation. The second trigger is that you ensure you are in a safe place so that you can be relaxed. The, the third trigger, the third accessing cue for entering safe, controlled relaxation, is that you say out loud in your usual speaking voice, or in your own mind the words:

Relax, relax, relax, lax.

There is no typo here, that last word is lax.

The state of safe, controlled relaxation can only be accessed by using these three triggers. Then, to make it really easy indeed, all you have to do to exit safe, controlled relaxation is to simply open your eyes.

It is as simple as that. You set the period of time that you want to spend in the state of safe, controlled relaxation and then you activate the three triggers, bask in your hypnotic relaxation without having to do anything (unlike in self-hypnosis) and then open your eyes to exit when your unconscious mind alerts you to let you know that period of time has elapsed.

You cannot deliver your self-hypnosis programmes while using safe, controlled relaxation; that is what your self-hypnosis is for of course. While you are in this state, you do not have the same kind of hypnotic contact with your unconscious as when you are in self-hypnosis; it is minimal. Keep your relax programme and Hypnosis programmes apart. You cannot enter one programme from another or go from safe, controlled relaxation to self-hypnosis or vice versa, you must exit each state before entering the other.

Really do your best to keep them definitively different and separate and you will reap the rewards. If you are using safe, controlled relaxation, you must come out safely before using your self-hypnosis programme. Remember, if you open your eyes, you are out of safe, controlled relaxation. So, go ahead and deliver this programme to yourself so that you can begin using safe, controlled relaxation as well as self-hypnosis.

Programme for Safe, Controlled Relaxation

This programme is called Safe Controlled Relaxation. Starting from this moment onwards and lasting throughout my entire lifetime, I know that there are three accessing cues that only I can use to activate my programme for safe controlled relaxation.

The first trigger is that I have the intention to enter safe controlled relaxation.

The second trigger is that I am in a safe place so that I can relax my body.

The third trigger is that using my usual speaking voice, or silently inside my mind, I speak the words:

Relax, relax, relax, lax.

On the last word 'Lax' I enter safe controlled relaxation, momentarily passing through hypnosis. This lasts for less than one fifth of a second, during which time I am fully protected from hypnotic influence. From the instant I enter into safe controlled relaxation and until I exit, I am fully protected from hypnotic influence upon my thoughts, images and feelings. Yes fully protected from responding to hypnotic influence.

During the relaxation nothing disturbs me, unless it is an emergency. An emergency is anything requiring my immediate attention. Should there be such a disturbance, I simply open my eyes and deal with it in the most appropriate manner.

Without such a disturbance I continue to relax, both mentally and physically deeper and deeper, until the time that I have set has passed by. At this point, my unconscious mind alerts me, and I know that it is time to open my eyes. Opening my eyes automatically ends this period of safe controlled relaxation. This programme is my control for safe controlled relaxation and every time I use it I automatically strengthen it. Each time I choose to enter safe, controlled relaxation, I go deeper and relax more profoundly, each time more than before, even if it does not consciously seem so.

I now ask my unconscious to take this programme and lock it away in the very deepest area of your mind, safe and secure, where it has a powerful influence and effect on my life and enhances my ability to be more and more appropriately relaxed in each and every aspect of my life.

If you would like to use your self-hypnosis sessions to enhance your relaxation and have a really nice relaxing hypnosis session, which many people find relaxing anyway, then you can use this kind of script to guide yourself into relaxing states and to keep and bring those relaxing sensations with you and incorporate them into your life. Again, you use this in conjunction with the self-hypnosis model or you can use it as a stand-alone exercise of enjoying the trance state generated by the script on its own.

Fractional Relaxation Script

So, in this comfortable position that I have chosen, the sound of my inner voice is reaching deep within me. With my eyes comfortably closed, allowing myself to begin relaxing easily and gently. Concentrating now, all my thoughts and my attention on my breath, and feel your breath easily and gently going deeper and deeper down. Note that a deeper breath is not necessarily a bigger breath or a larger breath; it is simply a breath that goes deeper and deeper down, a breath that relaxes me more and more and more.

I can and do imagine my breath as it moves from my mouth and nose into lungs, with each subsequent breath I can and do imagine my breath going deeper, reaching my stomach and then maybe later reaching the very tips of my toes.

Comfortable, calm, relaxed and at ease, so I concentrate all my thoughts, all my feelings, all my attention on my breath, feeling my breath coming in (when you are breathing in) and going out (breathe out). Relaxing, letting go more and more and more.

And I know that hypnosis is always good to me, always good for me, always a comfortable, relaxing and gentle experience and I know that should there be any reason that I need to come out of hypnosis, I know that all I need to do is simply to count from 1–5 and open my eyes. I can count aloud, or I can count silently to my self, whichever way, on 5, when I open your eyes you are completely out of hypnosis and fully emerged. Relaxing now though, more and more wonderfully deeply.

As I go deeper, I know that each time I enter into this deep hypnotic experience I am able to and do go even deeper than the time before, so that the effects of each hypnotic session are growing and working more and more effectively for me. Each session more and more enjoyable, the hypnosis more and more reliable, knowing that my hypnosis is of a progressively better and better quality.

And I know, as a result of each hypnotic session, of each deep, relaxing, comfortable hypnotic experience that each and every time I choose to enter hypnosis (each time I use my self-hypnosis), I am becoming even more relaxed, even more calm, my own level of hypnosis is becoming more easily and naturally deeper, of a better quality. Feeling and being more and more comfortable being in hypnosis, knowing all that I need to know to allow myself to drift blissfully into a deeper and deeper hypnotic peaceful state now.

And throughout this experience, throughout each and every hypnotic experience involving me responding to my own internal voice, the sound of my internal voice remains the most important sound that I hear. Even though my mind may wander, thoughts, images, sounds, feelings may come and go, the sound of my own internal voice remains the most important sound that I hear, and you react and respond hypnotically to the sound of my internal voice and the suggestions and programmes I deliver within this session. Of course, only those suggestions with which I have full agreement are for my better good and well-being. The now familiar sensation of self-hypnosis, responding to my internal voice, this familiar feeling of gently and easily, naturally relaxing, the familiar sound of my internal voice is the most important sound that I hear.

I know that throughout this session, throughout each and every hypnotic session I enjoy, I remain fully protected from random thoughts, random sounds and random images from having any hypnotic influence for me and to me. Random thoughts, sounds and images may continue to come and go and this is quite usual for me, quite comfortable for me. I may also be aware of the feeling of my eyelids fluttering, moving gently and this is also quite usual for me, and of course, I find it a gentle, and a pleasant, and a deepening experience.

And in my mind I may choose to imagine myself being somewhere where I can really relax, and I know that in this experience there is nothing that is required of me or from me, there is nothing that I need to do or have to do. This is an opportunity for me to be away from, separated from the outside world for a little while at least, to spend some time within, to spend some time deeper and deeper down, relaxing more and more and more.

And each and every word that I hear is relaxing me and taking you deeper and deeper down, and the gaps in between my words and the pauses at the end of my sentences continue to relax me and take me deeper and deeper down, into this wonderful hypnotic experience now. Comfortable, calm, relaxed and at ease, drifting deeper and deeper, letting go more and more and more and more.

(Maybe even imagine an audible sigh of enjoyment in your mind here, or even let go a nice sigh of pleasant relaxation)

Easily and gently, deeply letting go, with each and every gentle relaxed breath I take. And in your mind, choose somewhere to be where I can relax and let go, somewhere I have been before or somewhere I am creating especially for myself.

(The following paragraph is optional/ can be altered, added to etc. in keeping with that which you respond to the best.)

I can and do imagine myself lying on a beach somewhere in the world, the wonderful warm feeling of the sun coming from behind a cloud, that comfortably warm feeling, relaxing my body, relaxing my mind, gently and easily, more and more. The sounds of the birds overhead, the gentle feeling of the sea lapping against my feet, I can even hear the waves against the shore. So calm, so relaxed, every sound, every thought, every feeling, taking me deeper and deeper down.

I choose somewhere, I am somewhere where I can relax and let go, somewhere that is comfortable and calm for me to be, somewhere where I can leave the rest of the world behind for a little while at least, and every thought, every feeling, every emotion is taking me deeper and deeper down.

Knowing that each and every time I choose to enter into, I am also able to and do go deeper and deeper, relax more and more.

And I notice quite how wonderfully still my body is feeling, I become more and more aware of the sensations in my arms and legs, I notice the weight of my head more and more acutely. I Notice just how relaxed my body is feeling and being, and especially I notice this deep, heavy relaxation is already in my eyelids, I can and do imagine this deep, heavy relaxation as a beautiful crystal blue colour, or a wonderful azure green,, maybe as a golden, glowing colour. I feel it, visualise it, or just experience this wonderful, relaxing feeling spreading easily and gently and naturally from my eyelids out over my eyebrows to my temples and forehead, relaxing, releasing, letting go progressively more and more and more.

Spreading around my ears and over the top and over the back of my head, so that whatever it is that the back of my head is resting on, I find and can imagine more and more that the back of my head just settles a little deeper into whatever it is that my head is resting on. An increasingly comfortable gentle, easy feeling of letting go more and more and more. And this beautiful colour, this deep, heavy relaxation is spreading into my nose, my jaw and my lips, even into the muscles that allow the lower jaw to remain in place, I also do find that as these muscles relax even more now that my jaw, my lower jaw just hangs a little lower than usual as I am relaxing progressively more and more.

And this beautiful, deep relaxation is moving into my shoulders, releasing, relieving, massaging, letting go of any lingering tension or stress, so comfortable, so calm, so relaxed and so at ease.

And this relaxation is relaxing each and every part of my body, my entire physical being, it is relaxing the muscles and the tissues, the fibres and the tendons, the sinews, even the bones. Each and every system, muscular, skeletal, nervous, lymphatic, endocrine, vascular, urinary, reproductive, digestive, olfactory, visual and immune systems are all benefiting from this experience. Each and every cell, each and every molecule and each and every atom is benefiting from this deep, deep relaxation. Comfortable, calm, so wonderfully peaceful and tranquil.

And this natural, deep relaxation is spreading from my shoulders all the way down to my elbows and from my elbows to my forearms, and from my forearms to the backs and the palms of my hands, a wonderful, deep, easy, gentle relaxation, an easy letting go, all the way to the very tips of the fingers now, and I do notice that as this deep relaxation arrives at the very tips of my fingers, I really do notice a gentle tingling sensation in the tips of my fingers, a comfortable, calm, momentary experience of letting go even more.

And this relaxation is spreading easily, gently and deeply all the way along and down my back, around my sides, over and around my chest and my tummy. Bringing with it naturally, a better balance throughout each and every part of my body, each and every cell, each and every molecule, each and every atom is benefiting form this experience. And organically, that is to say within each and every organ of my body, there is a better balance and better unison a better harmony that is more appropriate to time and place, circumstance and situation, feeling and being healthier, fitter, stronger, more relaxed, comfortable, calm.

And this relaxation is spreading along and around my hips and my middle to the tops of my legs, and all the way down to my knees, then all the way along to my ankles, heels and across the soles and tops of my feet, all the way along to the very tips of my toes, so that there is flowing throughout my entire body, like a wonderful stream of pure, clean, clear water, a wonderful, gentle wave of pure deep relaxing hypnosis now. Spreading through my system.

And so in a moment, when I say the words **deeper down** to myself, I go to the very deepest level of hypnotic experience that is available to me, the very deepest level of hypnosis. The most enjoyable and profound depth of hypnosis as I say those words **deeper down** to myself in just a moment. I do even surprise myself at how deep I really do go, getting ready to go to the deepest level, in

3 . . . 2 . . . 1 . . . '**Deeper Down**'.

Deeper and deeper down now. Way down, deeper and deeper.

The information that you have learned and developed before this chapter in relation to creating your own programmes can be utilised to full effect in dealing with relief of stress. You can use imagination and visualisation to great extent to relax the body in that moment.

You can also begin to create new alternatives for your unconscious mind at the prospect of future events and circumstances. Take yourself into hypnosis, take control and deepen and then rehearse situations that in the past you may have avoided or found to be stressful; rehearse them in your mind to imagine yourself enjoying that circumstance and dealing with it wonderfully well, with an appropriate level of relaxation and mental calmness.

The more you envisage future circumstances as being less and less stressful, the more that your unconscious mind will accept that it has other options as to how to respond to those circumstances and situations.

When I say imagine it, really put some effort into it; imagine what you would see, imagine the sounds you would hear and the feelings that you would feel. Really step into a 'new you' in your mind and notice how others respond to you, get your unconscious mind to associate with a version of you that is relaxed and mentally calm in those circumstances. If you allow yourself to do this regularly, it simply begins to happen more and more often.

Other things that you can do with your self-hypnosis is to give yourself tools for dealing with situations and circumstances that in the past you found stressful. For example, when you are in hypnosis you can give yourself a programme that you have created so that every time you say a certain word to yourself, or think of a certain image you respond in a particular way. Maybe you can include in your programme that each time you enter those circumstances, your unconscious plays a certain piece of music in your mind that relaxes you, or you can imagine relaxing images in your mind, or maybe your unconscious alerts you to breathe more deeply and in a more relaxed manner.

As an example, instead of every time you hear your boss's voice, you respond with a stressful response, use your self-hypnosis to change the way you respond, so that your boss's voice serves as a trigger for you to feel alert, aware and relaxed. Maybe you can even reframe the response of your bosses voice, so that every time you hear it, you feel more driven and motivated and respond in whatever way your unconscious mind believes is the most conducive at that time. There really are so many things that you can do and create with your own self-hypnosis skills.

There are so many things that you can experiment with and ideas that you can develop for yourself, the resources really exist within you, the only thing holding you back is any limitation you place upon yourself. So go ahead and free yourself of stress as you used to know it.

2

Overcoming Pain

For all the happiness mankind can gain
Is not in pleasure, but in rest from pain.
John Dryden

And the Lord God caused a deep sleep to
fall upon Adam, and he slept: and he took
one of his ribs.
Genesis, The Bible

Before I launch into all the amazing stuff in this chapter I need to make something clear; be sure to get in touch with your doctor about your pain before altering your perception of it with self-hypnosis. Pain is usually there for a reason.

Pain is experienced by most as an unpleasant sensory and emotional experience as well as a physiological experience. It is commonly associated with strenuous activity, disease, injury and it can also be caused by toxins within the body's systems. Pain is there for a reason as I have said; it is a warning system.

Pain occurs in varying levels, I used the services of a physio-therapist following a running injury a while back and she referred to **low-level**, **acute** and **chronic** as levels of pain. Low-level pain often ensures that you will rest and recuperate, some people though, often work through low-level pain ignoring its important signs, I have read articles and heard about sportspeople who would take pain-killing injections before their sports regardless of the harm they might be doing. Chronic pain is often incessant and acute pain is somewhere in between those two.

Many ways have been used to alleviate pain over the years and I have experienced many myself and found self-hypnosis to be the best way of overcoming and altering my response to it.

Remember a time when you had a paper cut and you did not realise that you had it until later on that day when you saw it with your eyes? It was not until you saw it that it hurt. I remember I had been helping my father in the garden when I was young, I had been weeding (great jobs that Dads give you!) and my hands were covered in earth and when I washed them off later on in the day when I came into the house, I noticed that I had grazed my hand and having seen it, it began to sting a bit; it had not done so until then. This is naturally occurring anaesthesia.

There was a military doctor called James Esdaille who is mentioned in the enclosed history of hypnosis in this book and he would use hypnosis and auto suggestion with fellow soldiers for all manner of different ailments, he even carried out amputations with no anaesthesia other than that of the suggestions that he was delivering to his patient. This is perfectly within the realms of possibility as far as anyone is concerned.

Even more impressive and spectacular is the case of a dentist named Victor Rausch, who used self-hypnosis to undergo the surgical removal of his gall bladder, which is major surgery and he had no anaesthesia or analgesic (anaesthesia is total and analgesic is local).

Rausch's documentation of his experience in 1980 included the following:

> That from the moment of the first incision he 'felt a flowing sensation throughout my entire body . . . my eyes were open and the operating team said that I had no visible signs of tensing of the muscles'.

Rausch chatted with the team and enjoyed the process and even walked away from the operating theatre when it was all over. He had obviously had a lot of experience with hypnosis and hypnotherapy, but it really does illustrate what can be done with the correct belief system and application.

There are some important aspects to using self-hypnosis for the purpose of pain relief. Firstly, it is particularly important with pain relief that you practice. You really do need to continue to practice and experiment with the various techniques and strategies that are described in this chapter.

Secondly, think about what it is going to be like without your pain. Some people fear having no pain, they fear shutting off the pain. Thirdly, be aware that you create the pain. You and your brain create pain, it is not an external sensation, it is part of our ingenious survival system and ultimately, we have control over it. Then finally, ensure that you are driven to letting go of the pain; be comfortable with the idea of letting go of it. Some people have reasons, conscious or unconscious for keeping pain. So, really think about the notion of what benefit you would get from keeping the pain and make sure that you deal with that before using these techniques to free your self of it.

Your pain relief can be as long as you want, however, it is safe and healthy for you to use your self-hypnosis for pain relief almost as if it is a hypnotic tablet that you are taking that lasts for 2–4 hours. Set yourself a time limit for how long it is going to last for and allow your unconscious to work to that time scale. To enhance the length of time and the effectiveness and quality of the pain relief requires practice and requires your unconscious mind to get used to what it is being asked to do. If the pain has been a persistent pain that has been put up with for a long period of time, the pain may well be more difficult to overcome as you will have an unconscious pattern and memory of it and it will be well installed within your belief system, so it is likely to need a lot of persistent work and reworking by you.

Our belief system with regards to pain is where the root to success lies. We have had a certain belief system installed within us throughout our lifetime. With the emergence of modern medicine in the last few generations, we have learned to expect pain relief from an external source; through medicine or from someone else that would help us to overcome it such as a parent or a doctor and add to that the persistent media coverage and advertising from pharmaceutical companies, this further develops the belief that pain comes from outside our bodies, not from the inside.

When I was 13 years old, I had an in-growing toenail and it was a nightmare for me as it meant I would not be able to play football for a while. Now, the procedure for treating this in those days (not sure if it has changed these days) was to have a local anaesthetic in the toe, once it was anaesthetised; it was simply a case of lie back and have the toenail pulled out by the doctor.

Now, in those days I used to believe everything that doctors told me and just as this particular doctor was about to administer the local anaesthetic by injection, he held up the needle in the air before me and the doctor said to me, 'Brace yourself Adam, this is going to hurt.' You know what; **it did**! The reason it did was that he told me it was going to. Had he said to me 'A big lad like you won't even feel this' then I would not have done. The power of suggestion is powerful. The actual reason I mention this story though is that it leads on to an idea that doctors in those positions can use and sometimes do and that is the idea of distraction.

On some of my self-hypnosis seminars I have used the example of putting a pin through someone's arm to show how powerful hypnosis can be. All I do is get the individual that has been brave enough to volunteer, to focus and centre their attention elsewhere, or to really concentrate on how one arm feels while I put the pin in the other. They are often amazed.

One of the most embarrassing things that can ever happen to a young man happened to my younger brother when he was very young; he got the end of his penis caught in his zip when he had been doing up his trousers. I just know that some of you sniggered childishly then and some of you male readers crossed your legs. Now, my Mum had no idea what to do. She actually used a pair of scissors to cut around the zip area and removed the remainder of the trousers. It is hilarious in hindsight. My brother had the zip section of his trousers attached to his penis!

Now, my Dad was at work, so in her panic, my Mum took him to the hospital! I shall cut the story down. My brother was taken to the booths for a doctor to come along and examine him; here he was put on to one of those trolley beds that they wheel people around in (with his penis caught in his zip and some other trousers on top). The doctor came in and said to him that they were going to have to do a range of things and while he was talking about a load of complicated things to my brother, he suddenly yanked the zipper down and released him from the trousers, but not from his embarrassment. The doctor simply distracted him, pulled the zip and my brother felt no pain at all.

Distraction is something you can utilise with your self-hypnosis.

Prior to your self-hypnosis session, acknowledge the pain and where it is that it exists. Then, to use this technique, take your self into self-hypnosis, take control of the state and deepen it. Then, the first thing to do is to really focus and concentrate on a part of your body that feels really comfortable and well. Concentrate all your attention on the parts or a single part of you that feels fine and comfortable and then continue doing this for a few minutes. Think of this as spending some time separated from that pain.

Feed back to your self with your internal dialogue how good certain parts of you feel, for example you can say to yourself:

'As I am focusing my awareness on my toes, I notice how comfortable and good they feel, how calm those toes really feel, I may notice other sensations that indicate to me that they feel truly comfortable and well. These feelings can continue to last longer and longer and can spread through my body to other areas.' You can also add; 'As I remain focused on any part of my body that is feeling comfortable and well, the sensations stay for longer periods of time and spread out, maybe they even happen for longer than I thought would be possible.'

Then during this time, you are suspending your experience of the pain by distracting yourself from it.

Visualisation and imagery

Imagery and visualisation can be used in conjunction with this or as a separate method. Within your self-hypnosis session, you can imagine that the pain is made or formed entirely from ice. Imagine that your pain or discomfort is a physical thing and it is formed of ice. Really get into that idea in your self-hypnosis and even suggest that you can feel the coolness of it. Then, you can imagine pouring warm water on the ice, or imagine rays of sunshine melting the ice and melting it and subsequently melting the ice for a period of time that you set yourself.

Some people can imagine that they have the part of their body in ice to freeze pain away. One way to do this easily is to imagine that you have your fingers dangling into a bucket of ice, really sense the feelings in the tips of your fingers and imagine all the sensations that you would feel. Then spread that cool feeling along to the area where it is needed while you are in self-hypnosis.

You can also imagine the pain as a certain colour. Really colour the area of pain in your mind. Then imagine that you are sending soothing colours and accompanying soothing feelings to the area and that colour extinguishes the pain for the period of time that you want. You may even like to give it a shape and then change the shape of the pain to a shape that is comfortable and soothing. With visualisation and imagination, you can even go as far as to metaphorically represent your pain in a self-hypnosis session. For example, you could imagine your pain as a wilting flower in a garden and that when you pour sunshine and rain upon it, it flowers beautifully and as it flowers, your pain is relieved. Be creative and use what is the right kind of imagery for you. Use what appeals to you and use imagery that you associate with harmony.

I must admit that on the very rare occasions that I get a headache, one of the last things that I feel like doing is going into self-hypnosis. So, this is a good time to plan ahead and think about recording a pain relief session of hypnosis that you can use a hypnotic pain relief tablet whenever you need it.

The use of time with pain relief

There have been times in your life when you have been wonderfully pain-free. So, you can take yourself into hypnosis and when you get to step 'D', use this section of the session to recall a time when you felt really comfortable and well and free from pain. Compare and contrast how you felt then with how you feel today and have your unconscious absorb all that it needs to absorb to lock into place the conditions that were present within you when you were feeling really good and well.

Deliver the suggestion to your unconscious mind that it remembers how to feel comfortable and records all the information from being pain free and then installs those sensations and conditions within you again for a period of time. In addition you can add that your unconscious mind is getting better and better at doing this and responds more fluently and more effectively on each occasion that you do this.

You can also use time to reframe the experience where your body and mind learned to feel this pain. Especially if it was caused by a particular event, such as an injury. When you are in hypnosis, you can replay the incident and begin to alter it. So that each and every time you think of it, you can view it a different way. To take that a step further, you can actually begin to find solutions to avoiding the experience and offering those solutions to yourself immediately prior to the memory.

So, for example, you can take yourself back to before the incident occurred and offer solutions, then run the memory forward as if you had listened to the advice (the solution to avoid it) and run the memory over and over in your mind so that you are recoding the experience in your brain and responding to the memory in a different way. You can also add feelings of comfort and give suggestions of relief at the same time.

Of course, you can also use the time distortion methodologies from the chapter on time distortion, to increase the period of time that you experience relief, so that a period of time can just fly by where you are experiencing comfort. Utilise those methods from that chapter.

Here are some scripts for you to get ideas from and utilise in the best way for you.

Pain Release Script

I know that any pain is a warning device from my body. I can and do free myself from that warning for a period of time. I now know the problem is there and I am consciously and unconsciously correcting it.

If I need to know about a change, if I need to be warned further, my unconscious gives me a signal *(maybe a tingling in the area instead; you decide)*. I then know and see to it that any new problem is taken care of and addressed appropriately.

I am free from experiencing any pain connected with *(insert what was the specific pain problem here)* but this in no way alters my warning pain signals for any other reason.

I concentrate a healing light in the area where I desire that pain to go away and stay away. I naturally harness the innate healing powers of my body and set up rapid and instantaneous healing with the healing light. It is so wonderful as I feel all tension leaving the area. All pain is going and going from the area. That area is feeling and being more and more soothed, relaxed and painless; marvellously free from pain. It is as if that entire area has been anaesthetised leaving the area in my conscious minds control with its usual manoeuvrability as I have the right to expect. I have the usual muscle and motor response and the area is free from pain.

Thank your unconscious and expect it to take care of this for you. The next script uses the actual pain as the object. Use the idea in your own way.

Pain or anxiety as the object

As I am just relaxing deeper and even deeper, drifting way down now, deeper and even deeper relaxed, and I am just taking a moment to recognise and realise how many of us experience sensations that we regard as unpleasant, this is simply my perception of it and I have already learned one method of dealing with those things and that is to just allow deeper, conscious breathing to move deeply into those areas and remove all pain or discomfort.

And using another image now, another image that can and does bring me peace, comfort, contentment and deep relaxation, and that other method that is so powerful it can and does remove the symptoms of stress and strain and any pain, I now know and realise that the symptoms of stress and strain are all very subjective feelings, people feel them, however, as we know only too well it is difficult to consciously modify our feeling, and I know how much easier and easier it is to modify an object and so I am now changing old unpleasant sensations into objects, that's right, changing them in to 'things.'

(If you are experiencing pain or discomfort or if you feel tense or anxious, of course you need to modify the programme to meet your specific requirements.)

I allow myself to take that unwanted feeling, tension, stress or strained muscle and give it a shape, I really do, just imagine a shape, I allow myself to visualize that shape, it can be any kind of shape, it can be an abstract shape or a concrete shape, and it can be an object or a geometric design or it can be soft and it can have a colour, whatever shape or object first comes into my mind is the right shape or object for me, I just let that shape happen, it comes forward, I just let it happen, as I go deeper and even deeper relaxed, I am more and more peaceful, calm and very relaxed.

And just relaxing and going deeper and even deeper, I give that shape a colour, and I can and do just imagine the size of the shape, and I give it a size, either just by knowing the size or by picturing it next to an object I know the size of, and I am recognising and realising that the shape is the symbol of my discomfort, and the larger the shape is, the more severe the discomfort is, and the smaller the shape is, the less the discomfort is.

And so I practice now, first making the shape larger, and then making it smaller, and when I make the size of the shape bigger it is easier to make the shape smaller, I then can even begin to use a few tricks, if the shape is a balloon I can put a needle into it, or kick it away, I can and do throw it away, put it on a boat or an airplane or tie it to the back of a truck and let it drive away.

And as I am realising that as this symbol is becoming smaller, the feelings associated with it are becoming less intense and I can and do make it smaller, as small and comfortable as I want to make it, and I am making it smaller by practicing making it larger and then smaller, and I realise that these are skills and as with any skill, the more I practice the more powerful the skill becomes, and I am using these skills, and using these skills any time I desire, the more I practice the easier it is for me to allow these skills to be more and more effective, so very easy to use and so very powerful, anytime I choose to use this skill, and practicing making the shape smaller and the colour of the shape fade or change, and every time I do this it is easier and even easier.

I am going to allow myself to rest for a moment but when I emerge from self-hypnosis, I know that I can give the shape a size and a colour and then instantly, effortlessly and easily I make the shape smaller and the colour fade, and every time I do this it becomes easier and even easier, and when I emerge from self-hypnosis, the shape is fading and becoming smaller.

Thank your unconscious before you exit.

This next script is specifically aimed at freeing oneself of migraine. Please consult your doctor first to make sure you are not dealing with a tumour, poor eyesight, tooth decay, infectious disease, high blood pressure or a head injury. Please consult with them first and get checked first.

Migraine Release Script

I relax more and more and shape and form the headache and throw it away. As I relax, I know that I am free of this the headache. Anytime I feel a headache coming on, I release it. I instinctively place the tips of my fingers on the back of my neck and apply a very gentle pressure and the tension goes away. It is as if my fingers drain away the old headache.

Whenever the muscles start to tighten or I start to squint my eyes, I become more and more aware of it immediately and the relaxation begins immediately. It is like the signs now signal the relaxation to happen all on it's own.

If I have pressure behind the eyes, I very gently use my fingertips to brush my eyelids with an outward motion and the pressure subsides.

A deeper breath relaxes the muscles and the headache cannot materialize.

(Deepen by going down a staircase or something similar as in previous chapters.)

At the bottom of I staircase design a release valve for the escape of the tension or nervousness. Anytime I find myself in a situation that tension used to build in, like it used to do in the past, I imagine and see myself at the bottom of my stairs and I pull the release valve. I can imagine it releasing easily and gently.

If you really use your imagination to its best potential, you might want to start taking yourself into hypnosis and imagine bathing the painful area in some kind of analgesic, or a healing, soothing balm. Maybe you can give it a special ingredient that changes the quality of the pain to one that is perfectly tolerable. Use whatever you can from your own mind to work with; if you use the product of your own imagination, as much of the time as you can, there is often far greater benefit.

I sometimes even ask my clients what sort of treatment they wished existed – in other words, to invent their own 'miracle cure'. In this way, I tap into their inner resources – often more effective for them than my own might be. So think about doing that with yourself in your own way; invent a miracle cure.

I mentioned in the introductory chapters that a girl that came on my self-hypnosis seminar, Natasha, had her wisdom teeth removed without anaesthesia. Anyone can do that with the techniques here or with your own combination of them. Believe!

3

Time Distortion

Time will run back and fetch the age of gold.
John Milton

When I was at secondary school, I can remember being sat in my history class and being thoroughly uninspired and bored and watching the clock on the wall behind my teacher. Now, I swear to this day that as I yearned for the time to go past quicker, the second hands on that clock went by slower and slower. One hour felt as if it was ten hours. My experience of time during those lessons was painful. I often struggled to keep awake.

Now, I can contrast that experience to several occasions when I have had what can only be described as a fantastic night out. A really wonderful night out, whereby 8 hours of fun just seemed to zip by in a flash. I would talk to my friends the following day and it we would have done so many things during our night out, had so much fun, yet it all seemed to have flown by so very quickly.

I am sure that you have had varying experiences of time. Whereby time seemed to fly by or drag, depending on what you were doing. So, this innate occurrence is something that we are going to learn how to utilise instead of just letting it happen to passively.

Here is an exercise for you to follow:

In this hectic fast pace world, accelerated learning techniques are becoming increasingly more necessary. Many people are using time distortion for enhanced learning and this entire process is simply harnessing the unconscious mind through conscious direction, much the same as the overall ideology behind this entire book.

There are people out there who can calculate mathematics in an 'instant' mentally. There are fantastically successful baseball

157

players who, when focused, seem to experience the ball coming toward them much slower than others seem to. There are also high-speed readers, who can read over 2,000 words per minute and they all experience a sense of time distortion as information flashes through their mind in only seconds. Through self-hypnosis, you too can learn to review information in a time-distorted fashion.

As an example, there was a concert violinist that put herself into a self-hypnotic state and used her own self-induced time distortion with which she practiced her music in several different ways. By 'playing' the difficult spots mentally, it helped her finger memory to improve in speed and accuracy. She was able to review long pieces over and over in very brief 'real-world' time periods, and her technique and technical performance improved strikingly.

By repeating memorized material in a time-distorted fashion, valuable associative patterns can be firmly established and conscious recall becomes more available. Using time distortion, problems can be reviewed and approached from all angles in a matter of seconds. Hypothetical lectures, appointments and scenes can be laid out in your mind, prepared for and visualised in a brief amount of time.

Kinaesthetic body movements in gymnastics or the martial arts can be reviewed in this way as well. Doing 'instantaneous' calculations and high-speed mathematics can and has been learned with time distortion. In a similar way, solutions to everyday problems can be achieved effortlessly and quickly. By a simple trusting in your unconscious mind, you can establish a better awareness and faith in your own abilities.

As Einstein pointed out, time flows at different rates for each person. Some people have experienced their entire life flash before their eyes in a matter of seconds just prior to a sudden death-risking situation. Also, dream researchers have discovered that a one-minute dream sometimes feels like hours to a dreamer. In one experiment, hypnotised subjects were given imaginary tasks to perform in their minds – like designing a dress and preparing a complicated meal.

They were tricked into thinking they had an hour to accomplish their tasks, but they really had only 10 seconds. After 10 seconds had elapsed in world time, the hypnotised subjects experienced intricate and accurate detail in their inner perception that seemed to them to be a complete hour! Given the same tasks in the waking state often stymied them so badly that they could not think of a single dress design and actually prepared a meal in a very disorganised fashion.

In interviews after the hypnotic sessions, it was revealed that the subjects experienced no difference in their 'thinking' and that at no time did they feel hurried or 'speeded up'. Time distorted thought thus seems to have superior clarity to usual conscious thought beset with constant distraction.

The experiment was achieved by starting a metronome at 60 beats per minute while the hypnotist stated that he was slowing it down gradually. The subject was to listen carefully as he did so and when in the subject's opinion the metronome had been slowed down to the rate of one stroke per minute, the subject would acknowledge by saying, 'Now.' The metronome's beating always remained the same, but the hypnotist progressively encouraged the state of suggestibility in the subject by saying that the metronome was going still slower. The same suggestibility can be achieved in a self-hypnotic state.

Use an audible second-ticking clock or a metronome stroking at 60 beats per minute. Assume a comfortable position in a chair or a bed, and achieve a self-hypnotic state as we have been doing up until now. After getting into a deeply relaxed state, your heartbeat will entrain itself to the slow rhythm of 60 beats per minute. Concentrate on deep rhythmic breathing and clear your mind to allow your brain waves to also slow down. You can deliver suggestions to yourself to enhance the 'slowing down' of time.

As an important aside, when using suggestions to do such things, remember to use the words 'as if . . .' Instead of 'is' in certain suggestions. By that, I mean you can deliver a suggestion to say to yourself that 'time feels as if it is going slower and slower . . .' rather than 'time is going slower . . .' This is because you are not actually altering time. You are altering your perception of it.

Bear that in mind. If you start suggesting to your unconscious that time itself is slowing down, your unconscious will just respond by thinking 'no it isn't' and ignore the suggestion rendering it impotent. Be aware of using the most progressive and precise language and deliver suggestions to help slow your perception of time right down.

You can memorise and say the following statements to yourself or you can record them for playing back when you are in your self-hypnosis.

Now begin using the following suggestions on yourself, I would recommend that you develop your own, however, these give you an idea from which to start from.

I am feeling more and more comfortable. I am feeling more and more wonderful.

The beats are slowing now – slower and slower. They sound as if they are going slower and slower.

When you say those words, use the right kind of tonation to yourself; slow your words down and say it deliberately slower to enhance the experience. If you shriek at yourself with a high-pitched fast voice, you are unlikely to help yourself slow down your perception.

The time between each beat seems longer and longer.

I am more and more relaxed and I have lots and lots of time. All the time in the world.

Time is only relative to what I want it to be.

Each stroke is further and further apart now.

There is lots of time.

I feel so relaxed and at peace with myself.

Time feels as if it is slowing down.

Each beat of the metronome/clock feels more and more distantly separated and sounds as if it is too.

Then continue to repeat the above suggestions or similar ones over and over to yourself until you 'feel' that each click of the metronome is spaced between 2 – 4 minutes apart. Bring into mental focus the material you want to review and say something along the lines of the following:

I have plenty of time to review this.

Every time I do this, I improve myself and my performance.

I am more and more relaxed and taking my time.

The more I practice, the easier and better it becomes.

I am feeling better and better and experiencing no hurry.
I have all the time that I need to accomplish this review.
I am completing my review.

Obviously, you make the suggestions relevant to you and your circumstances.

Then, whilst in your self-hypnotic state and having a suggestive state of mind, you can review any material you wish in a matter of seconds over and over again. By being relaxed and saying to yourself that you have lots of time, your mind does indeed 'create' lots of time.

You can and do work at optimal levels of efficiency when you are relaxed and enjoying yourself. The more you practice this exercise, the easier it does become.

Bring yourself out of the self-hypnotic state in the usual way. Do your best to remember as often as you can to give yourself a post-hypnotic suggestion that the next time that you want to experience self-hypnotic time distortion, it is so much easier and faster to undergo. Once you have mastered doing this one way, you can begin to use it and apply it so many other things. I have worked with men and women who have learned to heighten their enjoyment of sex by slowing down their experience of their orgasms. I have also used these techniques to allow plane journeys to fly by, so that you step off the plane feeling fresh and free from jetlag. I tend to find that however comfortable they make planes these days, it is really difficult to do much that is constructive whilst on board, so I just get it to seem like it flew by.

You can also use past experiences to recall how to change your experience of time. If you recall one of those occasions when you had a night or an experience that just flew by really quickly, then recall how you experienced that time. Think about how you felt, what you saw, how you saw things, what frame of mind you had, what sounds were there, how you communicated with yourself, what feelings you had in your body and so on, and ask your unconscious mind to record that experience and apply that mode of experiencing time to whenever and wherever you want it. It really does take practice.

Sometimes you might just want to take yourself into a self-hypnotic state and speed things up and stay in that trance until the time has gone by and you bring yourself out of it. Again, I have done this. You will be amazed how well your unconscious minds clock can and does work.

5

Better Quality Sleep

To sleep: perchance to dream.
William Shakespeare

In my experience of life, I cannot say that I have met anyone that has not had a bad night's sleep. Come to think of it, most people have experienced a period of poor sleeping. These periods can of course be caused by a wide variety of different things; expectation of an event or anticipated occurrence, a new bed or different surroundings, a stressful period of life or a time with a lot of change, noisy neighbours or some kind of physical ailment or discomfort; the list goes on. I know how my sleep was interrupted when I began sleeping with current partner; her and I both had disturbed sleep for a period of time.

There are those people that spend eight or nine hours 'sleeping' each night, however; they awaken tired, drowsy and fatigued, having slept restlessly perhaps. There are then those others that sleep for 5 hours and wake full of enthusiasm and are fully refreshed and invigorated. It is the quality of sleep that varies. It is becoming increasingly better documented by medical professionals and researchers that poor quality sleep and sleep deprivation can lead to a range of detrimental health conditions, so lets get cracking on getting some better quality sleep.

It has been my experience through years of therapeutic work, that people that encounter sleep disorders have very active minds and they think a lot. Many of the contributory factors leading to sleep deprivation involve worrying, being tense or anxious, maybe being fearful or experiencing some kind of emotionally charged circumstances or situations.

There is a common thread to these causes and that is the constant thinking about these things whether or not anything can be achieved from that thinking. Over thinking about problems or issues in fact is like painting the insides of our minds with that problem; it is acquainting us with it more and more and we become better and better at worrying about it. It is important to be able to move away from that kind negatively focused mental activity.

You can use your self-hypnosis to being to distract your mind and move it away from those thoughts that cause the sleep disturbance. Entering self-hypnosis immediately prior to the desired period of sleep is something that can often send one to sleep without all of the applications mentioned within this chapter, however, use your self-hypnosis at a time when you are not about to go to sleep and when you arrive in self-hypnosis, take some time out to examine some of the disturbed sleep experiences; consider the causes of your sleep disruption.

Then begin to reframe those experiences; maybe by laughing about it or accepting the ridiculousness of your worries and then deliver more and more powerful suggestions and programmes for better quality sleep. You can of course use lots of the material and visualisation techniques described in earlier chapters and within the stress control chapter, also remember to add to your programmes and suggestions instructions for being in control of your sleep and choosing to drift into the state of sleep.

One way to be able to do this and to actually do it is to review several instances and occasions in your life when you have been in control and think about having the same kind of control over your sleep; think about the mental conditions that were in existence when you did so. You may also want to think about times when you have done something without disturbance for prolonged periods of time and begin to use those experiences also to really acquaint your unconscious mind about how to do these things, remember; create sensory rich experiences for your unconscious to move toward, instead of thinking about all the stuff you want to avoid.

So, in dealing with the symptoms of sleep deprivation or poor quality sleep, you can begin to use posthypnotic triggers for activating the processes of sleep within your mind. By posthypnotic triggers, what I mean is that inside of your hypnosis, you set yourself up with a trigger that you can use or 'fire off' when you are outside of hypnosis, that trigger is then a signal to your unconscious mind to begin getting ready for and into sleep.

One way of doing this is to write your self a programme that includes a suggestion like:

Every time I say the words sleep Adam' and I have the intention to enter sleep in a short period of time, my unconscious mind recognises this and begins the processes necessary to create the optimum internal conditions for sleep.

Or something along those lines. You can increase the power of this trigger so that every time you say those words to your self or out loud that you then create images of yourself in your mind enjoying a profoundly deep slumber. Then, in your programme write in a section that has you attach powerful imagery of you sleeping deeply and peacefully in your bed (or wherever you are going to be sleeping). You can then attach those images to your trigger, so that every time you activate your trigger and say those words, you also have your imagination pulling your unconscious mind in the same direction as your word and thoughts.

Please bear in mind that the word 'sleep' as an order to your unconscious mind may not resonate too well with you if you have been struggling to sleep for a while. The word may have negative connotations and you may well want to use the words 'deeply relaxed' or other words that resonate with you better.

You may not wish to create such an obvious trigger or instruction to your unconscious. Rather, you may wish to make other events or circumstances to act as posthypnotic triggers. If you think about your usual routine before sleeping (incidentally, if you have a routine that you associate with not sleeping well, I recommend you change it) then use those aspects of your routine to trigger the deep sleep process. So, actions like walking up stairs to your bedroom, or seeing your bed, or taking off your slippers all activate your unconscious minds ability to sleep. Let me give you an example of something you may include in a programme for better sleep:

Each step that I take toward my bed, when it is time for me to sleep, is another signal to my unconscious mind to begin the process of deep sleep attainment.

Or you may even want to use something like:

My unconscious mind knows that when I am brushing my teeth in the evening immediately prior to sleeping, that this is a signal to begin to relax my mind and create peaceful, serene thoughts, images and sounds in my mind that I consider to be conducive to peaceful and natural deeper sleep.

You get the idea. Remember to use caution and remember how literal your unconscious mind can be sometimes. If you add to your programme that you always wake with energy and vitality, this could cause an issue if you wake at 3am to go to the toilet and find yourself skipping vigorously to the bathroom and subsequently unable to return to sleep.

Despite some of those people that insist to me that they cannot remember ever sleeping well, there has been at least one night, even if it was when you were a baby that you slept well. If you are now racking your brain for an excuse that proves you have not, then please just imagine what it would be like and accept that I do not believe you. Your unconscious mind has memories and information of how it is to sleep well. Your unconscious mind knows how to sleep well.

You were born with it as a natural ability, just like you know how to breathe and let your heart beat. It has been changed or is perceived differently by you for whatever reason; just know that you know how to sleep well. You also know how to sleep better. The same way that you will trust your unconscious mind to instigate the healing process if you grazed your knee after a fall (as mentioned in an earlier chapter also), is the same kind of trust that you can begin to develop about your ability to sleep better and better now. Write this into your programmes.

Maybe even begin to write it into your programmes that your unconscious mind recalls occasions when you slept beautifully deeply and powerfully and it is now unconsciously remembering how to do that again and build upon that experience to sleep even better and deeper.

Another thing to begin to consider is stopping resisting your thoughts regardless of how busy your mind is. That's right, I said stop resisting them. Let them happen, even observe them and as long as you don't resist them, you may well begin to find that they go just a quickly as they came. You can even begin to imagine that you have a speed control for your thoughts and you can begin to slow your thoughts down; just imagine that you are playing your thoughts on slow motion. The material in the time distortion chapter and in the stress relief chapter can and does add to this much more comprehensively.

In addition, you may want to create tapes or CDs as demonstrated in earlier chapters for yourself so that you can just allow yourself to drift off to sleep naturally while listening.

Here are some scripts to get your imagination working and to begin to give you some ideas for your own programmes.

Script for better Quality Sleep

Using my imagination I can begin to imagine that you I am sponge being wrung of any stress and unwanted feelings, down and out through my toes. I take these 3 deeper breaths and as I say 'sleep now' so I do just that. I am aware of my own communication until my relaxation sensations are complete, then I do just go into a deep easy natural sleep.

Because I want to get a fuller nights sleep, and because I want to awaken at the time I set myself (in the morning or evening) feeling more and more naturally refreshed, rested and with more and more natural enthusiasm and energy for life, each night as I retire I relax every muscle in my body by taking those 3 deeper breaths. After each breath I say to myself **'sleep now'**. And I allow every muscle and nerve go looser and limp as if I was a rag doll. After the third breath I am so beautifully relaxed that I drift off into a deep and restful slumber with more and more speed, which remains unbroken until the time I set myself to wake, unbroken of course, except in the case of an emergency and an emergency is anything that requires my immediate attention and should such an emergency occur or exist, I wake and deal with it in the most appropriate way. Only an emergency awakens me and if this happens; upon returning to bed after attending to it, I return to sleep within 60 seconds. It is easier and easier for me to relax and go to sleep because I expect to sleep. Throughout my sleep, I am more and more contented and pleasantly relaxed.

I am finding it more and more easy to relax more thoroughly upon taking my 3 deeper breaths and at bedtime I drift to sleep more naturally as I relax. I sleep progressively more soundly and comfortably and without effort, it is just the way I am now. Throughout my sleep I feel naturally calm, contented and relaxed and I carry this calm, contented sense of relaxation over into my waking hours, installing this deep sense that I can and do sleep more regularly with a deeper quality. I awaken at my set usual rising time and feel more and more wonderful! I am increasingly, enjoyably relaxed, rested, alert and cheerful! I look forward to each new day ahead of me with a renewed sense of optimism and opportunity. I am more ready for another wonderful day and view it with freshness and awe; I feel like I am discovering each day. I thoroughly enjoy my deeper, more restful sleep and at bedtime I continue to just take 3 deep breaths and think those words of 'sleep now' after each breath, and I go to deeper sleep more and more naturally. These thoughts come to me when I relax and say, 'sleep now'.

I now am going to spread through myself the colours of the rainbow. The colours are red and orange, yellow and green, blue and purple, lavender, and white. As I go through the colours, imagining them working their way through my mind and body, I do go deeper and deeper into that wonderful natural sleep.

Just sensing the colour red and allowing it slowly evolve and turn into the colour orange, in my mind and in my body, slowly, calmly, easily and gently going into deep, usual sleep. That orange moving into the colour of yellow, filling my senses as it evolves through me into the colour of green, every nerve and muscle in my body is loose and limp and relaxed, as I go deeper and deeper into natural sleep.

(While thinking of each colour, you may want to picture things that are that colour, or sounds that go with them or spread soothing feelings that you might associate with them.)

The turning in the colour of blue, flowing through me, into every cell from head to toe I am feeling more and more sleepy, I feel more and more wonderful sensations flowing through my body and I go deeper and deeper into natural sleep.

Moving into purple now and then transforming into lavender, my mind and my body are now going into a very deeper and healthful slumber. I feel so good, and at the next colour, I gently and easily allow myself to drift right off, then I go into deep restful and natural sleep for the entire night as I think about white, the colour white permeating my cells, easily and gently now allowing my mind to go to that place that allows me to feel and be more and more peaceful, more tranquil and more and more serene. Sleep now. Sleep now. Sleep now.

Additional Better Quality Sleep Script

Now, I have actually used this kind of script in two distinctly separate ways; after an induction, as a deepener to be remembered later, and as a straightforward programme for better quality sleep. This kind of programme may not be ideal for those that may have any form of sleep disorder. It is a fairly well known idea in the field of hypnotherapy and not totally original, again, adapt it as you feel is best for you.

Now, I imagine myself on the top floor of a busy department store . . . at Christmas time . . . Christmas eve, in fact, with shoppers bustling everywhere, tills ringing, flustered counter assistants looking harassed and hot . . . there's noise and hassle and everybody's pushing everybody else . . . and patience is becoming strained as entire families rush about searching for those last-minute gifts that they had forgotten all about until now . . . and this is all too much for me and so I decide to go down to the next floor, via the escalator . . . and even the escalator is busy, loaded up to almost maximum capacity . . . but when I get down to the next floor . . .

I actually sigh with relief (you may want to actually let off a big sigh at this stage) because it is only half as busy as the floor above . . . only half as busy as the floor above . . . and it's maybe the cosmetics department, because there are women having makeovers and still people trying to buy last-minute gifts . . . worried young men sniffing at perfume bottles . . . older men looking at price labels . . . and it is still too busy for me, so once again I decide to take the escalator down to the next floor . . . and this time the escalator is only half as busy . . . and the next floor down is only half as busy as the one above . . .

The entire atmosphere is decidedly calmer and more easygoing . . . and this is the floor where they sell luggage and all sorts of things connected with holidays . . . and even though everything feels so much calmer here, I decide to see how things are on a lower floor still . . . taking to the escalator once again and being pleasantly surprised to discover that there is hardly anybody else on it at all . . . and when I step out onto the sales floor this time, I see that it is the furniture

169

department . . . sofas and chairs, tables and cupboards, bookshelves and display cabinets . . . furniture of almost all descriptions . . . and it's quiet and cool down here, hardly anybody around . . . and those that are here are just moving around quietly, gazing at things for a few moments before moving on . . . and I notice that the escalator has nobody on it at all . . . and I move towards it and soon find myself being transported gently down and down and down . . . with this wonderful relaxed feeling . . .

. . . and as I step of at the bottom, I am intrigued and interested to notice that I am in the bedding department now and there is no other soul around . . . just me . . . and in the peace and quiet of this place, I stroll casually to the largest most comfortable bed I have ever seen in my entire life . . . and I just flop yourself lazily onto it . . . marvelling at the sense of deep comfort that I suddenly experience . . . a deep comfort that seems to fill every pore of my entire body . . . relaxing me . . . calming me . . . lulling me into a deep and relaxing sleep . . . a deep, sound, beautiful sleep . . . the bed seems to mould and melt itself to the exact contours of my body and I feel as if I am settling a little deeper into it and as I sleep, I have a dream . . . I dream that I am on the top floor of a busy department store . . . at Christmas time . . . Christmas eve, in fact . . .

Additional ideas for sleep and its use

Lots of people firmly believe that sleep is a time that you recharge your batteries and that following your exertions of the day, you can then go to be to repair and recuperate. This can be a misunderstood concept. Bear in mind that your entire being is not resting while you sleep. All your vital functions are still going for it, you perspire, digest, your heart beats, your lungs breathe, you grow nails and hair; this is a lot of stuff that is going on. In the same way, your unconscious mind is not resting in sleep, it is controlling all the above-mentioned functions and processing experience and lots more besides. When you sleep, there just happens to be no interference from the conscious mind, so your unconscious mind can get on with things that it may not have had the opportunity to do while you were awake.

So, how about you use your unconscious mind while you are sleeping? Great idea. Before you sleep, give your unconscious mind some suggestions of things to get on and do or to let go of or to process during that time. Much nicer than thinking about running up a hill and your legs are not working, or monsters lurking in cupboards; or is that just me? A simple way to start is to begin to ask your unconscious mind to wake you up at the time that you want.

Ask your unconscious mind to repair more effectively and to forgive people and let go of anything unwanted while you are sleeping. Take yourself into hypnosis immediately prior to sleep or during the day before and ask your unconscious to do these things while you are sleeping. You may be seeking guidance, so you can request answers or understanding or to provide solutions more readily and naturally. What you can request from your unconscious while you sleep is limited only to your own limitations; hey, I even ask for wonderful dreams.

5

Stopping Smoking

Not choice
But habit rules the unreflecting herd.
William Wordsworth

Whether you are a smoker or not, lots of the techniques and strategies within this chapter are very useful in dealing with a vast array of differing things of varying natures. For some, it may be the main reason you invested in this book, because you have made a fantastic decision to stop smoking. For those of you that have done that, now is the time for me to tell you that there are no short cuts with this; it is really important that you are using your self-hypnosis and are acquainted with the programme writing ideology and the model of self-hypnosis.

Having been a therapeutic hypnotist and consultant for many years now, I know of and experience the benefits of hypnosis as a stand-alone treatment in helping people help themselves to stop smoking, however in order for it to be successful, it requires you to involve yourself in the stopping smoking process outside of hypnosis too. This chapter is a combination of the most modern and innovative psychological interventions.

As a smoker or a non-smoker, I am sure that you are aware that smoking has many facets, there is the physical aspect, the addiction to nicotine and the many chemical compounds and of course, the psychological aspect; the habitual processes. In order to achieve maximum success, you will be required to address both of those aspects to ensure a thorough ability to stop smoking and to remain a non-smoker for the rest of your life.

By now, and at this stage of this books journey, you are well aware of the difference between the conscious and the unconscious

172

minds. Your conscious mind, the analytical part of you, knows all the reasons that you should not smoke; the financial reasons, the health implications, the social pressures and all the rest. In fact, I encourage you to physically write down your reasons for wanting to stop smoking, have a look at them and read them. Your unconscious however, has learnt how to smoke and made it an automated process, so that you smoke on autopilot regardless of what you consciously think. It is like there is a civil war going on within you, your hypnosis is going to access that part of you and the way you feel about cigarettes or cigars or whatever form of tobacco it is that you may smoke.

Consciously, you may have been saying to yourself 'I will not smoke, I will not smoke' or 'don't smoke'. However, you now know that your brain and your unconscious mind cannot tell the difference between positive and negative. For example, as I said in the earlier chapter, if I said to you now that sentence 'Don't think about a pink elephant', in order to not think about it, you had to think about it, I know you just did. It is the same when you tell yourself 'I will not smoke'. You may as well be ordering yourself to smoke!

All habits are transferred from your conscious mind to your powerful unconscious, like with learning to read and write, to drive your car, tie your shoelaces and of course smoking. Once you have learned it, your unconscious mind stores it and cannot tell the difference between a negative behaviour and a positive behaviour. Having stored the behaviour, it then protects it for your safety, so you do not forget how to drive while you are at the wheel of a car! Your self-hypnosis deals directly with that part of you. In addition, you should consciously forge new habits too as we are coming on to.

Conscious changes

Use your self-hypnosis to get yourself to begin to do things differently. In neuro-linguistic programming, one of the really powerful presuppositions that is inherent with it, and I want to become inherent in your approach to stopping smoking is the sentence and the idea that 'If you always do what you always did, you will always get what you always got.'

So, if you keep on doing everything exactly as you always did do, even with all the self-hypnosis in the world, you might not make much progress.

To interrupt your patterns and instigate change into your life, you may want to use your self-hypnosis to incorporate some subtle changes before stopping fully. Others among you may just wish to go for it one go, either is fine. You know what is best for you.

If you want to prepare yourself hypnotically before stopping, you can begin to use your self-hypnosis to create some subtle changes in your habit, to lay some foundations before you free yourself of the habit for good in a later session.

You can do things like, over the course of a week, reduce the number of puffs you take from each cigarette. So for the rest of today, smoke 9 puffs per cigarette and then throw it away. Tomorrow you smoke 8 puffs per cigarette and so on reducing the number of puffs by one per cigarette, per day.

This can serve to interrupt the patterns, it is lessening the amount of nicotine that your body is absorbing and it is also heightening your awareness of your habit, so that it is no longer automated and happening without your awareness as it may have been doing in the past.

You can interrupt your patterns further by buying smaller packets, ensuring that you only buy one packet at a time and you can also switch brands every packet and do not buy your usual brand, buy a different brand each time and try your best to sample as many brands as possible over a set period of time before you stop. This way you will also be getting to know that you really do not smoke for taste or enjoyment, but continue to smoke, even if you don't like the taste; for the nicotine.

You could use your self-hypnosis to ensure that you do not offer or accept cigarettes or tobacco products, so that the people around you are getting used to you not smoking. Again, it is interrupting your old patterns.

To really interrupt and begin to break up your old pattern of your habit, change and alter where it is that you habitually smoke. If you used to always smoke in the car, do so before or after journey has happened and smoke in different places to that which you used to and be with different people. Avoid smoking in front of the television in particular.

All of these things are for interrupting your patterns, breaking them and developing a firm foundation for stopping smoking. Some people may want to get straight on with stopping and be mentally prepared for doing that.

Useful ideas and strategies for using in your programmes for stopping smoking

Deliver suggestions within your programmes to ensure that you are aware of how to relax without smoking. You may even want to deliver suggestions that smoking actually gets in the way of being able to relax naturally and deeply and that you are more relaxed without smoking.

Include suggestions that you feel more and more comfortable in social circumstances without smoking and that you enjoy social situations more and more when they are free from smoking.

You may well want to associate smoking with smells, tastes or memories that you find unpleasant. I shall give you an example; when I was at university, I had to take the bus each day to get to my lecture theatre. At the front of the bus there were seats that meant you sat parallel and facing another set of seats. On one particular day, a vagrant had got onto the bus and had been allowed on the bus despite how smelly and dirty he was. I had to sit opposite him while he sat there picking his nose, now if you are squeamish, skip on to the next paragraph; he also proceeded to eat the disgusting things he had up his nose and it truly made me feel sick, I had to get off the bus early. I could not bear it. If you happened to think about such a disgusting thing every time you put a cigarette near your mouth, it could enhance your ability to let go of that filthy habit.

You may want to deliver suggestions to yourself that if you ever have a craving, that taking three deeper breaths of clean, fresh air helps to free you of that craving and allows you to let go of it. You may want to use something else that when you do it, it will give you some other kind of good sensation or nice feeling.

There are many other techniques and strategies in other sections of this book that can also be utilised, just create more powerful programmes to do whatever you have to do to stop smoking with more and more ease.

When writing a programme for stopping smoking, there are lots of things to consider. Make sure that you deliver instructions to your unconscious to ensure that your unconscious mind is working in harmony with you. Tell yourself that your unconscious mind now begins to work with you to achieve the change you want.

You may want to consider ensuring that your unconscious mind now understands that cigarette smoking is a habit that can cause illness and/or even early death.

Then you might even want to consider that before you move on to delivering suggestions for stopping smoking, let yourself know that your unconscious mind is now activating its primary programming of protecting you against danger and begins to work with you to accept the suggestions that you be giving yourself and will completely erase all programming that now causes you to be a smoker.

Ask your self the important question. I do not want you to answer consciously to yourself. Get a gut feeling about the answer. Allow the answer to come into your mind naturally and easily as if it is coming from the deep level of your unconscious mind:

Is my unconscious now willing to accept and seal permanently within my mind, my body, my very spirit, the suggestions of change that will completely eliminate my present need to be a smoker?

Sit back and wait for the answer. Make sure that you are getting an undoubted 'yes' response before you proceed with using your self-hypnosis to stop smoking. If you are not absolutely 100% sure that you want to stop smoking, you may not enjoy the success that you would do if you really do want to. This could lead to doubts in your self-hypnotic skills and abilities.

If you get an answer of 'no', then this is not the right time for you to stop smoking. Go for it again when you feel ready.

Once you get a 'yes' let yourself know that you are really going to do this, consider suggesting to yourself something along the lines of:

Wonderful, now my inner mind accepts and seals in the suggestions I give, as long as I want to accept them and I know they are going to work. And I accept no laziness from any deep inner part of me.

OK, so here is an example of a script for stopping yourself smoking using your self-hypnosis:

The reason that I am here at this stage is that I have made up my mind. I have made a final decision to be a non-smoker, to stop smoking completely. I have made up my mind to stop smoking now, not tomorrow, not next week, not next month, but this very moment. I do not allow any exception to this decision, because I honestly and truly want to and do become a non-smoker for the rest of my longer, healthier life.

I reflect on the reasons that I want to be a non-smoker so strongly? I know them when I think about them. I think about the difficulty that smoking brings. Some people have their doctor tell them to stop. Some people have a chronic cough, or pains in the chest. Other people continue thinking about smoking and cancer or emphysema. It does not make any difference. The point is that I have made this final decision to stop smoking for myself, and that final decision is that I am stopping now.

My motivational factor is very important in any habit changing. I realise that I have no need of smoking; I am a non-smoker. What is it that I am freeing myself from? I am freeing myself of a cough, I am freeing myself of pain, I am freeing myself of trouble, I am freeing myself of all those things that I do not want, including smoking. I am freeing myself of the things I do not want in order to get the things I do want: naturally occurring relaxation, natural rest, a natural feeling of security, real natural happiness, all the things I do want, all the things I can and do find as a non-smoker.

I allow all these elements of this programme, my programme for being a non-smoker to have a more and more thorough and deep effect upon me, my mind, my body, my very spirit.

Now, nicotine is poison. It is one of the most powerful poisons on the face of the earth. A very tiny amount would be enough to kill a horse, let alone a human being. Fortunately, nicotine is not too concentrated in cigarettes, but it is present and I was taking poison, even minute amounts of poison. I was still taking poison every time I smoked. Now, I am freeing myself of that poison.

I am now choosing that I am going to do positive things from now on. There are many positive things I can do and positive things I can partake in. I enjoy clean, fresh air more and more, and enjoy the experience of the air in my body being cleaner and fresher. I can and do relax and enjoy your self more and more naturally. There are millions of other things I can do to maintain a wonderfully more and more relaxed, peaceful, calm, tranquil, placid existence without taking any poison. As a matter of fact, poison does not really make me more tranquil or placid; poison really makes me more nervous. Poison takes me closer to death. Poison isn't good for people at all. I do not need to punish myself. I am not guilty of anything.

Now, those ideas are gone and finished and I do not have to think of them ever again and just as those ideas are gone, that old supposed need for poison that I thought I had is gone right along with them. I do allow the entire thing to just drift away. I don't need any of that, I don't need any poisons. What I do need and what I bring more and more of into my life is natural relaxation, comfortable and cool relaxation. During this time I drift down deeper and deeper. I relax more and more, I enjoy life more and more as a non-smoker, I feel more comfortable in every way and I am free from the desire for tobacco in every way and any form, for its starting to leave and very soon I am surprised and amazed to find out that I no longer require tobacco in any form, nor do I need any type of poison in its place. I am through with poison; I literally turn my back on it. Poison in all its forms, you walk away from.

As I pay more and more attention to my inner realities and my internal voice, so I can feel the last remnants of that unwanted habit leaving. Now, every person who has smoked a cigarette in the past has connected smoking with other activities. Some people feel they have to smoke when they first open their eyes in the morning, or when they go to bed at night, or immediately after dinner, or when driving the car, or when at work, or when not at work, or when watching TV, or in any other situation.

They associate smoking with some activity or with something else they are doing, and because that other thing happens it triggers a mechanism which causes one to reach for a cigarette. Now we are breaking up all those mechanisms, destroying them, we're destroying them all right now. Each of those typical occasions in the past when I used to smoke that I think of, I can imagine that though shattering, smashing, being destroyed and so my unconscious destroys all association with those old mechanisms.

Everyone knows how dangerous smoking is, it's dangerous to my health, dangerous to my lungs and if there was any reward for living dangerously, that's different. Whatever situations were connected with smoking in the past are now completely revised, smoking for me is in the past.

From this moment forward there is no other activity that occurs in my life that requires smoking; there's no other activity in my life that goes better with smoking. In fact, every other activity in my life goes better with health. They go better with fresh, clean air in my lungs, they go better with a good blood supply, they go better without the coughing and spluttering, yes, everything goes better with health.

So from this moment on, it is easier and easier for you, because you are free of the urge for tobacco in any form, at any time, at any place, under any conditions, in any situation.

Not only have I stopped smoking, I am free of the urge, no matter how hard I try, I do not smoke. It is already set that I won't smoke. It is completely set and finished that I am through with smoking. I have a mind of my own and I have set it.

Because I have made this decision to break the smoking habit, and become an ex-smoker, become a non-smoker, and because it is my wish to become an non-smoker, that is why, I stop smoking, I stop smoking, for ever and ever, because it was my decision to stop smoking, and I have broken the smoking habit for ever and ever, because it is my decision, and I am more and more pleased that, I are now a non-smoker, I know, when I first started to smoke, when I first inhaled tobacco smoke, I felt dizzy, even nauseous, wanting to cough, because my body did not like, did not want that smoke.

But I persisted and finally my body accepted the fact that I was going to smoke and smoking became a part of my life, and when later on I wanted to stop I found it difficult to stop smoking, because my body did not know, did not understand that I was stopping, now though, my self-hypnosis and inner belief and desire, allows my unconscious mind to understand and now, I no longer smoke. And my unconscious can communicate that fact to every part of me, so that my body knows too that you I am a non-smoker and my body is more and more pleased that I am a non-smoker and since my body always knew how to enjoy life without smoking, there are no withdrawal symptoms at all, far from it, my body never liked that smoke, does not like it now and it never will, and now that I am a non-smoker, my body is more and more pleased that I am a non-smoker.

I allow these thoughts and I let those words sink into the deepest depths of my unconscious. I am a non-smoker and am for the rest of my life. I am a non-smoker and am for the rest of my life.

So I allow myself to understand that, of course, in the past, I used to smoke, and that as far as I am concerned, smoking for me is a thing of the past, no longer a part of me, just a memory, a gradually fading memory, I go through my daily life And for long periods of time, I forget about smoking, even if I see other people smoking, smoking means nothing to me, it is a fact of life that other people smoke, and other people smoking means nothing to me, and if anybody offers me something to smoke, or I am asked if I smoke, I are more and more pleased, more and more delighted to say, to think, to know 'I don't smoke' and each time I think it, I say it or know it, my determination and ability to remain a non-smoker is reinforced, in any event, I am suggesting to my unconscious mind that I have no desire to smoke, so I just allow my unconscious mind to make these suggestions a part of me, a part of my inner world,

As I am taking control of my own mind, I also have better control of my eating habits too, wherever I am, whatever I am doing, whoever I am with, I have no desire to and that's all there is to it, I know that I am an ex-smoker. That's right, I let those words sink in to the deepest level of being, which does reproduce in me my dominant thoughts.

I am a non-smoker, which means that I do not smoke, I do not touch tobacco in any form whatsoever, like every ex-smoker, I may have the occasional thought about smoking, but I treat that thought like a passing fancy, I let it go, my mind soon wanders onto something else, so I forget about smoking, sure in the knowledge that I am a non-smoker, which means that I do not smoke, as an ex-smoker, healthy alternatives to smoking come naturally to mind, just as automatic as my smoking was in the past, if I bother to think about it at all, I think of all the wonderful benefits that I am now enjoying as a non-smoker, the money I find in my pocket, the social advantages, the health implications, above all that wonderful feeling of well being that lets me know that I am free . . .

. . . free of the burden of smoking, the burden of smoking that I left behind in the past, and I enjoy that sense and feeling of freedom that comes from being an ex-smoker, no longer having to continually scratch that itch. And now that I am no longer deliberately introducing tobacco smoke into my body, my health receives a boost, in fact, I are physically fitter and healthier in every way, I have not given up anything, I have just left something unpleasant behind me. Another marvellous benefit is that my head clears, and that means that my mind becomes clearer and clearer, allowing my body to be more and more relaxed, every day, and I become so much more relaxed, not only in my body, I am more relaxed about myself, the world around, and the days and weeks and months go by and I become ever more clear in my mind, ever more relaxed in my body, now that I am a non-smoker, I find that I am coping better with anything, anybody, and any situation that I have to handle in my daily life, because I are coping more calmly, more relaxed, and more confidently, I have greater self-control, in other areas of my life too. Greater control over the way I think, feel, and greater control over the way I do things, over the way I behave, altogether, I feel as if a weight, a burden, has been lifted, and it has, the burden of smoking that I left back in the past, where it remains for ever and ever.

Of course, there may well be ways in which you would prefer to create your own programme for stopping smoking and I encourage you to do just that. Notice that the script includes a sentence that you are not 'giving up' smoking; note this when thinking of stopping smoking. You do not want to give up anything really, do you? Suggest that you are **becoming a non-smoker** rather than *giving up* smoking.

Now, here is a very powerful technique that I learned from the world renowned Tony Robbins on a training he did in the UK a few years ago. It is called the Dickens pattern, because it is loosely based on the experience of some of Dickens' characters in a story of his. The idea is that you are going to take your self into hypnosis and imagine two contrasting eventualities based on a decision that you could make today. Here, we are using it to compare your future as a non-smoker or a smoker; however, it can be used with anything that you want to use it with. The following procedure really is self-explanatory. You just take yourself into hypnosis and begin to do the following exercise:

Using your imagination, you imagine that you have reached an important fork in the road of your life today. Allow yourself to imagine that you are standing at that fork. As you look down the road that leads to the left, you notice that it is a cold, barren, unfriendly road. The sky is dreary and a cold drizzle is falling. The trees are barren of leaves and the grass has long been replaced with cold, hard rock. A cold wind blows the mist and drizzle. It is a dead place. This is the road of a smoker.

This road leads to pain, suffering and even early death. It is a sad road; it is cold, lifeless and dead. As you look closely, you can see, sense or just imagine a milestone ahead. It is of you in one years time if you continue with this unwanted habit; you can notice the damage that another year of smoking has made to your health, the increase in disappointment about how you feel about the fact that you have been unable to be in control of your own mind, then notice another milestone, five years in the future if you carried on down this road, the added damage that this has done to your health and the way in which you fell about your own inability to make a change, knowing that a simple decision you make at the fork today can create so much difference for your future.

You need to really emphasise this in your mind. Use sights, sound and images and really see, hear and feel what it is that you will experience in the future if you take this road as a result of the decision you make today.

As you turn from that road and look down the road to your right, you see a beautiful road. The sun is shining brightly in a deep, rich blue sky, the trees are full of leaves and the grass is lush and green. This is the road of a non-smoker. And as you begin to walk down this road now, you can breathe in the clean, fresh air. With each step you feel yourself feeling healthier and healthier, stronger and stronger. This road leads to a longer, healthier, happier life. With each step you feel yourself feeling more and more alive, more and more convinced that no one could ever again make you go back to that other cold, dreary deadly road of a smoker and no one can ever change that. You choose life.

Congratulate yourself on being a non-smoker for the rest of your life.

You may even want to create future versions of yourself in one weeks time, looking back on this moment as having been the start of you becoming a non-smoker and noticing how easy that week was as you look back on it, maybe see yourself in months time as a non-smoker, one years time, still a non-smoker.

Just build in to your hypnosis the correct anticipation and expectation about your future as a healthier non-smoker. Also, when creating your programmes for stopping smoking, think about that term 'give up' and realise that it is not very progressive. I would not want you to give up on anything. I know I mentioned it earlier; some people just say this expression without thought. Now you would have to be really silly to ignore this advice twice wouldn't you? Remember; you are becoming and non- smoker for the rest of your life.

Hints and tips for stopping smoking

I have had lots of people tell me all the marvellous ways in which they are stopping smoking. Of Course I am biased, I believe self-hypnosis and hypnotherapy are the best. This list of tips, techniques and strategies are sure to help anyone in addition to that which they do in self-hypnosis. These techniques are sometimes like self-hypnosis without the trance, and some of them are just practical advice that is essential to follow.

Anyone looking to stop smoking can run through these techniques, strategies and hints for aiding you in stopping smoking. It is up to you to ensure that you do these things to really enhance what you are doing, the more effort you put into these exercises, the easier it is to stop smoking for good.

Powerful Hint 1

Being a smoker is like cycling with stabilisers attached to the wheels, you can find it hard to be balanced without smoking. Now, when you cycle freely again, the natural balance returns.

When people smoke more than half of what they breathe is fresh air – pulled through the cigarette right down into the lungs. So if you feel any cravings you can instantly overcome them by taking three deeper breaths. Imagine breathing from that space just below your belly button. Whenever you do this you put more oxygen into your bloodstream. This means you can use deep breaths to change the way you feel instantly and give you power over the way you feel and help you let go of those old cravings.

Powerful Hint 2

Next, think now of all the reasons you don't like smoking, the reasons that it's bad and the reasons you want to stop. Write down the key words on a piece of paper. For example, you experience breathlessness, it's dirty, filthy and your clothes smell, your friends and family are concerned and it's expensive, unsociable and so on. Then, on the other side of the paper, write down all the reasons why you'll feel good when you've succeeded in stopping. You'll feel healthier, you'll feel in control of your self, your senses are enhanced; your hair and clothes will smell fresher and so on. Whenever you need to, look at that piece of paper.

Powerful Hint 3

Next, we are going to programme your mind to feel disgusted by cigarettes. I want you recall 4 times when you thought to yourself 'I've got to quit', or that you felt disgusted about smoking. Maybe you just felt really unhealthy, or your doctor told you in a particular tone of voice 'You've got to quit' or somebody you know was badly affected by smoking. Take a moment now to come up with 4 different times that you felt that you have to quit or were disgusted by smoking.

Remember each of those times, one after another, as though they are happening now. I want you to keep going through those memories and make them as vivid as possible. See what you saw, hear what you heard and feel how you felt. I want to take a few minutes now to keep going through those memories again and again, overlap each memory with the next until you are totally and utterly disgusted by cigarettes.

Powerful Hint 4

Have a think to yourself about the consequences of you not stopping smoking now, if you just carry on and on. Imagine it, what will happen if you carry on smoking. What are the consequences? Imagine yourself in 6 months time, a year's time, even 5 years time if you do not stop smoking now. Think of all the detrimental effects of not stopping right now and how a simple decision you make today can make such an impact on your future.

Imagine how much better is your life going to be after you've stopped. Really imagine it is months from now and you have successfully stopped. Smoking is a thing of the past, something you used to do. Keep that feeling with you and imagine having it tomorrow, and for the rest of next week. In your mind, imagine stepping in to that non-smoking version of you and feel how it feels to be a non-smoker.

Powerful Hint 5

Also, your mind is very sensitive to associations, so it's very important that you have a clear out and remove all tobacco products from your environment. Move some of the furniture in your house and at work. Smokers are accustomed to smoking in certain situations. So, for example, if you used to smoke on the telephone at work move the phone to the other side of the desk. Throw away ashtrays, old lighters and anything that you used to associate with smoking.

Powerful Hint 6

Smokers sometimes use their habit to give themselves little breaks during the day. Taking a break is good for you, so carry on taking that time off – but do something different. Walk round the block, have a cup of tea or drink of water, or do some of the techniques on this programme. In fact, if possible drink a lot of fruit juice. When you stop smoking the body goes through a big change. The blood sugar levels tend to fall, the digestion is slowed down and your body starts to eject the tar and poisons that have accumulated. Fresh fruit juice contains fructose, which restores your blood sugar levels, vitamin C which helps clear out impurities and high levels of water and fibre to keep your digestion going. Also try to eat fruit every day for at least two weeks after you have stopped.

Also when you stop, cut your caffeine intake by half. Nicotine breaks down caffeine so without nicotine a little coffee will have a big effect. Drink 8–10 glasses of water (ideally bottled and still rather than carbonated) to help wash out your system.

Powerful Hint 7

You were used to using cigarettes to signal to your body to release happy chemicals, so next we are going to programme some good feelings into your future. Allow yourself to fully remember now a time when you felt very deep ecstasy, pleasure or bliss, right now. Take a moment to recall it as vividly as possible. Remember that time – see what you saw, hear what you heard and feel how good you felt. Where about in your body were those feelings, imagine turning them up and spreading them through your body to make them more intense.

Keep going through the memory, as soon as it finishes, go through it again and again, all the time squeezing your thumb and finger together. In your mind, make those images big and bright, sounds loud and harmonious and feelings strong and intensified. We are making an associational link between the squeeze of your fingers and that good feeling.

OK, stop and relax. Now if you have done that correctly when you squeeze your thumb and finger together you should feel that good feeling again. Go ahead do that now, squeeze thumb and finger and remember that good feeling.

Now we're going to programme good feelings to happen automatically whenever you are in a situation where you used to smoke.

Next I'd like you to squeeze your thumb and finger together, get that good feeling going and now imagine being in several situations where you would have smoked, but being there feeling great without a cigarette. See what you'll see hear and take that good feeling into those situations without a need for a cigarette.

Imagine being in a situation where someone offers you a cigarette and you confidently say 'No thanks, I don't smoke'. And feel fantastic about it!

Powerful Hint 8

Get social support. Your commitment to stopping smoking for the rest of your life can be made much easier by talking about it to friends and family and letting them support you. They will congratulate you on doing so well too!

Powerful Hint 9

Be aware of making excuses for yourself. Some people talk themselves into smoking, especially if they encounter a stressful situation and in the past they used to deal with it by smoking. If those old thoughts pop into your head, shout the word 'STOP' in your head, to stop the thoughts from progressing. Nicotine just stresses your body more and is like that itch that can never be properly scratched; the more you smoke, the more you have to. So say, '**STOP**' and steer clear of old slippery slopes.

Powerful Hint 10

Reward yourself. Congratulate yourself. Treat yourself each time you get past a certain milestone; the first week or first month, the six-month target. Let yourself know that you did something really special here.

You actually need to do these things to make changes. Make sure you employ as many of these things into your days and take the time to demonstrate to yourself that you know it is important to do this for you. Write your programmes and enjoy becoming (and being) a non-smoker.

6

Weight Control

The highest possible stage in moral culture is when we recognize that we ought to control our thoughts.

Charles Darwin

When people decide to stop smoking, stop drinking alcohol, overcome an addiction to drugs or gambling for example, you can stop doing it knowing that you do not have to do it. However, you do need to eat.

When using self-hypnosis for taking control of your weight and achieving and maintaining the size, shape and weight that pleases you, it is better that you create a lifestyle programme to introduce yourself to a new way of life – leading to a fitter, happier, healthier you in whatever way is right for you.

This chapter is going to give you a lot of information to give you a very wide set of tools and techniques to help you to achieve your goals. The aim here is for you to create a programme or a series of programmes that are all flexible and that will allow you to focus on the elements that are key for you. However, you do want to make your programmes holistic programmes, again, in the way that is relevant to you and your situation. We know that diets on their own do not work in the long term, for a life free from dieting you will need to make changes on all key areas of your life.

However, the key to sustained weight reduction is the mental stretch, that's right, it's all in your mind!

I recommend that the main elements of the programmes you create are:

Firstly; **good nutrition.**

No one wants to be on a diet forever, and the good news is that you don't need to be! As long as you are aware of the basics of

188

good nutrition, and how the body responds to the different foods you put in. In this section, I am going toe give you basic advice about healthy eating, and hints and tips to help you regain control. I am not a nutritionist, so the information will be basic, but it will contain some golden nuggets for you to use in your self-hypnosis programme creation.

Second; **exercise**.

I encourage you to feel the physical and mental benefits of a regular routine. You can include your own exercise routine or fun activities to speed up weight reduction and increase your energy. I also offer you some simple and basic exercise targets. You can use your self-hypnosis to motivate yourself and drive yourself to enjoy extra activity and promote its effectiveness.

Third is the **Mental Stretch**.

Many diets and exercise programmes fail because we often lose motivation or ignore the fact that weight is a complex issue. The main cause of overeating for many is emotional; it is about our mood swings and often our self-image. Here, I have providing you with a range o'f tools to enable you to deal with the causes of weight problems and thereby avoid the yo-yo' effects of many diets. We are going to do this by teaching you new techniques to build confidence and get rid of negative self-beliefs. So here goes! – You've got nothing to lose except your former self! Remember, that word 'lose' is one I encourage you not to use. We do not want to lose anything and you certainly don't want to be a loser, do you? You are achieving and maintaining the size, shape and weight that please you.

Before getting too far into creating your programmes for change, it would be helpful to identify the areas you already have strengths in, and those areas where you may have to work a bit harder.

Have a think; with regards to **Good Nutrition**, do you eat regular meals? Do you eat only when you are hungry and stop when you are full? Is your food healthy and pleasurable?

With regards to **Exercise**; are you physically active? Do you take time to each exercise each day? Are you physically active? Do you notice how your body feels?

Then finally, with regards to **The Mental Stretch**; are you aware of your feelings? Do you recognise and meet your own needs? Are your thoughts positive?

As you think about these sets of questions, you can begin to notice which area needs more attention.

So, now you can begin to start planning how you are going to use your self-hypnosis to build on your strengths. You can assess your own profile in each of key areas mentioned.

Be aware of the strongest area for you and plan to make it stronger with your self-hypnosis and you can also begin to be aware of the areas that you need to improve.

Now look at the weakest area. The element will then provide you with the most challenge and opportunity as you move through the process of creating your own programme for change. Identify this area and begin to think about what you can do to ensure that you succeed, and also consider what support you will need from others to help you.

What support do you need? Make notes to your self of the areas that you require the most support and write your programmes with that focus in mind.

Good nutrition

Balance is the key to sustained and healthy weight reduction. Think about this entire creation of programmes as an education programme for yourself and your unconscious, it currently has habits that may require further education and updating, so that in addition you are learning more about the nutritional content of all the foods we eat, and what works for you.

One in five of us are extremely sensitive to carbohydrates, feeling bloated, lacking in energy and even having an allergic reaction. Many high carbohydrate foods are also high in fat, for example chips and crisps – the perfect combination for clogged arteries, let alone weight gain. Switching to 'Good Carbohydrates', as outlined in the next section on 'Low GI Foods', would also be a better option. Use your self-hypnosis to direct yourself in these directions.

We have always known that sugar, bread and cakes turn into fat – why? Because insulin turns excess energy into fat. Limiting your carbohydrate intake (remember, we said '**limiting**' not totally excluding, also remember that some simple carbohydrates are the same as eating refined sugar products; drive yourself toward more complex carbohydrates) does enable your body to keep insulin low, so that we stop turning excess energy into fat. Our bodies do then burn fat.

Therefore, you want to think about creating an energy plan that is about dissolving old beliefs and myths. In fact, your entire programme can be about changing beliefs that are no longer serving you.

Let's look at two dieting myths:

Firstly, that **Fat is bad for you**.

Do remember there are two types of fat, and it's those fats typically found in margarines and processed foods that have been chemically altered which are not natural to the body. By contrast, eggs, fish, olive oil, nuts and seeds are rich in omega 3 and omega 6, which are essential to health. Now, doesn't this remind you of the 'Mediterranean' diet? We have known for many years that the Mediterranean diet has lower incidence of heart disease and obesity. The benefits of omega 3 oils have been promoted recently as 'brain food'. You can obtain omega 3 in fish oil supplements.

Also; **Low Calorie diets shed weight**.

95% of low calorie diets fail. Why? Mainly because they are unsustainable, we cannot starve ourselves indefinitely. So when we go back to 'normal' eating, we gain more weight than before. Hence, the 'yo-yo' effect so common with low calorie diets. Our bodies soon learn that food intake is low, and this means reduced energy, so that our bodies turn down our metabolism, which means we just don't lose weight. Our bodies have a primitive defence mechanism against starvation whether that is by reducing calories or just skipping meals altogether.

We recommend that you cut back on your simple carbohydrate intake in order to achieve healthy weight management. This plan focuses on getting more flexibility into your diet, allowing you to eat carbohydrates, but 'good' carbohydrates! So use your self-hypnosis to make those kinds of carbohydrates more appealing to you and ensure that you are more and more consciously aware of them.

Here is an important question that you should learn the answer to: **What is Glycaemic Index?**

The body's preferred fuel is glucose, which it makes from the carbohydrates we eat. This is converted into energy. The glycaemic index is a measure of the speed that this conversion happens at. Foods with a high glycaemic index (high GI foods) convert rapidly into glucose, and those with a low glycaemic index convert more slowly. Use your self-hypnosis to heighten your attraction to foods with a low glycaemic index.

Here is the next question: **Why does speed matter?**

Speed matters because when glucose is released into the bloodstream, your body also releases insulin, which transports the glucose to the parts of your body where it is most needed. If glucose is released slowly there is no problem, however if there is a 'rush' of glucose entering the bloodstream the body releases higher levels of insulin to cope and high levels of insulin quickly transfer the glucose into fat stores. Not only can this result in weight gain, but it can also cause cell damage, contribute to the aging process, furring of the arteries and triggers type II diabetes.

So, the process of switching to a low GI diet reverses this process. You can begin to employ you self-hypnosis to get your diet on a low GI track.

Here are some simple guidelines for low GI foods.

Some examples of high GI foods are: Beer, alcohol, maltose, glucose, glucose drinks, sports drinks, dates, watermelon, instant rice, puffed rice, rice cakes, white rice, rice krispies, cornflakes, wheat cereals, crackers, cheerios, whole-wheat white bread, white bread, waffles, parsnips, baked potatoes, instant mash, french fries, pumpkin, corn chips, tortillas.

Here are some examples of medium GI foods: Soft drinks, corn syrup, sucrose, honey, chocolate, ice-cream, low fat ice-cream, cantaloupe melons, pineapples, raisins, bananas, apricots, mango, kiwi, rye crisp breads, shredded wheat, grape nuts, couscous, brown rice, basmati rice, pasta, muesli, pastry, oatmeal, buckwheat, all-bran, rye bread, cornmeal, sweet corn, beetroot, sweet potato, yams, carrots, green peas, crisps.

Finally, here are some examples of low GI foods: Flavoured yoghurts, low fat milk, butter, orange juice, grapes, apple juice, oranges, apples, pears, strawberries, unripe bananas, peaches, grapefruit, plums, cherries, whole wheat pasta, white spaghetti, barley, rice bran, peanuts, dried peas, pinto beans, canned baked-beans, chick peas, black beans, kidney beans, soy beans, lentils, tomato soup, Green vegetables, wholegrain bread.

Here are some tips for Effective Weight Management to consider including in your programmes for you to incorporate into your daily life:

- Plan your menus for the week ahead.
- Do not go shopping when you are hungry.
- Stick to regular meal times as best as you can.
- Your metabolism is always higher earlier in the day, so eat light at night.
- Drink 2 glasses of cold water before each meal and not immediately afterwards.
- Eat slowly, chew your food well, it takes 20 minutes for your stomach to let the brain know you are full!
- Do not eat whilst doing other activities like watching TV.
- Wait 5 minutes between each course, and if you are still hungry, then eat.
- Be aware of how different foods make you feel, full, bloated, energised?
- Stop when you are satisfied, not full. If you are full, you have generally eaten too much.
- Drink plenty of water throughout the day.
- Always picture in your mind how you want to be and tell yourself: 'I am achieving this'

Use these ideas in your programmes and within your self-hypnosis sessions. Incorporate them into your overall plan.

Here are some basics with regards to exercise and some core fundamental things that you should consider including in your healthier lifestyle regime. Please do consult your doctor and/or a physician before you embark on a new exercise regime.

So, what is the reason for exercise? **Our bodies are designed for movement**, and if we don't keep our muscles active, they begin to lessen in power. Strong muscles stabilise our posture, keeping us supported, which cuts the risk of joint problems, pain and discomfort. Strong muscles support the body, but also increase the activity of one very important muscle; the heart. This obviously reduces the risk of coronary heart disease. You are at greater risk of obesity, diabetes, high blood pressure, coronary heart disease and cancer if you don't exercise.

In addition to that, regular **exercise helps you to look younger**. Research from Tufts University in the U.S. has shown that you can reverse the effects of aging. A group of women aged 50 – who were given a twice-weekly weight-training regime, looked 15 to 20 years younger after 12 months! Their bodies were toned, fat had been replaced by muscle and their posture had improved.

Regular exercise is good for the brain and boosts your memory. It may also even help to delay the onset of Alzheimer's disease, according to a recent study published in the American journal *Exercise and Sport Sciences Review.*

Exercise improves your moods: Exercise causes the brain to release mood-boosting chemicals including serotonin, dopamine and endorphins. Just 10 minutes of vigorous activity will lift your spirits, although the best results are achieved after 20 minutes, 'according to a study in the US journal, Psychology'.

So begin to think of ways to use your self-hypnosis to address and incorporate these things into your life in a way that is congruent with you and your life. Find a type of exercise that suits you and do it regularly!

The recommended amount of exercise we should be doing is 30 minutes a day for at least 5 days per week. However, this can be split into 15-minute sessions, so find a way to increase the amount you do gradually to a level that fits with your lifestyle. This could even be as simple as walking up and down your stairs at home, or going for a brisk walk. You are not expected to run marathons and sometimes expecting too much of ourselves too soon can be demoralising, you just want to get your heart rate above its usual rate for those prolonged 30 minutes. There are small changes you can make which would make a big difference in the long term, write programmes about these kind of things:

- Walk rather than use the car when you can.
- Use the stairs rather than the lift.
- Add a 10-minute exercise routine that focuses on your stomach muscles every other day.

The power of your beliefs

How many times did my Mum say to me; 'Don't leave food on your plate. There are starving children in other countries!'

Who hasn't been influenced by others? We have all been influenced every day since birth. From the earliest moments of our life we absorbed suggestions from our parents, teachers and friends. Their opinions provided important information, which led to lifelong habits, attitudes and behaviours, without which we could not function.

Suggestions from others led to the creation of many of our own beliefs. 'These beliefs then became the guiding principles in our lives. Why? Because we have to be true' to our own beliefs. These early beliefs form what is known as a self-image. It is as if we have an 'internal picture, an inner voice or just a strong sense of who I really am'.

Many of our beliefs were instilled in us during childhood. As babies and young children we were highly suggestible. The mind of a young child is often described as being like 'a sponge' or an 'open book'. In our formative years we accepted almost everything we were told as true, then, at about age 4 to 6 we started to develop a critical faculty. We started to disbelieve in Father Christmas and the Tooth Fairy, I am sorry to those of you that are hearing this for the first time.

Each positive and negative suggestion moulds our self-image, and, because we have to act in accordance with this self-image, such suggestions tend to influence how we feel and then, how we act. Right now you may be subjected to many external suggestions (from helpful friends perhaps) such as:

'It takes willpower to lose weight'
'It's hard to keep the fat off'
'Dieting causes the yo-yo effect'
'Exercise is boring'

Also, the media bombards us with images of eternal youth, of 'perfect bodies', which in turn promotes unrealistic expectations and the pressure to conform. If that were not enough, we may also be struggling with 'emotional baggage', negative beliefs about ourselves (typically adopted in early childhood) such as:

'I'm not good enough'
'I'm not worthy'
'I'm not attractive'
'Nobody loves me'

Many of us learnt to use eating as a way of tranquillising or stuffing down' uncomfortable emotions. Many of us were given food as a substitute for love.

Even if you have a legacy of dis-empowering beliefs or emotional baggage, your mind has a tremendous capacity to change. Recall a story of someone who has triumphed over great difficulties. Think about it, what one person can do, you can do. You can erase past negative influences and establish new beliefs and positive behaviours. You are not imprisoned by self-sabotaging patterns forever. I often remember what the famous hypnotherapist and renowned psychiatrist, Milton Erickson, once said: 'It's never too late to have a happy childhood!' You self-hypnosis can be utilised to let go of old programming and create a new you with new patterns.

Always remember that your unconscious mind is trying to protect you. Your unconscious mind is trying to protect you from physical harm and from emotional pain. At the unconscious level of habit, your mind actually believes that your current eating and exercise habits are benefiting you.

Your unconscious mind is a creature of habit and, like a computer it will keep running old, out of date programmes until it gets new instructions. Some people say that it takes 21 days to create a habit. That means, you need to keep taking your action for 21 days. Keep driving your self to take that action; your results will be amazing.

Your unconscious mind may well believe that over-eating is protecting you from emotional pain. By numbing your emotions, tranquillising your anxiety, it thus protects you from raw emotions. Use your self-hypnosis to d'eal with any painful emotions and limiting beliefs, which are the true cause of the yo-yo' effect. Change your outmoded ways of responding and thus transform your life.

Useful ideas to employ in your self-hypnosis for achieving your ideal weight

Within your self-hypnosis sessions, create a vision of your self, as you want to be, create a rich image, include sounds and feelings and then keep that image in your mind and deliver it to your unconscious mind about how you choose to be. There is a more detailed way of doing this in the wealth creation chapter.

When in hypnosis you can create a hologram of your body, as you want it to be and imagine locking that hologram into your unconscious as a blueprint of how you want your body to develop. This can be done in a vast manner of ways; be creative.

You can use your self-hypnosis and create a programme that relates to how you respond to hunger. You can begin to reframe what hunger means to you; each time you feel hunger get your unconscious mind to remind you that means your metabolism is working and you are reducing weight and that you will enjoy your food more the next time you eat as a result of that hunger.

Use all kinds of mental imagery for stoking the fires of your metabolism. You can create a metaphor of some kind as something that you are 'turning up' or 'firing up' deep inside you. You may even relate your unconscious to the times in your younger years when your metabolism worked extremely efficiently and effectively and that it now remembers how to metabolise all excess.

Remember to keep within the realms of safety and ensure that you do eat sufficient for your physiological requirements.

You can write a programme for heightening the taste and sense of satisfaction with that which you eat; so that you are eating like a gourmet chef that gets the utmost satisfaction from the tiniest amounts of food; bring in to play the thousands of taste buds, observe the smell and colours of the food and ensure that you find smaller amounts more satisfying as a result of this newer, slower way of eating; like a gourmet. You can even include in your programme suggestions for always putting your knife and fork down in between mouthfuls and that you chew more thoroughly and slowly to get more nutrition from your food.

You can include suggestions that let you free yourself of old beliefs that might have been limiting you. When in hypnosis, you can imagine old beliefs that are written on a wall or on paper and you are knocking the wall down or ripping (or burning the paper).

Remember to reward yourself for achieving the goals that you set yourself and do your best to set easily achievable goals and then you can promote your success and build upon it.

I am really reluctant to give scripted examples of weight reduction programmes here, as it is one area that really does

THE SECRETS OF SELF-HYPNOSIS

require a lot of personal consideration from you. I have however, included a programme for better health at the end of this chapter. Apply all the in depth learning from the book so far and create programmes that are relevant and appropriate for you.

I have also outlined some further considerations for you when using self-hypnosis to achieve and maintain the size and weight that pleases you. A lot of the information that follows is very technical; however, it leads to a thorough understanding of the physiology behind cravings and will heighten your awareness of your own physiology and allow you to really create the changes that allow you to achieve and maintain the size, shape and weight that pleases you.

Use your self-hypnosis to ensure that you are truly aware of what we shall refer to as **Stomach and Mouth foods**.

People eat for many different reasons. The prime biological reason for food is simply to provide resources and energy. Your body needs to eat in order to have fuel so you can move your muscles and allow your internal organs to do what they need to do. You also need vitamins, minerals and proteins in order for the body to repair itself and grow in a natural and healthy way.

Eating, however, also has an important social role to play. We eat at weddings and birthday parties to celebrate. In fact whenever there is a celebration of some kind to be had, food will very often feature as part of the reward. The opposite is also true. Food is also used in order to mark solemn occasions. You eat at a wake after a funeral. You have farewell dinners and some in honour of people that have passed away. These are ordinary social functions in which food will be involved.

The problem is that your mind has extended the categories in which food will serve as a reward or as a remedy to cheer you up. So people begin to eat because they are bored and have nothing else to do. They will eat to cheer themselves up when they are depressed. Some people will even eat to punish themselves for being to fat! This is where food begins to become a substitute or crutch for something else.

The good news is that when you learn to identify what these underlying conditions are, you can do something else about them. When you learn to do something else, you instantly regain control over your eating habits. It means you can be free to enjoy the celebrations you attend. It means you can participate in solemn occasions. And in between such events, it means you can be free to choose the kind of food that will fuel your body and replenish the resources of vitamins, minerals and proteins that your body requires in order to function at its best.

So foods can essentially be put into two categories; mouth foods and stomach foods. Mouth foods satisfy the cravings for a certain taste of something. It's the chocolate rush or the creamy taste of ice cream to round off a meal. Mouth foods satisfy a need in your mind only. Stomach foods, on the other hand, are your body's way of telling you what kind of fuel it needs right now.

Does it need sugar to give you energy or does it need more protein to build muscles? Your body is so delicately balanced and sophisticated it can even recognise what minerals and salts it can absorb from different foods. That is why pregnant women often have cravings for unusual foods; because they need to replenish very different stocks inside their body. Include in your self-hypnosis programmes a heightened awareness of highlighting to yourself whether you are eating for psychological or physiological reasons; is the food you are about to eat a stomach food or a mouth food?

Eating protein with each meal

Use your self-hypnosis to ensure that you are including some kind of protein with each meal. Protein provides the raw materials to help your brain and body heal. Most important for you, protein provides the tryptophan your body needs to make serotonin; the feel good chemical. Protein also helps to slow down your digestion. Proteins are very complex foods and your body has to work hard to break them down into a simple form that can be used. They also help to stabilise your blood sugar levels so you won't have the steep peaks and valleys that can be so disastrous.

Vegetarian rice and beans or soy and oats each contain incomplete proteins. But if you eat both, they provide all the essential amino acids your body needs.

Many people ask for the exact number of grams of protein they should eat. Counting calories or grams of fat focuses on the measurement, you are going to focus on the relationship to what you are eating. When you eat protein, which is a complex food, at the same time as you eat a simple food, it will slow down the digestion. Remember you do not really want to lose weight, but to look and to feel good.

Adjusting carbohydrate intake towards more complex foods

Carbohydrates include some alcoholic beverages (beer, wine and drinks mixed with fruit juice), sugars such as sucrose (table sugar) fructose (fruit sugar) and lactose (milk sugar), and starches like bread, pasta, cereal, beans, grains. A carbohydrate can be simple or complex depending on how many molecules it has. Sugars are considered simple carbohydrates while starches are complex carbohydrates because they consist of three or more sugars joined together to make a long chain of molecules.

Remember that a certain food can be slower or faster to break down depending on how it is prepared too. Digesting a jacket potato with skin takes longer than digesting mashed potatoes, because the skin of the potato contains fibre. Digesting cooked broccoli is faster than digesting raw broccoli because the cooking breaks down the fibre before you eat it. Your body has less work to do. When using carbohydrates, choose the slowest ones.

Sugar-free products

Many so-called sugar-free products are free from certain kinds of sugars. If a manufacturer uses a trisaccharide (a sugar with three parts in it), it does not have to be called a sugar since legally it is a starch e.g. Maltodextrin. But you will respond to it as if it where a sugar. Other sugar-free products use Aspartame as a sweetener. Aspartame is made from phenylalanine, which is an amino acid. High doses of a single amino acid can throw off the balance of amino's in your brain and body. Just as you shouldn't substitute sugar for fat, do not substitute fat for sugar. Look and know what you are eating and notice the effect it has on your body.

Most bread contains white flour even though it's labelled as brown or whole grain. e.g. breads with wheat flour or flour at the head of the ingredients list is still made with refined white flour.

Unless the first ingredient is wholewheat flour, think of it as white. Also check food labels for the amount of fibre. Look for 2 or more grams of fibre in each serving. You will see white things are white because they don't have much fibre, the more fibre, the longer the digestion process and the slower the flow of sugar into your bloodstream will be. If you do eat white things try not to eat them alone, have them with other slower digestible foods. Remember, we are looking for solid long-term success, not dramatic short term results.

'I'm too busy'

When you feel you are too busy to prepare food or to pay attention to your food, think about what is really important to you. Being too busy can reflect an unfocused mind, which is one of the symptoms of low serotonin. You may find that by taking the time to make changes to your food, you end up being able to get everything done and in significantly less time.

How you choose to use this information is up to you. Tune in to your physiology. Use the information in whatever way you choose with your self-hypnosis to take control of your body and mind and achieve and maintain the size, shape and weight that pleases you. Do your own research and find out as much as you can and then utilise that knowledge with your self-hypnosis to deliver change to your life.

Here is a generic script for better health. I have not wanted to spoon feed (excuse the pun) you scripts in this chapter as weight reduction is so very personal to you and your own life; everyone is so different and you should address your own situation and aspects of your own life accordingly. You know what they are. Anyway, here is a generic better health script.

Healthier Lifestyle Script

My increasingly healthier and healthier body requires a healthier and healthier mind. Thinking of illness and unhappiness can make a person feel just that – however, I am better and better now at focusing my mind on these positive, progressive and healthier thoughts that do increase my resistance to illness more and more every day and night, night and day.

I Imagine myself brimming with more and more health and vitality, just the way I want to be and I keep this image focused in your mind as I direct my awareness to my health. I Feel and experience a newer, healthier energy beginning to flow into me and within me as my nervous system becomes and is more and more stable and I become so much calmer and more relaxed than ever before, naturally.

All the organs and systems of my body are functioning at higher and higher levels of effectiveness as I direct my mind to improve my health and appropriately increase my energy levels. My metabolism is becoming finely tuned to my individual needs, I can even imagine that the fires of my metabolism are being stoked deep within me. My digestive system uses the food that I eat more and more effectively and I limit the quantities of food to the appropriate and healthier levels so that I am eating just the right amount of healthy, nutritious food that you require to give you proper nutrition. The correct amount that is sufficient for my physiological requirements. I am more and more attracted to the foods that my body and mind knows are good for me and am drawn to them more and more and I find that they satisfy more and more naturally.

And because I am becoming so much calmer inside and so much more relaxed, my entire outlook on life is improving and I begin to take each day as it comes, being more excited at its prospect. I feel a growing an developing sense of acceptance, an increasing feeling of peace and serenity deep within me. My metabolism during my resting periods becomes much more natural and is adjusted for my relaxed state and because of all these improvements to my system, my heartbeat becomes steadier and my breathing becomes more natural because of the increased oxygen intake in my lungs, energising my being.

And my entire nervous system begins to function more efficiently and effectively, along with my autonomic nervous system, which controls my heart rate and my breathing without me even needing to be conscious of it doing so; they are working in peace and harmony together.

Because of the improved effectiveness of me nervous system, my digestion and kidneys begin to function more and more effectively and I feel a tremendous improvement to my entire being. The blood supply to my vital organs such as my liver, my pancreas and my spleen do nourish these organs more effectively as all the chemistry in my body becomes more balanced and stable.

My brain waves are becoming better balanced and this indicates a more peaceful and restful nature and because of this I am sleeping more soundly and experiencing beautiful dreams that create more good feelings within me. And when I wake up at the time I set myself, I do so with a refreshed and invigorating feeling with a growing sharpness and alertness.

As a result of my improved biochemical and metabolic system, my general resistance to infections and diseases improves and my blood pressure is at its optimum healthy level and I go about your day-to-day activities with a deep, inner calm serenity.

The tone of my muscles improves and I have more energy and vitality with which to carry out my daily tasks and activities, my skin and my hair take on a healthy glow, which radiates out from within.

And all these things are beginning to take place deep within you, right now.

Here are some additional scripts to give you more ideas on formulating your own.

Weight Reduction Script

I have begun a positive approach to obtain the appropriately slimmer, healthier, more attractive body, which I desire. I continue to give my unconscious mind more and more of the right kind of suggestions that do make this a progressive change in my living. These suggestions are going to and do take complete and thorough effect upon the deepest part of my unconscious mind, sealing themselves in the deepest part of my unconscious mind, so they do remain there forever, and become an intrinsic part of every cell of my brain and body. I may well be surprised and amazed just how effective these suggestions are going to be, how effective they are and how much they do become a part of my everyday life, giving me a brand new pattern, brand new thoughts, a brand new method of action, to make me the more and more effective and successful person that I know I want to be.

I do make use of a brand new method that I have not used as much as I should have done in the past when I used to be that way. I have now begun the first progressive approach for obtaining the more and more healthy, attractive body, which I desire and achieve. I have chosen to utilise my hypnosis as a positive means to attain this goal, because my hypnosis is a better and better aid in permanently changing my emotional reactions to food and eating and putting me in control of my own mind for the rest of my life. I do now realise that hypnosis is a new positive, progressive approach – a new positive approach to obtain what I desire and I do achieve that.

For one of the first times in my life I do really initiate a good positive approach toward food and eating. As I initiate this better, positive attitude toward food, enjoying the right foods, liking the right foods, eating the correct food for me and my goal. I now create an increasingly progressive positive change in my eating habits. From now on, I do prove to my own satisfaction that eating all I physiologically need does entirely satisfy me; just like drinking all the water I need. Instead of trying to kill my appetite, treating it as an enemy, I work within the framework of my natural inborn usual reflexes, making a friend of my appetite, paying attention to it; for this is a good thing. Slim people have appetites. They pay attention to them. Attractive people have appetites. They pay attention to them. My own hypnosis makes a friend of my appetite, rather than an enemy.

In the past, I was been paying attention only to half the signal from my appetite. Namely, the signal that says, 'Eat. I'm hungry.' From now on, I am making a friend of my appetite. I listen to all of what my friend's advice is. When it says 'I'm hungry,' I eat. When the hunger feeling first disappears, and my appetite says, 'I'm satisfied,' I stop. I stop long before I am full, because once I have this full sensation, it means that I have grossly overeaten. I know that it is not important to feel full and I stop that from happening.

I am more and more aware that I haven't really been paying attention to my appetite at all because my eating has be OK en driven by emotions rather than hunger. That has changed right now, here today. It isand usual to eat when my appetite says,' I'm hungry.' In the past I was eating when I have not been sufficiently hungry. I have been eating out of habit when my body had no physiological need for food. I have been eating to satisfy psychological, emotional cravings. I have not paid attention to my appetite when it says 'I'm done. I'm satisfied. Stop eating.' I haven't paid attention to it either. My appetite doesn't need killing off. On the contrary, it needs reinforcing. My self-hypnosis is helping me to make a friend of my appetite. I pay attention to the advice of my new friend. I tune in to my body and it's sensations. If I eat too much against the advice of my new friend, I know that I am violating my usual reflexes.

I know that it is important that I do eat all I physiologically need to replace my energy stores for immediate use and to store my body's sugar. I do now ban any and all plans that I used to have for dieting. I just do so, I let them go now. Otherwise, I bring into play an old instinct for self-preservation. This can spoil all of the positive results that I am gaining from my hypnosis. It is important that I develop the habit now and that I take action to develop these habits; that I do eat with more regularity, more of what it is that my mind and body know that I need. Within my hypnosis, I do and can reinforce the usual feedback mechanisms, the checks and balances that tell me when I need food and when my appetite is satisfied.

However strong I know my hypnosis is, it cannot overcome basic instincts for survival. One of my most strong instincts is that of self-preservation. The old concerns about being overweight that I used to have leads to sporadic dieting. This in turn suggests starvation. Starvation, in turn, demands defence. It brings out the instinct of self-survival. This instinct is responsible for others maintaining their excess weight. Slim people eat all they want.

Slim people do well. Slim, attractive people say to themselves, 'I eat all I want and I maintain my ideal size, shape and weight.'

I imagine myself as this slimmer, more naturally attractive person; the slim, healthy, attractive person that I soon am. I soon am saying and experiencing the very same thing. As I begin to talk and act like a slim, healthy, attractive person, I do become one, I am that version of me as I imagine it more and more. I do resolve right now to stop dieting forever. I do form a habit pattern to eat all I need when my body needs it. Paying attention to my appetite, trusting my own reflexes, reinforcing the sensation, reflexes and feedback patterns. I enjoy being slimmer, healthier, and more attractive. I do just feel increasingly more wonderful in more and more ways. The word diet and dieting are removed from my mind and all the plans I may have had for dieting are now let go of and removed from my mind thoroughly. Dieting just makes me think of growing hungry and giving up food, which in turn starts the anxiety about starvation, which brings forth the instinct of self-preservation. So I am through with dieting; through with dieting forever.

Through using my self- hypnosis more and more effectively I do restore usual reflexes that keep me more comfortably satisfied and bring into play that wonderful feeling of well-being. My natural association now is that the word diet is a negative word; it threatens me with denial of food and happiness. Hypnosis is a more progressive word; it helps me be more and more relaxed, comfortable and alive. Diets fail; hypnosis succeeds. Diet brings about starvation, which leads to overeating and obesity.

Hypnosis brings about a more natural satisfaction, which leads to relaxation and brings about a more naturally appropriate slim, healthy, attractive body, a relaxed mind and a satiated spirit. Those old urges to diet are now removed from my mind for now I really do realize that the real answer is in restoring usual reflexes. I concentrate on it, allowing every suggestion I give myself to sink to the deepest depths of my unconscious mind, for my hypnosis is a positive approach. Hypnotic suggestions, which I give myself, rapidly and effectively bring about a change which is necessary to insure a naturally slimmer, healthier, more attractive body, which I so desire.

Yet Another Weight Reduction Script

As I go deeper and deeper into this relaxation, even deeper and deeper down with every breath I exhale, all the sounds fade away in the distance. I pay attention only to the suggestions, which I deliver to my unconscious mind and the goals that are inherent within those suggestions, noting carefully the suggestions that I am delivering to myself. One thing is very important for me: I am not only going to reduce weight to the level that is right for me; I also keep it off. This program is designed so that I let go that old inert fat, and become a more lean, alert and vigorous person. I free myself of the extra weight and keep it off, easily and comfortably. That means that I am now reconditioning myself. I am a new person, in a new lean form, with new eating habits. Not only do I have these new eating habits, I am more and more wonderfully content and happy with myself and with these new eating habits. I am enjoying life more and more, eating the way nature intended, eating only when I have physiological needs for food and no other time; not only now; for the rest of my life.

In the past, I was eating more than my body needed for its energy requirements, so that I stored this extra energy as inert fat. Now in order to reduce weight and reduce this inert fat, I burn it up as I meet my daily requirements for energy. I eat less than I burn each day. Later, when I am lean, I then eat only that amount that I need for my physiological needs each day. Right now though, I am developing habits to eat less than I am using. I am not giving myself a measured diet, for that amount will vary from day to day and depend greatly on my activities. I eat less than I need for the storage will make up the difference. This restriction does cause me no trouble or inconvenience for the fat stores of inert fat are burned and I reduce weight. I do eat a great deal less than I used to eat in the past, and this is enough to satisfy me healthily. I do eat less, and I do burn the extra fat. I turn this inert fat into energy. From now on I am forming an eating pattern; a pattern that is almost a compulsion.

Fat by its very nature contains an extremely big amount of stored energy. So, as I do burn a little of it each day, I reduce a little weight each day. Nature designed the fat stores to last a long time so the weight reduction may be gradual, but it needs to be consistent. It matters not how long it takes to regain lean proportions, for I do surely get there and do stay there, as long as I continue to rearrange my thoughts about eating and my emotions about food. The important thing is that I have changed my habits my. When my excess weight is off, it is off for good. I am a new person; about to emerge from a cocoon that I shed. I am more and more happy with my new form. I emerge as a new person with thoroughly changed ideas, a thoroughly changed image of myself and who I choose to be now.

I continue to relax and let all of these suggestions sink into the deepest part of my mind's eye as an image. This image is of good and wonderful food. Food I like. There is plenty of it all around me. There always plenty of it. For me, there always is enough food. I no longer have to worry about starving. For me there is plenty of food everywhere. With all this food readily available, I let go of any need to store any more food inside my body. There is plenty of food. There are plenty of the right kinds of food, all the kinds and varieties that my body needs when it needs it. From now on I eat only the very things my body needs, one day at a time. I am through with storing pads and rolls of fat. There is plenty of food all around me. I stop the need to store food in my body that is more than my body needs.

I now know that there is in my central brain a small area which, regulates the biochemistry of my body and it controls the amount of fat I store in my body. This control is located in the hypothalamic area of the brain. My unconscious mind, through the hypothalamus, controls my weight by changing the body's chemistry. Using my self-hypnosis I can and do influence my unconscious mind to alter the control of both my appetite and storage of food in the form of fat.

Now while enjoying this beautiful state of hypnosis, I am giving myself the suggestion that I do change my body's chemistry so that I can and do break up these large storage houses of fat and prevent the recurrence of any new and unneeded storages of fat. Fat that has been putting an extra burden and overload on the body's machinery. Right now it begins, I break up and eliminate forever the unneeded fat stores. Change fat to energy and burn it up. Also, I free myself of it by excreting it. Free myself of it through my body's natural resources. It mobilizes more and more easily and readily and I can and do experience the fat melting away as I use it and excrete it. The globules of fat storage are leaving the normal cells and being carried away. The fat is being burned up and excreted.

I now use this stored fat to supply energy. This is extra energy to make me more vigorous. As I am eliminating the excess, I do eat far less than I need each day for the extra calories are coming from the food I ate yesterday and last year. I eat nothing to replace these stores. Nothing and no one can force me to eat so much that I replace this inert fat. I stop this fat from being replaced. These stores are going and gone. I am freeing myself of them, just as an overloaded ship needs to get rid of excess cargo. I only eat small amounts until I have used all of this stored energy and all those old storehouses that I used to have are gone. From this moment on, I eat less, and I move more and more lively and I feel more and more active, for I feel better than I have felt in along time. I am free of the desire for all but a small amount of food until my size, shape and is the lean size I want to achieve. Then I continue to eat more and more sensibly and correctly for the rest of my healthier, happier life.

Now that I change my chemistry, I have changed my entire body and my entire feeling to that of a wonderful sense of well-being. I eat more sensibly, get plenty of exercise, drink adequate liquids to always make myself feel increasingly more and more healthy, lean, trim and desirable.

I am progressively reducing my weight towards the ideal weight steadily every day. I am slimmer and shapelier. The excess weight is melting off me, just melting away and disappearing. I have a stronger feeling every day that I am now more and more in control of my eating habits. I picture yourself more frequently the way I know I am soon to be; slim and shapely and sexy in the way that is right for me.

So now as I relax and let all these suggestions take complete and thorough effect upon my mind, body, and spirit, as I allow my unconscious mind to correct and enhance my hypothalamus to change my body's chemistry. I let the monitor of my unconscious mind influence the hypothalamus to make this favourable body change. I let my appetite control centre be safely reduced so that excess storage of fat is utilised by excretion and burning of stored energy. I eliminate all that extra fat, I set myself free.

Weight Reduction Perspective Variation

Think about starting a programme with an idea like this:

Although sometimes we are quite fearful of change or something new, we are well aware there is no chance for improvement unless there is change. If we have had difficulty in some area, we must change the old patterns. So today, I am suggesting that I allow myself to do something entirely different from what I usually do. Today, I am allowing myself to see myself in perspective. I see myself as others might see me or as I might be seen in history.

Just an additional note here, when you are away from yourself, even for a few moments, you begin to see yourself in an entirely different light. Temporarily, if you separate yourself in time as well as in physical distance, you can see yourself not only as you are at the moment, but as you were yesterday or even far back in childhood. It is quite possible for you to see yourself proceeding through all the stages of growing to the present time, and even projecting your view of yourself into the future.

You are capable of doing this. It is a safe procedure. It is possible because your conscious mind calculates time and distance differently from the unconscious mind. In the conscious mind, everything is very concrete. The minutes progress in orderly fashion to form hours and days, weeks and years. The unconscious mind works very differently. You live in the present, but if you are suddenly, greatly stressed, you call forth experiences from the past. Your natural learned defences and reactions respond instead to the similar stresses of last year or five years ago.

In other words, in the unconscious mind, your frame of reference is entirely different. You can be in the present, but if something provokes or excites you, in a fraction of a second you can revert to childish or infantile behaviour and relive an incident with all the sound, fury and emotion you had the first time you experienced it. In other words, in a fraction of a second you can span the years and relive an incident as vividly as you did the first time.

In exactly the same way, it is possible for you to see some of the future. See yourself as you might be behaving a year or five years from now. Predicting the future is possible because the attitudes you hold about yourself determine your behaviour, the friends you choose and situations you create. Even though you may not be able to fill in the names of other people or the precise location, you can predict the kind of situation you may well place yourself into because of the attitudes you hold about yourself. Time and place in the unconscious mind is only relative. Your attitude and natural learned defences remain almost unchangeable and they interact with the environment in very much the same way throughout you life.

You can quite easily project yourself temporarily outside of your body as if you were a third person and look back at yourself and your surroundings freed of the usual physical limitations. It is very safe to project yourself in spirit out and beyond your normal physical limitations so you can look back at yourself and understand exactly where you are. This projection is entirely at your control.

You will find it quite easy to separate much of your spirit and intellect from your body so that you can momentarily be free from your body limitations. From this vantage point, you can see yourself in prospective from birth to present. You can become acutely aware of the program you had to adopt to keep your physical body alive in a world that is so threatening.

Best of all, from this detached, safe, vantage point, you can plainly see the defences that you needed when you were younger. You have now outgrown them just as you have outgrown the need for nursing bottles and wearing nappies.

Projection experience is common to everyone who dreams, for dreams change all the usual limitations of time and space. A good example is awakening abruptly from a very sound sleep and being momentarily confused about where you are. You have had the experience of looking in a three-way mirror in a clothing store and seeing yourself in profile and back view and getting an entirely different perspective of yourself. Another way to get a projection of yourself is to look into a mirror that shows your reflection in another mirror.

Then, by changing the angle slightly, you can see one mirror reflecting in another in a whole row of mirrors, almost on to eternity. Now to this picture, you add photographs of yourself in the same pose, but each at a different age of your life. You line them up so that you see yourself in these mirrors at all ages from infancy to the present time. Depending on the angle of the mirrors, you can see yourself projected either into the past or into the future.

Now picture yourself intellectually outside your own body with a clear view of your entire life in perspective (hey, do this all in hypnosis!). You have in your possession all of the wisdom, all the learning and all the understanding that you have ever gained. In this position, you're now able to influence your own destiny by re-programming and upgrading your attitude and defences. You let yourself change wherever you see the need for growth and maturity so all your reactions may come up to your expectations as you relinquish your hang-ups.

Hear yourself encouraging your entire self to accept yourself and approve of what you do. Especially see yourself reinforcing the correct usual eating patterns, to eat only when you are hungry, to see that your appetite is easily satisfied. Picture yourself, or just imagine enjoying food immensely but only in quantities you need to fulfil usual physiological requirements. Be aware of yourself overcoming the temptation to eat any extra food. Give yourself further suggestions like:

As you observe yourself it becomes easier and easier to pass up unneeded food and drink. Especially note carefully how your need to seek approval from everyone else is disappearing very quickly and progressively. More and more you are approving of what you do.

See yourself also using self-hypnosis as a very powerful and safe force for you. Its effectiveness increases as you let part of yourself be projected beyond your usual body limitations so that you can give yourself suggestions much more effectively as if you were a third person. Again and again you are accepting the suggestion that you eat only when you truly need food and that you are satisfied with basic nutrition. See yourself being increasingly happy with your eating pattern and showing approval of what you do.

There is a lot of information in this chapter as it is a very large and complex topic. What's more, we are all unique that I wanted to provide as many takes and ideas on this subject as possible. Take your time now to craft your own strategy and craft your own programmes and series of programmes to really ensure that you get some great changes into how you take control of your weight and all the related issues.

7

Creating Wealth

We have no more right to consume happiness
without producing it than to consume wealth
without producing it.

George Bernard Shaw

It may seem obvious to you what this chapter is about. Let me tell you to ensure that you really do know; it is about using self-hypnosis and related tools to allow yourself to be creating the kind of wealth that you want in your life. My definition of wealth is very different to the next person and that person's definition of wealth is very different to the next person. This chapter is not about money-making schemes other than those that exist within your own mind. It is about letting go of old conditioning and programming and installing and creating new beliefs, attitudes and behaviours. Please use your self-hypnosis over and over and involve yourself in the change and updating process more and more.

I have worked with many people that have fears that block wealth attraction, some think that money creates problems, that it will alienate them from family or friends, that you become a target or that it makes them a bad person or that it is sinful or that it is wrong to make it too easily or that rich people are unhappy. Rich people and comparatively poor people can be either you know. It is my personal viewpoint that is you are happy, you will be happy rich or poor and if you are unhappy, you will be unhappy whether you are rich or poor. This is not about what I think though. This chapter is about you finding the right tools to attract the kind of wealth that you want in your life.

In order to unlock the secrets of a millionaires mind for example, it is important that you are sure that you realise what real wealth is to you. I have encountered many multi millionaires that are not happy with their lives. When we are fulfilled, experiencing happiness and the kind of life that we want to live, that is real wealth. Appreciating what we do have, now that is real wealth.

I worked with a man once whose main goal in life when I first worked with him was to earn one million pounds. Once he had successfully earned his first one million pounds, all he had to say to me was that he wanted 100 million pounds and would not be happy until he got there. He was always feeling poor, with that kind of attitude, it is near on impossible to feel happy and experience a wealth consciousness.

When discussing the issue with another therapist and friend of mine Sam, she told me that her husband has been gifted with the love he attracted into his life from others, and that was real wealth. The fact that they realised that is the real gift and what many consider to be real wealth. It was the Indian guru, Swami Mktananda who, upon arriving in the United States of America said; 'They live in paradise yet they'll never know it.'

Some people have what is often referred to as a poverty consciousness; maybe they don't feel that they deserve wealth or do not feel worthy of it, and there are wide ranges of things, which seem to get in the way of accumulating wealth. Some people fear poverty and so plague their minds with such thoughts, another example of a poverty consciousness. We are going to look at those and other factors so that you can emerge from the cocoon of fears and outmoded beliefs, and transform your ability to attract and create the kind of wealth that you want.

Research has shown that many people who inherit money or win money often lose it, or end up being much worse off a few years later, they do not perceive themselves as wealthy. So they need to look at changing the fundamental thoughts and processes about wealth and toward wealth, as the saying goes; 'Give a man a fish he eats for a day, teach a man to fish and he eats for life.'

Have you heard the expressions; 'Filthy Rich' and 'Hard-Earned Money' and 'Money doesn't grow on trees' and people referred to as 'Fat Cats'. All the time our language and the in-built association to it install the belief that it is hard to be wealthy. What about that phrase 'Money is the root of all evil', what a whopper that is. If you allow yourself to believe that way and think of wealth as bad, you will unconsciously sabotage your ability to create it in your life. Our attitudes affect our ability to have money.

Lets get a few things straight about money and wealth, lets begin to create a new understanding of abundance; firstly, many people I have encountered believe it does but being wealthy does not deprive someone else from having wealth, your success does not prevent someone else from being successful, if you load up your bank account, it does not mean someone else's is going down, there are no shortages, there is plenty to go around. During war-times with rationing, in England, a belief was established by some that there was not enough to go around, this belief is often passed down through generations. It was Abraham Lincoln who said 'You can't help the poor by being one of them.'

Historically, we seem to have had the belief that wealth is seen as something only the rich had and that there was only a certain amount to go around. It is not too dissimilar when you look at modern corporations where the power is top heavy and everyone competes for their positions to scramble up the corporate ladder, further reaffirming the belief that wealth is limited.

Money and wealth needs to be separated from morality. There are a lot of good, hard-working Christian people who go through their entire lives needlessly poor and sadly disappointed because of a belief that the way to attract money is just to deserve it through 'clean living' or worse, by sacrifice. Poverty is sometimes seen as a Christian virtue. It was Joseph Heller who said:

> Money goes where it will increase fastest rather than where it is needed.

So it is a valuable way to develop a wealth consciousness by realising that moralizing does not trouble money and wealth. As Lewis H. Lapham said about money:

> Men can employ it as a tool or they can dance around it as if it were the incarnation of God. Money votes socialist or monarchist, finds a profit in pornography or in translations from the *Bible*, commissions Rembrandt and underwrites the technology of Auschwitz.

And it was P.T Barnum who said:

Money is a terrible master but an excellent servant.

So if wealth does mean having money to you, then begin to look at how you experience money and how you perceive it and have perceived it in the past, then of course, how you are going to learn to perceive it in your future.

With a negative attitude to money we hinder our ability to attract it. The resentment of another's wealth for example, really does come from a place of low self-worth; it keeps people stuck. It is far better to wish others well. You can include those kinds of notions in your self-hypnosis programmes for wealth creation; that you wish others well. It is sometimes perceived as a rather more esoteric concept, however, I recommend heightening your awareness of and working with the law of attraction; when **something** seems to be going on in the universe. Whatever your beliefs on these kind of subjects, the really wealthy people do often know this to be true; some say that the stock market runs on those kind of notions.

Whether you believe in attraction or not, many wealthy people do and so allow yourself to keep focusing on what you want, not what you don't want. Allow it to dominate your conscious thoughts. A bit like creating your own luck, for example, what you believe to be the truth will be the truth for you, so the thoughts you have transmit into the universe and into your unconscious mind, so keep those thoughts focused on what you want, with a relaxation, excitement and anticipation of achieving it. One of the key things that US Wealth Attraction guru Dan Kennedy mentions is that we should learn to attract wealth not pursue it.

So make a decision to consciously do things differently. Think different thoughts. If you worry about the bills or worry about money; your thoughts are on poverty. Of course it is fine to be financially aware and organised, however affirming a poverty belief day in and day out is problematic and further sets old beliefs in stone within you.

Allow yourself to feel rich inside. Imagine having a full bank account, imagine yourself as wealthy, act as if you are (within the realms of common sense here please!). Just affirming things in your mind can be impotent if your unconscious mind does not have more and more sensory rich experiences and thoughts for it to associate with. Imagine yourself as wealthy over and over again for the next few months. Play the part. Walk, talk, look, feel as if you were much wealthier, think about the luxuries you have. Be that person; attract it to you. Think about this every day. Even study and model wealthy people, think as they would think, feel like them, adopt their physiology and approach to being wealthy. This all conditions the mind for successful wealth creation.to enhance your ability to do this, you can get a scrap book and fill it with the things you want in your life, see the things, imagine having them, being in them and around them. Look at it regularly. See your desires, hear the sounds, feel the feelings, keep delivering to yourself heightened sensory experiences for your unconscious mind to assimilate within you. Use your self-hypnosis sessions to firmly implant those thoughts and give your unconscious mind instructions and suggestions to move you towards those things that you want to have in your life.

You can even go out there and test drive the car you want, to really get an idea of what you want, so that you have really good experience in your mind to integrate into your neurology. Get pictures of that house, and then imagine it over and over again.

Choose to step out of your comfort zone. Stretch yourself; again choose to do things differently. As I have said before already in this book:

If you always do what you always did, you will always get what you always got.

Do things in a new way, in every way. Invite change into your life by doing things differently. You can choose to use your self-hypnosis and deliver programmes for wealth creation and expect it to magically transform you, or you can amplify it effects by helping yourself and really doing new things, in new ways as well. This combination is what will make it happen now.

If wealth is money to you, then get comfortable with money, feel it about you, get used to it, to its smell, its touch, what it looks like. Be relaxed with money, at ease with money, even casual about money. Regularly deliver all the different components and ideas generated in this wealth creation chapter. Use your self-hypnosis with more and more regularity; use it repeatedly, over and over to deliver your message. Get this stuff into your brain; hard wire it into your neurology.

In addition; **keep going**. Keep on at it. I am sure you know the story of Colonel Sanders who after his retirement took his chicken recipe to 1009 restaurants before anyone took him up on it. He got 1008 'no' responses. Take action, the author of 'Think and Grow Rich', Napoleon Hill said, 'Your ship can not come in unless you first send it out' and then think, how many ships have I sent out today? What have I done today to create more of the kind of wealth that I want in my life?

Here is an example of a script for use in generating financial wealth. Again, I recommend that you create your own and that rather than creating one script as a panacea to create wealth all in one go, address separate areas of wealth creation with different programmes. This kind of script is for use with step 'D' in the self-hypnosis model, you have to still do the other parts of the structure.

Wealth Creation Script

*Prior to starting, you may even want to give yourself the kind of suggestion that you allow these words to become your words, your beliefs, your thoughts, that's right, your **dominant** thoughts.*

As I travel deeper into my own inner realities, moving through the corridors of my mind. I imagine myself walking into a vast library, that exists at the very centre of my unconscious mind, where all the books are about me, those nearest to me represent this year and as the books go back, they go back in your time, back to early learnings, earlier experiences, where I learned to do so many things, learned and forged so many beliefs, just imagine finding a book. I Search through my own library of every experience of my life and find that book called 'My Poverty Consciousness.'

As I locate it, I can and do rip it up, destroy it, whatever it is that I want to, I free myself of it and I do this now, and as I do, I let go of those old beliefs, old values, old limitations. In that space I place a new book, 'The Book Of Wealth', my very own book of wealth, and its messages spread and coarse through my system, like electricity through circuits, making deep fundamental changes in my hard wiring, in my deeper circuitry. Installing and creating more and more new beliefs, new attitudes, and a new expectancy throughout my entire being.

My natural state is that of wealthiness and abundance, I deserve to be wealthy, I release and let go of old emotional blocks to wealth, I release any old fears about money and wealth, release them out, even things that I am not consciously aware of I am letting go of, creating new wonderful states within me, I release any old limits about earning power, I allow money to flow into my life, it flows smoothly and naturally, I can and do imagine that I are surrounded in great wealth right now here in this moment, I smell the money, I see it, I touch and feel it, I have more and more of a wonderful intuition about money, I invite wealth and abundance into my life, I am more and more instinctively and intuitively astute and wise about money, I attract more and more of the kind of abundance I want in everything I do, I increasingly enjoy that sense of freedom that money brings me, more and more opportunities just flow into my life more and more as my unconscious mind opens me to them, with or without my conscious awareness, my increasing love of life is rewarded more and more abundantly, it really is as though I have a way with money.

The next part of this script can be adapted too. So that you can identify and understand certain parts of your mind.

I allow myself to really get in touch with that part of myself, that part of myself that I know very well, the part of myself that had those old beliefs, that had that old poverty consciousness, I know, that part of me that held those old beliefs had a positive intention all along, a positive intention that was trying to help me or do something progressive for me all that time, the only way it knew how to get that thing was by having that poverty consciousness, I now allow my unconscious mind to generate more powerfully wealthy ways of achieving that positive intention, using all the power of those old beliefs and values, keeping positive lessons and learnings and I let go of the old, outmoded and non-useful beliefs, I allow my unconscious to shift my circuits, alter those neural pathways, so that I allow my unconscious mind to achieve those positive intentions in ways that enhance my wealth and brings more and more abundance into my life.

I am more and more motivated to succeed with less and less effort, I succeed in seemingly effortless ways, and when I apply more effort, it really increases my wealth in ways that I have not even imagined, I am an inspiration to others, others are progressively more inspired by my passion for life, money flows into my life from many varying source, again, even sources that I have not imagined it would, I have more and more trust in my natural ability to attract wealth, I move progressively more easily towards my goals and outcomes, I have more and more good fortune

I am more and more worthy and deserving of wealth, I really know that, I really think that, I deserve this, I appreciate others who have wealth and I wish them well, I love the feelings of getting things done now, my natural state is one of abundance and wealth, it is just who I am now, I allow money to flow into my life, I deserve to be wealth, I invite more and more of the right kind of abundance into my life, now as I u breathe in, I take in these words and let them become the electricity in my circuits, powering and energising my goals and desired outcomes which I am more and more aware of, my unconscious just makes these thoughts my dominant thoughts, my new beliefs of who I choose to be now, of who I am now, I am the new me that is now emerging with a growing and expanding enthusiasm as I find that I am naturally and holistically releasing all old limits, I am letting them go, they are fading, fading, fading, like a light going out in the distance.

I expand my awareness, a far reaching awareness of wealth in my life, I know from this deep inner space within me there is a vastness of infinite knowledge here, I use that now, I are more and more grateful for who I am, I act and behave like I am so wealthy, I take on the role, knowing that the more I behave like it, I acquaint your unconscious and conscious minds with who I choose to be with more and more authenticity, I am stepping into a new me, the wealthy me and I imagine feel how it feels, wearing this new me like I am wearing a new coat, I act like I am exuding wealth, I resonate wealth, I ooze optimism, I notice how others feel to be around me, it is like there is a light or warmth radiating from me that feels so good to be around, and a deep silent joy spreads into my system more and more and I recognise that I am that wealthy person, I deserve this, I choose to be this way now, I am this way now, I allow that feeling to spread, I release the old limitation, those old beliefs that I used to have, I now have new attitudes, I have new progressive beliefs, these are new beginnings in my new life, I see and experience money as my servant, it is progressively more exciting to know it is flowing my way.

Remember to thank your unconscious.

Here are some additional ideas and ways of using your self-hypnosis for creating wealth with what we refer to here as

Mind Projection. It is a powerful way to utilise your unconscious resources.

The difference between successful people and non-achievers begins with the way those people think about themselves and their abilities. Take for example two men who live five thousand miles apart. Each one independently comes up with the same brilliant innovative idea that could make a small fortune. The first man thinks to himself: 'This will never work, it's just too good to be true'. However he's prepared to give it a chance and half-heartedly sets out to sell his idea to the public.

When he fails, as he ultimately must, he is reaffirming what he knew would happen all along. The second man however is totally enthusiastic about his new idea and infects everyone around him with his optimism, the passionate belief that this idea is the best thing since sliced bread and he is as excited as a child on the night before his birthday.

In the previous script, I included the term 'I deserve this' over and over again, it is important that you think that way with regard to generating wealth. Believing in oneself is not always as easy as we would like it to be. Some people experience years of criticism, put-downs, negativity from others and self-doubt that may have done an excellent job in dampening any prospects for achievement that was our original birthright. Remember that, it is your birthright; you deserve this.

So, I return to that earlier mentioned sentence – 'if you always do what you've always done, you'll always get what you've always got' – which is why – if we want to get something different – we can begin to look to the future instead of drawing on past experience. The past is where we learned how to be like we are today, and if you are not entirely happy with that, then the future is where the new you is at.

Because the future has not yet happened, you can play about with it and design your own destiny. That's what this notion of wealth creation with **Mind Projection** is all about. So first of all, you need to take a pen and paper and design your ideal future.

Where would you like to see yourself in ten, twenty or thirty year's time? Depending on your age, set yourself a time span by which you'd like to have achieved affluence. Be realistic about this, but not pessimistic. Very few people manage to create millionaire status (if that is what you want) in the space of 7 days! You don't have to wait ten years, but next week could be a bit soon to give yourself chance to get these new wealth creation notions, ideas and strategies reaping the rewards.

What would you like to be doing? If your goal is to own your own business empire, have two cars, a house by the sea and one in the country, have a hundred thousand pounds in the bank – write it all down. Design your future now.

Who would you like to be with you? What would you like to be wearing? Again, be as specific as you can.

When you've designed your future, read through it a couple of times and evaluate what you've written. Are these the things that will really make you happy? What details can you add to your design?

The next step is to use the self-hypnosis model; access hypnosis, take control, deepen as you have learned how to do. Then at step 'D' instead of delivering a programme you have written, you create an environment, a reality where you project your mind to that future date and really see yourself very clearly, doing all those things that you wrote down. This is creating the sensory rich experiences for your unconscious mind to know what to move towards.

You don't have to have picture perfect images really clearly at first, instead concentrate on other aspects of your design. For example, hearing people congratulating you on your success, feeling yourself sitting in an elegant sports car or walking around your country mansion, arranging flowers in the vase, smelling the expensive aftershave or perfume, looking at your bank account – or whatever you've decided you want to achieve.

When you have spent a few minutes in self-hypnosis really absorbing that experience, heightening your unconscious awareness of the things you wrote down, give yourself a key word to summarise your goal, that summarises this future outcome, then thank your unconscious, and count yourself up to five, and open your eyes.

Aim to use this technique with more and more regularity; every day if possible. Use the images and experiences from your real life too, and use all your senses as much as you can. If you find yourself thinking negative thoughts, or being drawn back towards the old poverty consciousness that you used to have, simply say your key word to your self, repeat it in your mind with power and authority.

The very act of replacing negative thoughts with your progressive key word and additional progressive wealth creation programmes in your own mind with self-hypnosis, combined with the powerful imagination of wealth creation, makes your conceivable goal believable and achievable. Then your unconscious mind and you start moving toward what is rightfully yours – a wealthy life.

8

Enhanced Confidence

*In quietness and confidence shall be your
strength.*

Book of Isaiah, The *Bible*

Lots of people that I work with in a therapeutic context, those I
teach and attend my workshops, seminars and trainings often
comment to me 'Adam, you are one of those confident kind of
people' and that 'these things must just come easy to you' or they
even say 'but I am just not that kind of person'. What powerful
statements they are telling themselves and the world around them.
There is a story told in Oriental tradition;A king was watching a
great magician performing his act. The crowd were enthralled and
so was the king. At the end the audience roared with approval.
And the king said: 'What a gift this man has. A god-given talent.'

But a wise counsellor said to the king, 'My lord, genius is made,
not born. This magician's skill is the result of discipline and
practice. These talents have been learned and honed over time with
determination and discipline.'

The King was troubled by this message. The counsellor's
challenge had spoiled his pleasure in the magician's arts. 'Limited
and spiteful swine. How dare you criticise true genius. As I said,
you either have it or you don't. And you most certainly don't.'

The king turned to his bodyguard and said, 'Throw this man
into the deepest dungeon.' And he added for the counsellors
benefit, 'so you won't be lonely you can have two of your kind to
keep you company. You shall have two piglets as cellmates.'

As I tell you this story, it reminds me of a man called Milton
Erickson, a real hero of mine that I have mentioned already in this
book, a well renowned psychiatrist and hypnotherapist, who used

to tell lots of stories. He tells a story about how one summer he spent the entire summer grubbing up brush on ten acres of land. His Father ploughed it that autumn and replanted it, reploughed it in the spring, and planted it with oats. And the oats grew very well and they hoped to get an excellent crop.

Late that summer, on a Thursday evening, they went over to see how that crop was getting along, when they could harvest it. Erickson's father examined the individual oats stalks and said 'Boys, this is not going to be a bumper crop of thirty three bushels per acre. It will be at least a hundred bushels per acre. And they will be ready to harvest next Monday.' So, Milton Erickson and his fellow family workers were walking along happily thinking about a thousand bushels of oats and what it meant to them financially. But then it started to sprinkle with rain.

Now, later in his life as a full time psychiatrist, Erickson commented that he used to go into trance states so that he would be more sensitive to the intonations and inflections of his client's speech. He felt that it helped him to hear them and see them better; he would go into trance states and forget the presence of others. Erickson mentioned a patient he had called Rodriguez, a professor of psychiatry from Peru. He wrote to Erickson stating that he wanted psychotherapy from him. Erickson knew that Rodrigues was far better educated than him, far more quick witted than him and Erickson regarded him as far more intelligent than he himself was.

Erickson wondered, 'How can I handle a man who is brighter, better educated and quicker witted than I am?' Rodriguez was Castilian Spanish and extremely arrogant-arrogant and ruthless, very insulting to be with. He was booked in for a two o'clock appointment. Erickson took down his address, marital status; the official information. Then he looked up to ask him a question and saw that the chair was empty. As he looked at the clock he saw it was four o'clock. He noticed that he had a manila folder with sheets of paper inside. So Erickson realised he must have gone into a hypnotic trance to interview him. Now before I continue, I recommend that you ensure that you set time limits and awareness controls with your own self-hypnosis trance sessions!

It's interesting, the first half of the story, the part I have just told, fascinates me as it reminds me of an exert from a book by

John Burton and Bob Bodenhamer called **Hypnotic Language**, they write about the fact that it seems that one of the main ways a person feels certain emotions and behavioural feelings is to look at the present through the past. Doing this is sort of like using a mirror to look at the present, all you see is what's behind you and then mistake it for what is before you. Of course the next thing you know is just what you knew before, so history repeats itself.

So it is important to take control of your own states, your own beliefs about yourself and using your self-hypnosis you can do that. You can allow yourself to be more and more confident, with a growing self-esteem.

Now, what I really recommend to anyone that is making powerful and progressive changes to their confidence is that they begin to start taking control of their thoughts, instead of allowing all their previous programming to control them. Begin to imagine people who you believe to be confident, hold your body like them, think like you imagine they would think, talk to yourself as you imagine they would.

You know that voice in your head, your internal dialogue that I have referred to on many occasions in this book, well get it talking to you in a voice that you find motivating and confident, really assured, maybe someone you truly know to be confident, instead of insisting on using that same internal dialogue that you had when you were not as confident as you wanted to be.

Imagine yourself, as you would like to be and step into that version of you. Do different things consciously stopping those old thoughts in your head, say the word 'stop!' to those old thoughts, just '**Stop**' them. Then take a deep breath, relax, feel good, play confident sounds in your mind, make confident pictures in your mind, remember a time when you felt confident, or how you imagine your self to be and make that picture larger, brighter and bring it nearer and wrap it all around you. Do this in and out of self-hypnosis, work it into your programmes that you do it in and out of hypnosis.

Think about the things that you used to say to yourself or others that were statements of 'I am such and such'. 'I am this'. 'I am not this'. You delete all opportunity to be anything other than that. So '**stop**' those statements, '**Stop**' those old thoughts; that is how you used to be and think. Think of how you used to be before you became more and more in control of what you allow yourself to think to yourself, before you had self-hypnosis and now that you believe in yourself and your ability to be more and more confident.

How you think is how you allow yourself to be. What you believe to be the truth is the truth for you. You are the most powerful influence in your life. Now as you consciously start changing your thoughts, grab them by the scruff of the neck and think, 'I am going to choose how I feel, and what I think from here onwards' and notice how good it feels to be feel so good.

Now I wonder, and you may wonder also, in relation to that mirror I was talking about earlier, what will happen when you step through that mirror? Stepping through the mirror immediately removes the past view and now all you know is the present and the future, you look forward to the future. This might sound confusing, read it over and over to get it into your mind comprehensively.

Now, looking forward to the future, just what of the infinite possibilities do you notice? What do you want to notice? Now just notice how and what new ideas come into your mind in the present about the future. Feel these ideas become a fuel that propels you toward them so you just naturally want to move closer and closer don't you now?

So anyway, Milton Erickson had had spent 13–14 hours of therapy with Rodriguez and in one session, Rodriguez jumped to his feet and said:

'Dr Erickson, you're in a trance!' Erickson awoke and said 'I know you're brighter than I am and more intelligent, quicker witted, much better educated. And that you are very arrogant. I didn't feel I could handle you and I wondered how I would handle you. I didn't know until after the first interview that my unconscious mind decided to take over the job. I know I've got sheets of notes, in the folder. I haven't read them yet. I will read them today.'

Rodriguez looked at him angrily and pointing to a photo said 'Are these your parents?' Erickson replied 'yes'.

He said 'Your Fathers Occupation?'

Erickson replied, 'He is a retired farmer.'

And Rodriguez said scornfully, 'Peasants!'

Now Erickson knew that he knew a lot of history and said, 'Yes, peasants. And, for all I know the blood of the bastards of my

227

ancestors runs in your veins.' He knew about Vikings over running Europe. Rodrigues was far better behaved after that exchange. Now that took rapid thinking on Erickson's part. Erickson trusted his unconscious throughout the entire process.

So, returning to Milton Erickson and his field of oats. You know, it rained all night Thursday, all day Friday, all night Friday, all day Saturday, all night Saturday, all day Sunday, all night Sunday and in the early morning Monday when the rain ceased, when they were finally able to wade through the water to that back field, the field was totally flat; there weren't any upright oats. Erickson's father said 'I hope enough of the oats were ripe enough so that they will sprout. In that way we will have some green feed for the cattle this autumn-and next year is another year' And that's really being oriented to the future in the way that is important for many people to do.

So, back to that original story; from the very first day of his imprisonment, the Wise Counsellor practised running up the steps of his cell to the prison door carrying a piglet in each hand. As the days and weeks and months went past, the piglets grew steadily into sturdy wild boars. And with every day of practice the Wise Counsellor increased his power and strength.One day the King remembered the Wise Counsellor and was curious to see how imprisonment had humbled him. He had the Wise Counsellor summoned.

When the prisoner appeared, a man of powerful physique, carrying a wild boar on each arm, the king exclaimed, 'What a gift this man has. A God given talent.' The Wise Counsellor replied, 'My lord, genius is made, not born. My skill is the result of discipline and practice. These talents have been learned and honed over time with determination and discipline.'

Here is a technique for use inside or outside of your self-hypnosis sessions, it can even form part of a daily practice to develop confidence, it is the **Circle of Confidence**, which can be used for many things as well as confidence. You can adapt it to suit your own requirements. I recommend you do that in fact.

Circle of Confidence

Right now, right in front of you, create and imagine a circle of excellence, whether you see it, sense it, imagine it or just know that it is there is the way that is right for you. Really notice; really imagine a circle in front of you on the floor. This circle is yours and allows you to create all that you desire about yourself. Now step into the circle, as you step into the circle, imagine a light shining down upon you that is going to integrate new learning and abilities into your reality. Every time you step you step into this circle of excellence, this light shines upon you, really imagine it there.

Now we are going to anchor this state, by that I mean hold your thumb and forefinger together on your dominant hand. Each time you step into the circle, you are going to hold your thumb and forefinger together on your dominant hand, so then, you can learn that when you press them together and you are outside of the circle, you can draw upon those resources and feel really confident and good about yourself.

Each time you step into the circle you will speak to yourself or out loud these words and allow them to become your thoughts, your reality and your feelings. 'I am more and more deeply, profoundly confident, confidence radiates from me, oozes from my pores'. Hold your body in a way that is congruent with these words. Now really allow that light to shine down upon you, allow it to illuminate your being, illuminating and permeating every cell of your being and as it does, it integrates new learning's in a way that is harmonious with your mind, body and spirit. Say those words to yourself again; 'I am more and more deeply, profoundly confident, confidence radiates from me, oozes from my pores' So now, step out of the circle and release your anchor; release your thumb and forefinger that you were holding together.

Imagine your circle and again look at your circle, imagine it getting brighter and brighter, more and more powerful each time you step in. So now step in again and speak these words in your mind to yourself or out loud as they become your reality. 'I love my body, my mind and everything that is me, I care for myself, nurture myself and love myself and love being myself.' Bring the light in and press your anchor together again by pressing your thumb and forefinger together. 'I love my body, my mind and everything that is me, I care for myself, nurture myself and love myself and love being myself.' Let that light flood your system. You can take some time to really use the light, imagine it spreading into your body and mind. Then step out of the circle and release your anchor by releasing your thumb and forefinger.

Now step into your circle and press your anchor again. Let the light come down upon you, with each breath that you exhale, imagine that you are pouring more energy and light into the circle, giving it more and more power as you speak these words in your mind or out loud; 'I love my personality more and more, I am more and more spontaneous and more and more confident in my ability to communicate myself better and better with others and myself'. Lighting up your self, with your anchor pressed, feel the feelings of that statement and what it means to you, imagine the sights, the sounds with the light coming down onto you; 'I love my personality more and more, I am more and more spontaneous and more and more confident in my ability to communicate myself better and better with others and myself'.

You can pause and absorb the light and those words and when you are ready, step out of your circle and release your thumb and forefinger. You can do this exercise in your mind during a self-hypnosis session at step 'D'. Or you can do it out side of hypnosis while standing up and actually step into an imaginary circle. You can of course create new suggestions to deliver to yourself when you are in the circle. Suggestions, that resonate with you and include language that seduces your unconscious mind to move toward the more confident version of you.

Here is a script for developing and growing confidence. As with all the scripts in this book, I recommend that you use it for ideas and inspiration and then create your own for delivery to your unconscious mind using your kind of language, imagery and likes.

Confidence Script

We've all had that special moment when we felt really proud of ourselves for something we'd said or done, or not done, or it may have been a complement that someone paid us that triggered off those wonderful feelings, just have a think about that before running through this script.

I allow my unconscious mind to provide me now with a memory of a time when I felt really good about myself – a time when I had accomplished something I was really proud of or maybe I was complimented for my effort – the content of the memory is not important – what is important now is the feeling that this memory generates within me.

As I develop and recall this wonderful memory, I expand upon it – I see the situation that I am in, who is with me, what I am doing and where I am, I then fill in the details, the time of year, spring, summer, autumn or winter, the time of the day, morning, afternoon or evening – what I am wearing and feeling and seeing and touching – if anything – I hear what it is that is being said – if anything is said – or any other sounds – or smells – and now I focus on the feelings, and I can and do really remember how it felt inside – those good, positive feelings, strong feelings – confident and self assured feelings – and I can and do allow those good feelings to grow stronger and more positive whilst I take in a really long, deep breath in through my nose and press together the thumb and the middle finger of the right hand.

Then, in the future, whenever I take in a really long, deep breath through my nose and press together the thumb and the middle finger of my right hand, I can and do feel those good, strong, confident feelings – and I can feel these good feelings anytime I wish, anywhere, in any situation. Because these good, strong, confident feelings are becoming more and more a part of me and I are becoming that stronger, more confident person. And I remember, anytime I want to feel even more confident, all I need to do is to breathe in that really long, deep breath through my nose and press together the thumb and the middle finger of my right hand, and I feel those good, strong, confident feelings filling my body and my mind. I can and do feel more and more wonderful. Calmer, more relaxed, and much more confident than ever before.

I know what it is like to feel those good, strong, confident feelings – and I can really enjoy remembering and re-experiencing those feelings, which are becoming more and more a permanent part of me.

Self-Confidence Script

I am more and more relaxed now, and because I am so wonderfully relaxed I begin to feel free from any unwanted feelings and spread all those good feelings throughout my entire system. I now realise that I am more confident and sure of myself because I am taking these enormous first steps to helping myself.

I begin to feel and experience this strength from within, motivating my self to overcome any and every obstacle that used to stand in the way of my happiness, social life and home life. I find that from this moment on I am developing more of the right kind of self-control. I do now face increasingly more situations in a calm and relaxed state of mind. My thinking is more appropriately sharp at the times when I need it to be so.

I begin now to feel and know that my self-respect and confidence are expanding more and more each day in every way. I do realise that in the past I felt helpless and overwhelmed and I am now replacing that with confidence, strength and self-control. I am a more and more happy person now with a more progressively positive attitude towards life. I am succeeding now in more and more of the things that I do and I discover more and more the abilities necessary for my own interpretation of success.

I realise that unhappy relationships can be caused by value judging and resisting others and myself. So I find that love is a natural state of being for me and I am naturally in a state of loving when I accept others and myself totally and unconditionally. So from this moment forwards, I realise that I do not have to approve of anyone's actions, behaviour or appearance in order to willingly accept and love them or myself. Our actions are but the means we choose to satisfy our dominant needs to feel good. I feel more naturally warm and loving towards others and myself.

Additional Self-Confidence Script

From this moment forward and lasting throughout my entire lifetime, I now realise that my number one responsibility is to fulfil my fundamental human need to feel really good mentally, physically and emotionally about myself, and so I do. I now realise that I have the freedom and the authority to do anything I feel necessary to satisfy this basic need. So, I do also realise that I am in charge of my own life and my own well being, for people benefit or suffer, feel good or bad, according to the consequences of everything they think, say, do and feel. I know that I am in charge of my own life and my own mind. From this moment on, my number one responsibility and priority is to fulfil my fundamental need to feel better and better about myself mentally, physically and emotionally. I stop resisting the reality of any unwanted circumstances and I accept the unwanted realities in my life and willingly allow them to be.

Additional Self-Confidence Script

I now become more and more aware of the self-confidence growing within me. I am more and more self reliant, self confident and filling up with more natural independence and determination. I have opened my mind to the inner security that was lying dormant within me in the past; I have awoken it and continue to develop it and build upon it. I am updating myself, as I am more and more self-confident. I think confidently, I talk confidently, and I project an aura of natural self-confidence. I am more naturally independent and filled with more and more genuine, appropriate inner security. I am more and more self-confident internally and externally. My inner confidence has emerged and continues to emerge and grow.

I am creating a new positive and progressive reality for myself. I now experience increasing levels of warmth and joy in my life while detaching from old, outmoded ways and letting go of them. From this moment on I see the positive, progressive side of things that happen in my life, as long as it is appropriate to do so. I am more and more positive in being aware of opportunities in more of my life experiences. I possess more useful positive thinking and that now results in a more positive and progressive life. I experience a feeling of overall well being and growing mental calmness. I am at peace with myself, the world, and more of those things and people that are in it. Each and every day I experience more and more positive results of my positive thinking.

My self-esteem is increasing. My self-confidence is increasing. I feel and am more appropriately enthusiastic about my life and look forward to any of the challenges that may present themselves. I now breathe life with new optimism, with new enthusiasm. A happy, self-assured inner me has emerged and continues to emerge. I am a more positive individual who sees any problems that may arise as opportunities. I am more patient, calm and harmoniously centred more and more of the time.

I keep my mind like calm water; tranquil and serene. I enjoy remaining centred more and more of the time; this means to be physically relaxed, emotionally calm, mentally focused and alert. I am more and more confident and secure about things in my life and my reality. I maintain a calm mind and I think more and more positive, progressive thoughts. I let go of things that I cannot change. I am increasingly confident and secure, mentally at peace.

9

Healing

*The twentieth century will be remembered
chiefly, not as an age of political conflicts and
technical inventions, but as an age in which
human society dared to think of the health of
the whole human race as a practical objective*
Arnold Toynbee

Let me refer you to that example that I have used a couple of times already in this book; ff you fell over and grazed your knee would you then concentrate on the graze and try to use your will to instigate the healing process? No. You just accept and expect your body to know how to heal it. Despite whatever state of health you are in, your unconscious has the ability for you to be well. In the most part anyway, some people are born with severe illness or disability and I could end up writing 100 more books on that topic; that is not what is being discussed here.

You can trust that your unconscious knows how to be well. In your self-hypnosis, one way of healing is to imagine your body as a hologram; in fact you can create a hologram of your being and then amend it to be the way that you want it to be. You can concentrate on the specific area that you want to work on and even go into deeper detail with your hologramatic representation of yourself in that area.

You can also ask your unconscious to go to the time in your life when you were at the optimum state of health and ask your unconscious mind to make a record of the conditions that were present at that time and almost create a blueprint of it. Then ask your unconscious to examine your condition of today and compare the two and notice the differences and of course then to lock into place the healthy blueprint. These kinds of things do need to be done with a fair degree of regularity to really install the message in your unconscious mind of how you choose to be now.

Some physical problems may well be amplified or even created by psychological aspects. It is very well documented these days in all kinds of health journals that when we are stressed for example, our immune system is often less as effective than usual. You may also want to consider other meanings to your symptoms and what they may tell you about, in the wonderful book *The Healing Power of Illness* by Thorwald Dethlefson, you can get a far deeper understanding of this notion. For example, for someone that has psoriasis, sometimes you can think that it may be trying to provide some kind of armour plating for the body to protect them from something or from begin hurt again, sometimes with irritable bowel syndrome or constipation you can look at the idea that the individual may not want to let go of something. These are just ideas to aid your understanding of healing more than just your physical symptoms; this is not the case with everyone of course.

The scripts at the end of this chapter focus on ideas of instigating the body's natural healing abilities. Please, please know that I always recommend that you see your doctor for any physical problems you have, but conventional medicine wrangles with me somewhat because sometimes it suppresses symptoms; it takes the symptoms somewhere further inside often, they don't necessarily go away, they are just temporarily abated. Sometimes we can release causes of illness and let them go. Self-hypnosis is a great way to create a really healthy internal environment within our bodies. By communicating with the unconscious, you can get straight to the root of the issue; the start and cause of it.

The effect of placebo is far better known these days and used in many scientific and research studies and can often illustrate the body's own ability to heal itself. With hypnosis you are channelling directly into that wisdom and letting your body do what it really does know how to do.

Use of metaphor and visualisation

Metaphors of healing are used in many types of alternative and complementary healthcare. Earlier in the book, I suggested imagining your unconscious mind as a garden or landscape where you are sowing powerful seeds in the form of thoughts and suggestions. You can take this notion a step further and imagine yourself as something in particular such as a tree that is poorly or mal-affected with rot of some kind. Then the rain and sunshine heal it and it transforms into a healthy, strong tree. You can use all kinds of ideas on a regular basis to create metaphors that represent you and within your self-hypnosis sessions, you can replay the metaphor and create the healthy transformations.

Although we have used visualisations already in this book, we are going to really mature the notion here. There have been cases in the world whereby individuals have had brain scans showing that they have a golf ball sized lump on their brain and then 6 weeks later it has disappeared using only visualisation techniques. I cannot go into a full in depth study of this; there is a lot of additional literature out there that can give you a more thorough understanding of this.

If you think that certain emotions or psychological things are contributing to your illness or unhealthy condition, then you may want to visualise yourself as letting go of them. Maybe you can imagine them as baggage that you put on an aeroplane and send away, you can imagine that the plane is carrying that baggage into the past even.

In the later chapter of manifesting your unconscious mind, you learn how to start dialogue with your unconscious mind and you can even then consider asking your unconscious mind what it requires to create a healthy state in the body.

You can also use visualisation and suggestions to create 'hypnotic medicine.' You can imagine taking a magic tablet or some elixir that stimulates your healing while you are in your state of self-hypnosis and suggest that it is having. You can also hypnotise your body and mind into believing that something you are about to eat, such as a grape or an orange has a more and more powerful effect on you and heals you, and then eat the grape or orange. Write programmes to enhance your immune system and use your self-hypnosis to prevent illness rather than fire-fighting it when it happens.

The following scripts are ideas; these are scripts for using the body's natural healing abilities. They involve a lot of conscious and unconscious concentration to really channel into the unconscious healing abilities and also should be done with some real regularity. In addition to these kinds of programmes, you can write additional programmes to include suggestions that you are healing faster and better and more thoroughly.

Healing Visualisation Script

I allow myself to focus . . . all my attention . . . on that area in the middle of my forehead . . . so that my entire concentration . . . becomes more and more focused . . . on that point . . . in this area of my forehead . . . and I allow myself to imagine . . . this point . . . as a tiny, white ball of light . . . now hovering just in front of my forehead . . . just floating in mid air . . . right in front of my forehead . . . and this tiny white ball of light . . . is in every way . . . the size and appearance . . . of a tiny distant star . . . a shimmering glowing star . . . shining brightly in the night sky . . . radiating energy and light . . . and I do soon . . . feel a slight sensation . . . or feel a warm comforting glow . . . as I become more aware . . . of the radiant vibrations . . . coming from this tiny white ball of light . . . that shines ever more brightly . . . as it hovers just in front of my forehead . . .

. . . and now . . .

I allow myself to . . . imagine this tiny white ball of light . . . slowly begin to float upwards . . . just gently lifting up into the air . . . higher and higher . . . until it reaches that point . . . about a foot above my head . . . and as it hovers there . . . just above my head . . . I allow myself to imagine it beginning to grow in size . . . and as it begins to expand . . . shining more and more brightly . . . I do become more aware of the radiant quality . . . of this illustrious object . . . I imagine the purity of its colour . . . like the pure white of freshly fallen snow . . . I can and do feel its radiant warmth . . . like a gentle heat from an open fire . . . I can imagine hearing its faint vibrations . . . as it grows larger and larger . . . giving off a more brilliant light all the time . . .

. . . and as it grows to the size of large ball . . . I am instinctively more aware now . . . of its healing qualities . . . sensing that its radiant energy can heal all that it needs to . . . instigating the natural healing abilities that exist within my unconscious mind. it revitalises and energises anything it touches . . . and as it hovers there . . . just above my head . . . glowing even more brilliantly . . . I can feel myself drawn to this healing energy . . . more and more . . . as I sense its purity . . . and its inherent goodness . . . knowing that it has these healing qualities . . . without limitations . . . and knows no boundaries . . . when it comes to seeking out . . . and destroying . . . any disease or discomfort . . . and I allow myself to immerse myself . . . in this radiant energy . . . to bask in its purity . . . knowing that I can and do only benefit . . . from its wonderful healing properties . . .

As I think of this and concentrate more deeply on my own inner resources . . . the ball slowly begins to open . . . showering me with its pure healing white light energy . . . energy that revitalises me . . . and balances me . . . energy that cleanses me and heals every part of me . . . and as this free flowing stream of energy . . . begins its downpour . . . I allow myself to feel and experience this stream of healing energy . . . freely flowing down into every part of my body . . . down through the top of my head . . . clearing out any old negative thoughts, beliefs or emotions . . . and installing new feelings of well being and balance as it goes . . . down my neck and shoulders . . . relieving any tension or stress there . . . and all the way down my back . . . entering every muscle fibre and nerve in my spine . . . clearing away any toxins that may have gathered there . . . and as this fountain stream of pure healing white light . . . continues cascading down . . . pouring into every last cell . . . in my entire body . . . cleansing and revitalising me . . . healing and rejuvenating me . . . I do begin to feel more and more uplifted . . . more and more alive . . . than I have felt in a long while . . . as feelings of health and well being . . . begin to resonate through my entire system . . .

As the constant stream of energy . . . continues to pour into my body . . . I can imagine this pure healing white light energy . . . freely flowing into every organ . . . in my chest and stomach . . . cleansing every artery and vein . . . purifying the air in my lungs . . . strengthening every muscle and bone . . . as it continues its free flow . . . down into my lower body . . . into my legs . . . and all the way down . . . to the tips of my toes . . . clearing any wastes or debris on the way . . . and at this point . . . I really notice and concentrate the flow of energy . . . on a certain part of my body . . . a part that maybe needs a lot of healing . . . and I just allow that to happen for a short time . . . so that I can direct the flow of energy . . . to where I need it the most . . .

As I continue to allow this pure healing white light energy . . . this free flowing radiant white light . . . to permeate every part of me . . .

clearing any blockages . . . cleansing and purifying every part of me on every level . . . and I can imagine . . . that the ball above my head . . . has now grown even larger in size . . . to about three feet in width . . . so that its endless downpour of healing energy . . . has now completely enveloped my entire body . . . so that I am now immersed . . . from the top of my head . . . to the tip of my toes . . . in this radiant healing white light energy . . . completely bathed in this pure source of radiant energy . . . that continues its free flow in and around my body . . . bringing me wonderful feelings of health and vitality . . . and the knowledge that any time . . . I can visualise this white light energy . . . entering my body . . . and healing every part of myself . . . I do just continually encourage . . . feelings of health and well being . . . in my mind, body and spirit . . .

As the healing process is completed for now . . . I imagine a beautiful mass of energy above my head . . . shrinks to the size of a large ball again . . . and the downpour of energy . . . begins to slow down . . . slower and slower . . . until it finally comes to a stop . . . as the large ball above my head gently closes . . . leaving me radiating with feelings of health and vitality . . . and a feeling of well being all over . . . and at this point I can and do notice . . . how much better I feel . . . both physically and mentally . . . as well as a feeling of being emotionally uplifted . . . and as this wonderful healing process comes to its conclusion for now . . . I allow myself to imagine the large ball . . . still floating above my head . . . slowly begin to shrink in size . . . smaller and smaller . . . back to the size of a tiny distant star . . . then let it begin to descend . . . gently floating down . . . back to the area . . . just in front of my forehead . . . where it is absorbed again . . . back into my consciousness . . . and I am more aware and more aware . . . of how uplifted . . . and revitalised I feel and am . . . as my entire system . . . my mind and body . . . has been purified and cleansed . . . in this wonderful holistic healing process . . . that I can continue . . . as and when I need to . . .

Additional Healing Script

I am surrounded by a divine blue healing light, which is flowing through all of my cells, healing me more quickly and thoroughly. I have the power and ability to accelerate the healing of my own body. My body is filling up with positive healing energy and my natural healing process is now accelerated.

Each breath of air that I take into my body contains this divine healing process. My mind is all-powerful and I now use it to heal myself of more and more imperfections, which may exist body *(Be specific about your own situation here).* I am now healing more and more profoundly and my body is returning to a higher state of well-being.

From this moment forward I choose only progressive better and better health, mentally, physically and spiritually. This deeply powerful level of health is my divine right and I now manifest better and better health. Each moment, each second, and each hour I move more rapidly and more thoroughly toward total healing of myself. I am more and more healed.

Further Healing Script

At the count of 3, I imagine myself projected through time and space to the most famous healing temple known. 1 – 2 – 3. I am now standing outside the most famous healing temple of all time.

(Pause here and really develop this in your mind; sights, sounds, feelings.)

I now enter the temple and meet the physicians and priests who will be working with me.

(Again, take some time out to really create this in your mind; interact.)

I am now going through all of the diagnostic tests.

Now the diagnosis has been completed and I can and do see myself being wonderfully healed, participating with the priest and physicians in the healing process.

I experience myself being beautifully healed, leaving the ancient healing temple; being projected back to the present time and bringing with me the feelings and the energies, which I have created.

As I now take a nice deep breath, I am comfortably feeling and imagining the healing energy flow throughout my body.

Be creative, consider using techniques from other chapters too and create programmes for your self to use in hypnosis and that work inside and outside of hypnosis to create optimum health and healing.

10

Manifesting Your Unconscious Mind for Direct Communication

The meeting of two personalities is like the contact of two chemical substances: if there is any reaction, both are transformed.

Carl Jung

So, throughout this book, you have been continually thanking your unconscious minds at the end of each self-hypnosis session and delivering suggestions and programmes to yourself and who knows; maybe you even starting to hug your unconscious mind as I do. Many people that I have worked with on my self-hypnosis trainings and seminars have even named their unconscious mind.

On one of the two-day courses, we had a man attend who was an airline pilot, he was from New Zealand and played rugby and drank beer and was the real epitome of what a 'real man' should be! I was running through the self-hypnosis model with them all again and I went around the room asking everyone how they enjoyed deepening their own state of hypnosis the most.

This particular man told us all that he liked to imagine that he was a snowflake floating through the air. As you can imagine, there were a few sniggers because he was such a man and surely men like him didn't imagine being snowflakes! So, I was very sensitive from then on and decided to call him 'snowflake' for the rest of the course and he actually named his unconscious mind just that. Joking aside, it established a really deep, fond and loving relationship between him and his unconscious mind. Have some fun with your unconscious and really befriend it. Your success will improve as you do.

Now is the time to really power up the relationship that you have with your unconscious mind. Within this chapter, we are going to learn how to actually manifest and create your unconscious mind in a way that is best for you and a way that you find to be most easy and responsive. The script at the end of this chapter walks you through a great way of doing this.

When you get in touch with yourself in such a way, you can examine issues and problems or obstacles in your life in such a way that you do not associate with them too much and can learn from them. You can then also ask your unconscious mind for information and guidance on certain issues. This may lead to things that you have not been aware of or things that you already know but did not realise the importance of. At the end of a day, you can then even consult with your unconscious mind or request assistance from it.

Of course, at this stage, I hasten to add that there may well be things that are not always dealt with best on your own and of course, at that stage do consult with a professional therapist or your GP. Therapists can be located through the larger, professional Associations that can easily be found on the Internet or in your phone book.

If you are going to use your unconscious mind almost as if it were your own specialist counsellor, maybe consider taking some time out to have a good long discussion with yourself about whatever it is that you want to work on. You can discuss emotions and feelings and you may well experience more of them, so it is a very good practice to ensure that you do protect yourself from that stuff having any further influence upon you. Depressed people get more depressed when they keep running over the reasons why they are depressed. So if you are going to spend time allowing your unconscious mind to counsel you, protect yourself from the emotions having any further influence upon you.

You can even create a special place inside your mind which you use as a meeting place to meet up with your unconscious mind and have these discussions and the room prevents all that goes on within it from spreading anywhere else.

As you have been discovering and as I have been mentioning, self-hypnosis opens the door to your unconscious and your unconscious sure knows you better than anyone or anything else. Seeking information and guidance from your inner self, your unconscious mind is a very direct way to receive information, guidance and assistance and it all comes from your accumulated life experiences, interpretations of the world and life, your influences, thoughts and feelings; remember what a storehouse your unconscious mind is.

Your conscious mind will have filtered all your experiences and interpreted them very differently and so the perspective from your unconscious mind, your inner self may well shed new light on matters arising in your life.

People often ask me if hypnosis can work with children. You know what, hypnosis works so much better with children; when they use their imaginations, they are there, in that place, living it. Can you remember playing games as a child? You lived those experiences. It shows how much more in touch we all are with our unconscious mind when we were younger. As we progress through life, we often lose touch with ourselves, and so getting back in touch with yourself and with your unconscious self can be wonderfully uplifting and nurturing if you allow it to be so.

While tuning in to your unconscious with your self-hypnosis, you can get better feedback and honest interpretations of your behaviours and actions in circumstances and situations. You can heighten your awareness of your interactions and actions that may have been clouded by your rational and logical conscious mind.

Before you begin to communicate with yourself in this way, ensure that you note down in your mind or ideally on paper, your objectives. What do you want to achieve from doing this. What goal are you moving towards? What do you want to know? Be really specific. Be honest and open with yourself. This is so important that I am going to say it again; be honest and open with your self. You will get nowhere with this if you are not honest with yourself. You simply cannot fool yourself, so treat your unconscious self with the honesty it truly deserves.

Make this important and show yourself how important it is by taking the right time to do this. Any results and insights that you gain from the communication you can then start writing programmes to deal with and work through and enhance or whatever is relevant to it.

Some basic guidelines for doing this is that firstly, you go over the period of time that you want to reflect on if that is what you are doing; examine your reactions, interactions and the behaviours you did. Trust your unconscious mind in the session and listen to it, be aware of it, notice it, really observe what it communicates with you.

Let your unconscious guide you, if you are not going to ask specific questions (outline for that session is coming up) then let it guide you and wander to whatever is right for you, just go with it and take what you need from the experience. Give yourself suggestions to the effect that even if you are not sure of the relevance of what your unconscious has shown you, then it is still unconsciously working for you and helping you. Do your best not to consciously guide what you want, do your best not to force what you consciously think is the solution; remove your conscious mind from the process as much as is pertinent to do.

OK, so bearing all that in mind, here is a wonderful script for manifesting your unconscious mind and beginning to communicate with it in a direct way, you can begin to alter it to your own requirements as usual;

Enter hypnosis in your usual way. I would especially think about using your breath here as you shall be using your breath later in this session too, so get tuned in to your breathing and allow it to be steady.

Then, having entered hypnosis, take control and deepen your hypnosis in whatever way is right for you, maybe give yourself suggestions like:

Each time I inhale and exhale, I do find myself twice as relaxed as I was in the moment before . . . Twice as comfortable . . . Twice as peaceful . . . For with each breath, every cell of my body becomes at ease . . .

Then, begin to use your imagination to create a favourite place or a favourite setting and follow the script. Make it as vivid as you can with images, sounds, smells and feelings.

. . . As I allow myself to enjoy this nice state of deep, peaceful relaxation, I return in my mind's eye to my personal place . . . *(Describe the characteristics of a personal spot if to yourself in your mind.)* I allow my imagination to become re-acquainted with every detail of this beautiful spot . . . I Sense the peaceful beauty all around my . . . I easily stretch out . . . Relax . . . And enjoy it.

As I relax in my favourite spot, I put a smile on my face . . . and I gradually look around me . . . Somewhere, nearby, some living creature, some being or essence is waiting for me . . . smiling and waiting for me to establish eye contact . . . This creature, this person or spirit may immediately approach me or it may wait a few moments to be sure that I mean them no harm . . . I look up in the trees or behind bushes, since my advisor may be a bit timid . . . But even if I see nothing, I can and do sense his or presence and so I introduce myself . . . I tell my advisor my name, and that I mean no harm, for I have come with only the friendliest intentions. I Find out my advisors name . . . The first name that comes to my mind . . . Right now . . .

I ask my advisor if they are willing to come over and talk with me for a few moments . . . Often advisors have been waiting a long time to make this kind of contact . . . Until now my advisor has only been able to talk to me sporadically through my intuition . . . I tell my advisor that I shall be listening to them more and more in the future . . .

If you feel silly or it feels unusual talking in this way, tell your advisor that just that; that it is hard for you to begin this unusual process, but if you sincerely want your advisor's help, make that very, very clear. Get the communication going.

I tell my advisor that I understand that, like in any friendship, it takes time for feelings of mutual trust and respect to develop . . . Although my advisor knows everything about me, since my advisor is just a reflection of my inner life, I tell my advisor that I won't push for any simple answers to important questions that I may be dealing with . . . Rather, I am going to establish a continuing dialogue . . . so that any time I need help with a problem or when I need guidance or meaningful reflection, my advisor can tell me things of great importance . . . things that I may already know, but I may have underestimated their significance . . .

At this stage, you should be talking fluidly or communicating with your inner self (your unconscious mind). If there is a problem that has been bothering you for a while or whatever it is that you wish to discuss with your inner self (your unconscious mind), ask your advisor if he or she is willing to give you some help with it; Yes or no? Your advisor's response is the first answer that pops into your mind.

Then, continue to pose your questions as you exhale, the first response that comes into your mind as you inhale (on any subsequent inhalation) is your advisors reply, an inspiration. So now ask your questions and continue asking them for a while and get yourself into the process.

Think to yourself about what and how your advisor replied. Ask any other questions that are on your mind. Continue your dialogue for a few moments, asking your questions as you exhale, and listening to the response that pops into your mind as you inhale.

Remember, your advisor knows everything about you, but sometimes, for a very good reason, they may well be unwilling to tell you something. This is usually to protect you from information you may not be ready to deal with. If and when this occurs, ask your advisor what you need to do in order to make this information available to you. Your unconscious advisor will usually show you the way. So, if there is something that you would like your advisor to be thinking about between now and the next time you meet, tell this to your advisor. If there is anything your advisor would like you to think about between now and the next time you meet, find out what that is now.

Then, set up a time to meet again, a time that is convenient for you and a time that is convenient for your advisor, remember to be specific as to exact time and place, you can even let your advisor know that although these meetings are important to you, part of you may be lazy or even reluctant to follow through. Now, one way your advisor can help motivate you to continue to meet periodically is by giving you a clear demonstration of the benefits you can gain.

If you are willing to do your share of the work, by relaxing yourself, entering self-hypnosis and meeting periodically to set things straight, there is no limit to your advisor's power. You might be, for example, somewhat forgetful and although you want to continue these meetings with your advisor, you might forget the exact time and place that you agreed to meet. If so, ask your advisor to help you by coming into your consciousness just a few moments before it is time to meet, to remind you of the meeting.

Before leaving, tell your advisor you are open to having many different kinds of advisors if you wish that to be so. If so, let them know that you will leave this totally up to your advisor's discretion. As I mentioned that I embrace and hug my unconscious at the end of each self-hypnosis session, you may well want to establish physical contact. For some this is very important; just about every person in the world likes to be embraced or hugged, even if your conscious mind doesn't think so. Then, check to see if there is anything that you would like to tell your advisor before you leave or that they would like to tell you and prepare to end that particular session. You can take as long as is necessary with the questions and answers part of the session of course.

Then, thank your unconscious as you usually do and you may even want to tell yourself that when this experience is over, you feel relaxed, rested, and comfortable, energized with such a powerful sense of well being that you will be able to respond easily to any demands that may arise. Just give yourself some support before you exit hypnosis in the usual way from 1 to 5.

This is a simple structure whereby we have created and manifested the unconscious mind as an advisor. Some people don't like that word; it conjures up images of a financial person. So, do what is best for you and work out a session that is right for you.

The natural high

This communication does not have to be only about dealing with profound or reflective things either; you can have some fun too. Having befriended, nurtured and enjoyed the relationship with your unconscious mind, you can even begin using it to get high. That's right, high and intoxicated without drugs or alcohol. How wonderful. We have all experienced times when we felt giddy and excited and one simple way to recreate those sensations in self-hypnosis is to remember past experiences of joy and happiness and feel them again.

One thing you can do is to ask your unconscious mind for bursts of good feelings. I have even manifested my unconscious mind as a specialised, internal barman, who dispenses me with shots of feel-good chemicals like serotonin or beta-endorphins. If you are a recovering alcoholic, then this kind of imagery is not advised of course. What I want you to do is to allow yourself to be creative and use your imagination; stretch your brain a bit, in fact, stretch it a lot. It is far, far more capable of making you feel amazing than you can ever imagine.

When I was younger, I put my headphones on that were connected to my stereo, I took myself into self-hypnosis and made sure I protected myself from random thoughts, sounds and images in the way shown in this book and then asked my unconscious mind to produce for me a wonderful light show and inspired, uplifting images in my mind as I blasted out the music from 'The War of the Worlds' in my headphones. Make sure that you do protect yourself as always, I still always do. It was quite an amazing sensation and tremendous experience. Just let go and let your unconscious mind provide some real fun and joy for you. You don't need a playstation when you let your unconscious mind entertain and stimulate you.

Get that relationship developed better with your unconscious and you are really on the right path, the golden path of achievement, happiness and discovery.

Section 5

Summary

I have given many specific ideas and applications in this book and they have all given indicators on how techniques and ideas can be applied to other areas of your life. I hope that you use your own imagination to create your own solutions. We are all so very individual; likewise, our experience of hypnosis is going to be so very individual and unique to us, so use self-hypnosis in a way that is unique to you.

There are so many applications of self-hypnosis; one of the first programmes I suggest you write is a programme for better programme writing. You may be finding it difficult to remember everything that is in this book, however your unconscious mind has it all in there; you have read the information and it is all in your unconscious mind, it may not all be at the forefront of your conscious mind, so within that programme you can include ideas and concepts to promote relying on your unconscious mind's ability to write programmes that can have a reliable, intended and profound effect on your life in the way that you want it to.

You may well want to consider writing programmes for developing your ability to communicate non-verbally and congruently and for enhancing your enjoyment of life or even for enhancing your memory. Really, the only limits are those that exist within your own mind, so reach out, stretch out with your brain, use your brain, use your unconscious resources and be sure to let me know of your successes.

When you are sure that your unconscious mind has accepted the structure of the self-hypnosis model, you may well then want to experiment with your own structures and abandon that which I have given here. Really let your self-hypnosis become free-style! Only when you know that you really are ready to do that now though.

1

Conclusions

In addition to all of the material in this book to do with self-hypnosis, I want to have you think about a concept that is lacking in many these days and that is the concept and idea of gratitude and acceptance. Your self-hypnosis will thrive in a nurtured environment. Remember all that time ago when I suggested that you think of your unconscious as a metaphoric landscape that you are sowing seeds within? Well, you will make that land far, far more fertile with a better internal environment and it becomes better and more fertile with acceptance and gratitude.

Throughout the pages of this book, I have written about many different techniques and approaches for using your self-hypnosis for getting what you want. This notion about gratitude is up there with one of the more esoteric ways I have mentioned. I started using the idea of gratitude for getting more of what I wanted a while ago, and it has really worked for me, whether you want more resources to achieve the changes you want to make, more money more clients, more time or anything else.

The word gratitude is something so many overlook and I recommend that you introduce it into your life properly and for good.

It is very true indeed that if you want more of something in your life, be grateful for what you already have. As what you have increases, you can allow yourself to become even more grateful. You can be grateful to whatever you like, for example;

To the Universe, To God , To All That Is, To universal love, To your own brain, To the process of evolution, To some kind of a higher power, To the natural world, To some kind of energy or chi, To natural law, To your unconscious, To a guardian angel, To a spirit, To all or several of the above, To things not mentioned above.

You can be grateful to any or all of these, as well as anything else you can think of.

I mention on lots of my courses, seminars and workshops the idea of, 'what the thinker thinks, the prover proves' so you can make up something to be grateful to that has all the qualities and attributes you would like in a deity.

For those of you that are currently unaware of that notion of 'What the thinker thinks, the prover proves', here it is in a nutshell;

Whatever the thinker is thinking, the prover will sort for evidence to support it. If a person thinks that all homeless people are lazy, the prover will sort through their experience to find evidence to support that idea. If they think all homeless people are victims, the prover will find evidence to support that idea. If a person considers himself or herself to be stupid, the prover will find evidence to show that it is 'true'. If a person thinks they are brilliant, the prover will show that to be true. What the thinker thinks, the prover proves. While it is easy to see that this is the case for everyone else, it is not so easy to recognise that it is also the case for us. While it is easy to identify the ways in which someone else is limiting themselves, the things we believe, are 'really true' – aren't they?

So, here are some practical steps to take to implement this into your life.

Gratitude is one of the most powerful ways to focus your mind. The pattern of gratitude in your consciousness gets you into receiving mode, and receive you will. Stuff you can feel grateful for includes:

Money, Love, Awareness, Friends, Loved Ones, Books, Fun, Health, Knowledge, Family, Your Home, Feelings or pretty much anything else.

Remember, what you focus on increases: if you only have £5, be grateful for that and you'll get more. If you haven't been in love since you were 10, be grateful for the love you had then; you'll get more. If you only have present moment awareness for 30 seconds a month, be grateful for those 30 seconds, and more will be on its way.

OK, so secondly, make a list of the stuff you want more of. Then, be grateful for whatever amount of it you've already got. Obviously (and I know the ironic amongst you will be thinking this), if what you want is a Ferrari, and you don't have one, you can't be grateful for it. But you could be grateful for your existing car, or your bicycle, or your legs, or your wheelchair. Be grateful for what you've got, and it opens the way for you to get more.

So, how does this work? The brain likes its patterns as well as familiarity; this is often born out when we have learned how to do something that at first seemed tricky and demanding (like learning to drive) and then we learn how to do it and we do it as if by auto-pilot. I mentioned this right at the very beginning of the book, funny how things seem to loop like that isn't it?

If a person reinforces a pattern of shortage or lack, it becomes familiar. Often they start to filter incoming data to support the idea of lack. If a person reinforces a pattern of plenty, then they will filter incoming data to support that idea. You may ask 'Will that really change the reality of the situation?', but bear in mind that you are creating your own perception of the reality of your situation in every single moment. What the thinker thinks the prover proves.

Let me give an example of this; Many people working in businesses or corporations today perceive a shortage of one sort or another, whether it's a shortage of capital, clients, time or staff. The more you focus on the shortage, the more of an issue it can become, especially if it's been going on for a while (remember, the familiarity factor means that even the most intolerable situation eventually become the status quo.). I have written before on the differences of moving towards what we want rather than away from what we don't want. This is verging on the same.

One way to shift the shortage pattern is to start being grateful for what you do have. If you only have 10 clients and you want more, be grateful for the 10 you have – more will come. If you only have 1 member of staff and you want 5, be grateful for the one, and more will appear.

Think this is hippy, new-age nonsense? Well, you are the ones reading a book about self-hypnosis! If you want to, be scientific about it: experiment with gratitude for a month and record your findings. If you are unwilling to do so because you think it is 'silly' or 'new age', congratulate yourself on the strength of your own belief systems, and don't become too curious about just how quickly you can harness their power to give you even greater benefits.

Creating the right fertile environment for your self-hypnosis to bloom and blossom will really enhance your results with self-hypnosis.

Someone on my course once said something to me that really stuck. When I was telling a group of my former students how they must practise and practise to ensure they get the most from self-hypnosis, she said to me 'I think knowing all that I know now and not using it would be like owning a Ferrari and keeping it in the garage all the time.' I could not sum things up better.

2

History of Hypnosis

To establish a depth of understanding with hypnosis, it is often useful for you to understand its origins and how it came to be that which it is today, there is far, far more than has been covered here, this brief history can help to add depth and understanding when using hypnosis for yourself.

Evidence of hypnotic-like phenomena appears in many ancient cultures. The writer of Genesis seems familiar with the anesthetic power of hypnosis when he reports that God put Adam 'into a deep sleep' to take his rib to form Eve. Other ancient records suggest hypnosis was used by the oracle at Delphi and in rites in ancient Egypt (Hughes and Rothovius, 1996). The modern history of hypnosis begins in the late 10s, when a French physician, Anton Mesmer, revived an interest in hypnosis.

1734–1815. Franz Anton Mesmer was born in Vienna. Mesmer is considered the father of hypnosis. He is remembered for the term mesmerism which described a process of inducing trance through a series of passes he made with his hands and/or magnets over people. He worked with a person's animal magnetism (psychic and electromagnetic energies). The medical community eventually discredited him despite his considerable success treating a variety of ailments. His successes offended the medical establishment of the time, who arranged for an official French government investigating committee. This committee included Benjamin Franklin, then the American ambassador to France, and Joseph Guillotine, a French physician who introduced a never-fail device for physically separating the mind from the rest of the body.

1795–1860. James Braid, an English physician, originally opposed to mesmerism (as it had become known) who subsequently became interested. He said that cures were not due to animal magnetism however, they were due to suggestion. He developed the eye fixation technique (also known as Braidism) of inducing relaxation and called it hypnosis (after Hypnos, the Greek god of sleep) as he thought the phenomenon was a form of sleep. Later, realising his error, he tried to change the name to monoeidism (meaning influence of a single idea) however, the original name stuck. 1825–1893 Jean Marie Charcot a French neurologist, disagreed with the Nancy School of Hypnotism and contended that hypnosis was simply a manifestation of hysteria. There was bitter rivalry between Charcot and the Nancy group (Liebault and Bernheim). He revived Mesmer's theory of Animal Magnetism and identified the three stages of trance; lethargy, catalepsy and somnambulism.

1845–1947. Pierre Janet was a French neurologist and psychologist who was initially opposed to the use of hypnosis until he discovered its relaxing effects and promotion of healing. Janet was one of the few people who continued to show an interest in hypnosis during the psychoanalytical rage.

1849–1936. Ivan Petrovich Pavlov – Russian psychologist who actually was more focused on the study of the digestive process. He is known primarily for his development of the concept of the conditioned reflex (or Stimulus Response Theory). In his classic experiment, he trained hungry dogs to salivate at the sound of a bell, which was previously associated with the sight of food. He was awarded the Nobel Prize for Physiology in 1904 for his work on digestive secretions. Though he had nothing to do with hypnosis, his Stimulus Response Theory is a cornerstone in linking and anchoring behaviours, particularly in NLP.

1808–1859. A surgeon, James Esdaille, performed 2000 operations – even amputations – with the patients under hypno-anaesthesia and feeling no pain.

1857–1926. Emile Coue, a physician who formulated the Laws of Suggestion. He is also known for encouraging his patients to say to themselves 20–30 times a night before going to sleep; 'Everyday in every way, I am getting better and better.' He also discovered that delivering positive suggestions when prescribing medication proved to be a more effective cure than prescribing medications alone. He eventually abandoned the concept of hypnosis in favour of just using suggestion, feeling hypnosis and the hypnotic state impaired the efficiency of the suggestion.

Coue's Laws of Suggestion

The Law of Concentrated Attention

'Whenever attention is concentrated on an idea over and over again, it spontaneously tends to realise itself'

The Law of Reverse Action

'The harder one tries to do something, the less chance one has of success'

The Law of Dominant Effect

'A stronger emotion tends to replace a weaker one'

These points really are worth bearing in mind when we come on to using the right kind of language and belief strategies in self-hypnosis.

1856–1939. Sigmund Freud travelled to Nancy and studied with Liebault and Bernheim, and then did additional study with Charcot. Freud did not incorporate hypnosis in his therapeutic work however because he felt he could not hypnotise patients to a sufficient depth, felt that the cures were temporary, and that hypnosis stripped patients of their defences. Freud was considered a poor hypnotist given his paternal manner. However, his clients often went into trance and he often, unknowingly, performed non-verbal inductions when he would place his hand on his patient's head to signify the Doctor dominant, patient submissive roles. Because of his early dismissal of hypnosis in favour of psychoanalysis, hypnosis was almost totally ignored.

1875–1961. Carl Jung, a student and colleague of Freud's, rejected Freud's psychoanalytical approach and developed his own interests. He developed the concept of the collective unconscious and archetypes. Though he did not actively use hypnosis, he encouraged his patients to use active imagination to change old memories. He often used the concept of the inner guide, in the healing work. He believed that the inner mind could be accessed through tools like the I Ching and astrology. He was rejected by the conservative medical community as a mystic. However, many of his ideas and theories are actively embraced by healers to this day.

1932–1974. Milton Erickson, a psychologist and psychiatrist pioneered the art of indirect suggestion in hypnosis. He is considered to be the father of modern hypnosis. His methods bypassed the conscious mind through the use of both verbal and nonverbal pacing techniques including metaphor, confusion, and many others. He was a colourful character and has immensely influenced the practice of contemporary hypnotherapy, and its official acceptance by the AMA. His work, combined with the work of Satir and Perls, was the basis for Bandler and Grinder's Neuro-Linguistic Programming (NLP).

Bibliography and Further Reading

Bach, Richard:
Illusions: The Adventures of a Reluctant Messiah
(Dell; Reissue edition; October 10, 1989)

Bach, Richard:
Jonathan Livingstone Seagull
(Avon; January 1, 1976)

Bandler, Richard and Grinder, John:
Frogs into Princes: Neuro Linguistic Programming
(Real People Press; June 1, 1979)

Bandler, Richard and Grinder, John:
The Structure of Magic: A Book About Language and Therapy
(Science and Behavior Books; June 1, 1975)

Bandler, Richard and Grinder, John:
Trance-Formations: Neuro-Linguistic Programming and the structure of hypnosis
(Real People Press; July 1, 1981)

Bodenhamer, Bob and Burton, John:
Hypnotic Language: Its Structure and Use
(Crown House Publishing; January 1, 2001)

Chopra, Deepak:
Quantum Healing: Exploring the Frontiers of Mind/Body Healing
(Bantam; Reprint edition; May 1, 1990)

Coelho, Paulo:
The Alchemist
(Harper Collins, 1995)

Dethlefson, Thorwald:
The Healing Power of Illness
(Vega; October 28, 2002)

Dilts, Robert:
Changing Belief Systems with NLP
(Meta Publications, 1984)

Elman, Dave:
Hypnotherapy
(Westwood Publishing Company, 1964)

Erickson, Milton and Rossi, Ernest:
Hypnotherapy: An Exploratory Casebook
(Irvington Publishers Inc., 1979)

Gibran, Kahlil:
The Prophet
(Arrow Books; Reprint, 1998)

Hammond, Corydon (ed.):
Handbook of Hypnotic Suggestions and Metaphors
(W. W. Norton and Company; October 1, 1990)

Hilgard, Ernest R. and Hilgard, Josephine:
Hypnosis in the Relief of Pain
(Brunner/Mazel Inc., 1994)

Hill, Napoleon:
Think and Grow Rich
(Vermillion; Reprint, 2004)

Hoff, Benjamin:
The Tao of Pooh
(Methuen Childrens Books Ltd., 1982)

Hogan, Kevin:
The Psychology of Persuasion: How to Persuade Others to Your Way of Thinking
(Pelican Publishing, 1996)

James, Tad et al.:
Hypnosis: A Comprehensive Guide
(Crown House Publishing, 2000)

Murphy, Joseph:
The Power of Your Subconscious Mind
(Bantam; Revised Edition, 2001)

Overdurf, John and Silverthorn, Julie:
Training Trances: Multi Level Communication in Therapy and Training
(Metamorphous Press; 3rd edition, 1995)

Robbins, Anthony:
Unlimited Power: The New Science of Personal Achievement
(Free Press; Reprint edition; December 22, 1997)

Rosen, Sidney:
My Voice Will Go With You: The Teaching Tales of Milton H. Erickson
(W.W. Norton, 1982)

Yapko, Michael:
Trancework: An Introduction to the Practice of Clinical Hypnosis
(Brunner/Mazel Inc., 1990)

Adam Eason

Adam Eason is a developing talent in the world of NLP, hypnosis and personal development. Very qualified in his field, highly academically recognised as an author, motivational speaker, therapist, consultant and trainer in the fields of hypnosis, NLP, Personal Development and human potential. Adam has worked with thousands of individuals, has featured in national, international and local media and appeared on television. He brings a refreshingly ready wit and contagious enthusiasm that permeates all of his work and spreads to all who experience it.

Eager to demonstrate the array of benefits of the many varying techniques he employs, Adam has a passion for leading by example and personal experience. His competitive nature is amply demonstrated by successfully competing in marathon, half marathon and various other running events and the successful businesses he runs.

Adam has worked with many of the worlds most famous trainers in the field of human potential, and continues to be a student in this fascinating field. Continually researching, studying and working toward discovering and understanding human happiness, achievement and excellence. Adam encourages innovation by seeking out and employing cutting edge technologies from across the world.

Those all over the world who have bought his products, consulted with him, attended his Seminar's, workshops and trainings continue to be moved deeply; they learn profoundly and laugh loudly.

www.adam-eason.com